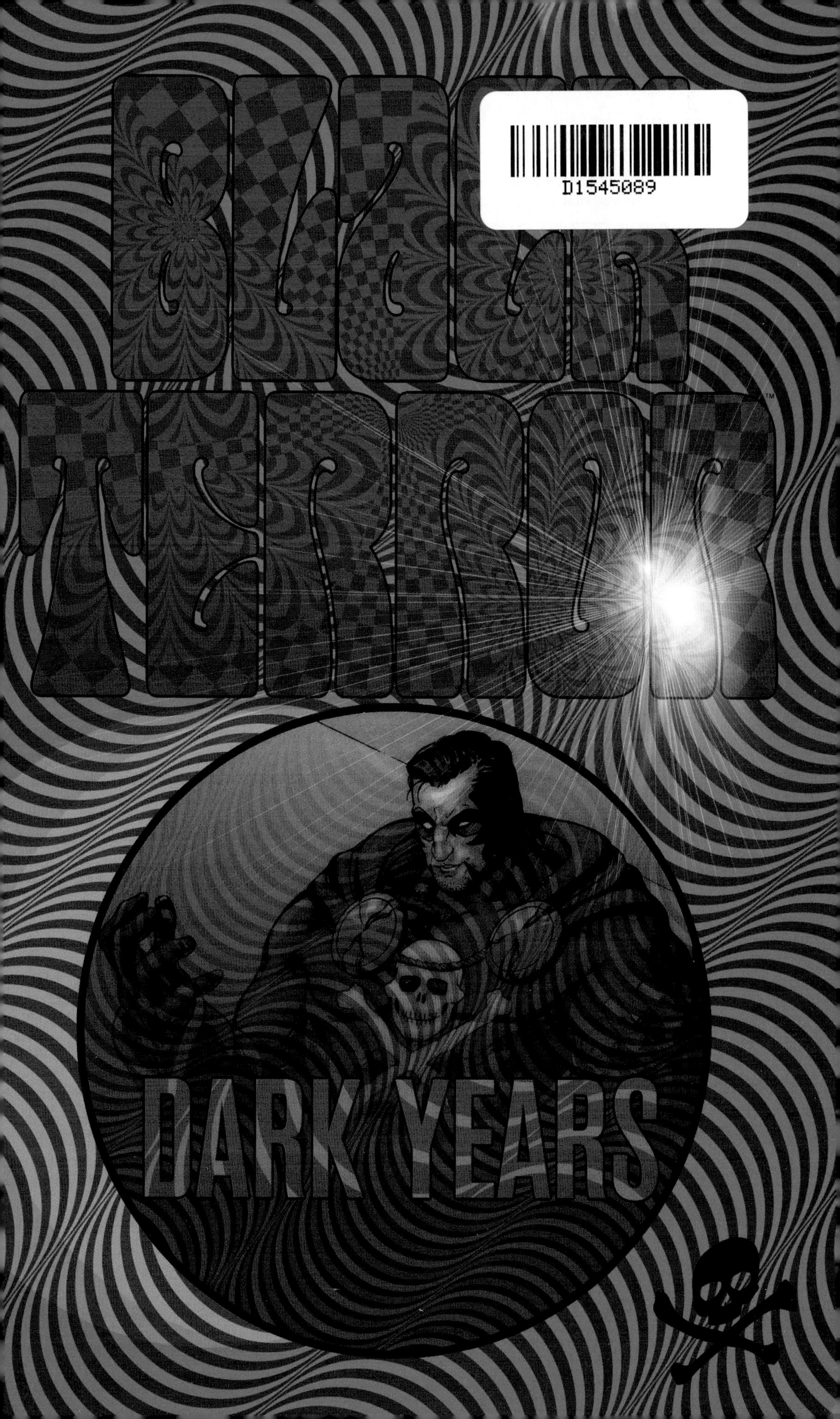
BLACK
TERROR™
DARK YEARS

WRITER	**MAX BEMIS**
ARTISTS	**MATT GAUDIO** (ISSUE 1)
	RUAIRÍ COLEMAN (ISSUES 2-5)
COLORIST	**BRITTANY PEZZILLO**
LETTERER	**TAYLOR ESPOSITO**
COLLECTION COVER	**FRANCESCO FRANCAVILLA**
EDITOR	**KEVIN KETNER**
COLLECTION DESIGN	**CATHLEEN HEARD**

DYNAMITE®

Online at www.DYNAMITE.com
On Facebook /Dynamitecomics
On Instagram /Dynamitecomics
On Twitter @dynamitecomics

Nick Barrucci: CEO / Publisher // **Juan Collado:** President / COO // **Brandon Dante Primavera:** V.P. of IT and Operations // **Joe Rybandt:** Executive Editor // **Matt Idelson:** S
Editor // **Alexis Persson:** Creative Director // **Rachel Kilbury:** Digital Multimedia Associate // **Katie Hidalgo:** Graphic Designer // **Nick Pentz:** Graphic Designer // **Alan Payr**
V.P. of Sales and Marketing. // **Vincent Faust:** Marketing Coordinator // **Jim Kuhoric:** Vice President of Product Development // **Jay Spence:** Director of Product Developme
Mariano Nicieza: Director of Research & Development // **Amy Jackson:** Administrative Coordinator

CK TERROR™: DARK YEARS. First printing. Contains materials originally published in magazine form as BLACK TERROR™, VOLUME 2: ISSUES 1-5. Published by Dynamite Entertain-
nt, 113 Gaither Dr., STE 205, Mt. Laurel, NJ 08054. PROJECT SUPERPOWERS™, THE OWL™, PYROMAN™, THE ARROW™, THE MIGHTY SAMSON™, SCARAB™, GREEN LAMA™, HOLY
RROR™, BLACK TERROR™, DEATH-DEFYING "DEVIL™, THE CRUSADERS™, ATOMAN™, THE "F" TROOP ™, THE FLAME™, THE AMERICAN SPIRIT™, MASQUERADE™, MR. FACE™,
AMIC FAMILY™, all characters featured in this book, the distinctive names, images, elements, logos, symbols, and likenesses contained therein and associated therewith that have been
oduced (collectively "intellectual property") are ™ and © 2021 Super Power Heroes, LLC. All rights reserved. "Dynamite" and "Dynamite Entertainment" are ®, and the "DE Logo" is ™
©, Dynamite Entertainment. All rights reserved. All names, characters, events, and locales in this publication are entirely fictional. Any resemblance to actual persons (living or dead),
nts or places, without satiric intent, is coincidental. No portion of this book may be reproduced by any means (digital or print) without the written permission of Dynamite Entertainment
ept for review purposes. Printed in Korea.

information regarding press, media rights, foreign rights, licensing, promotions, and advertising e-mail: marketing@dynamite.com

N13: 978-1-5241-1498-5   First Printing   10 9 8 7 6 5 4 3 2 1

ISSUE 1
COVER ART BY FRANCESCO FRANCAVILLA

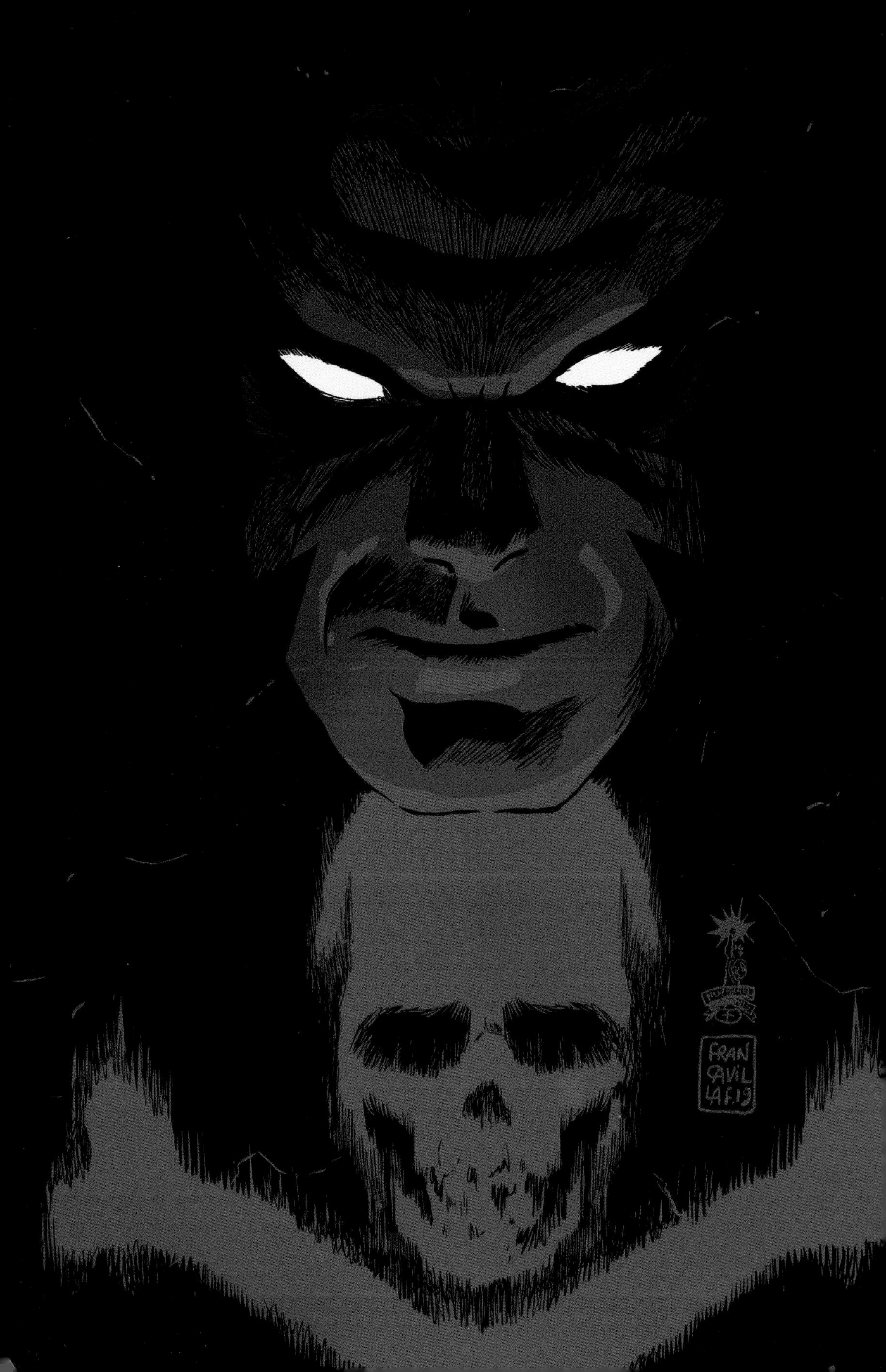

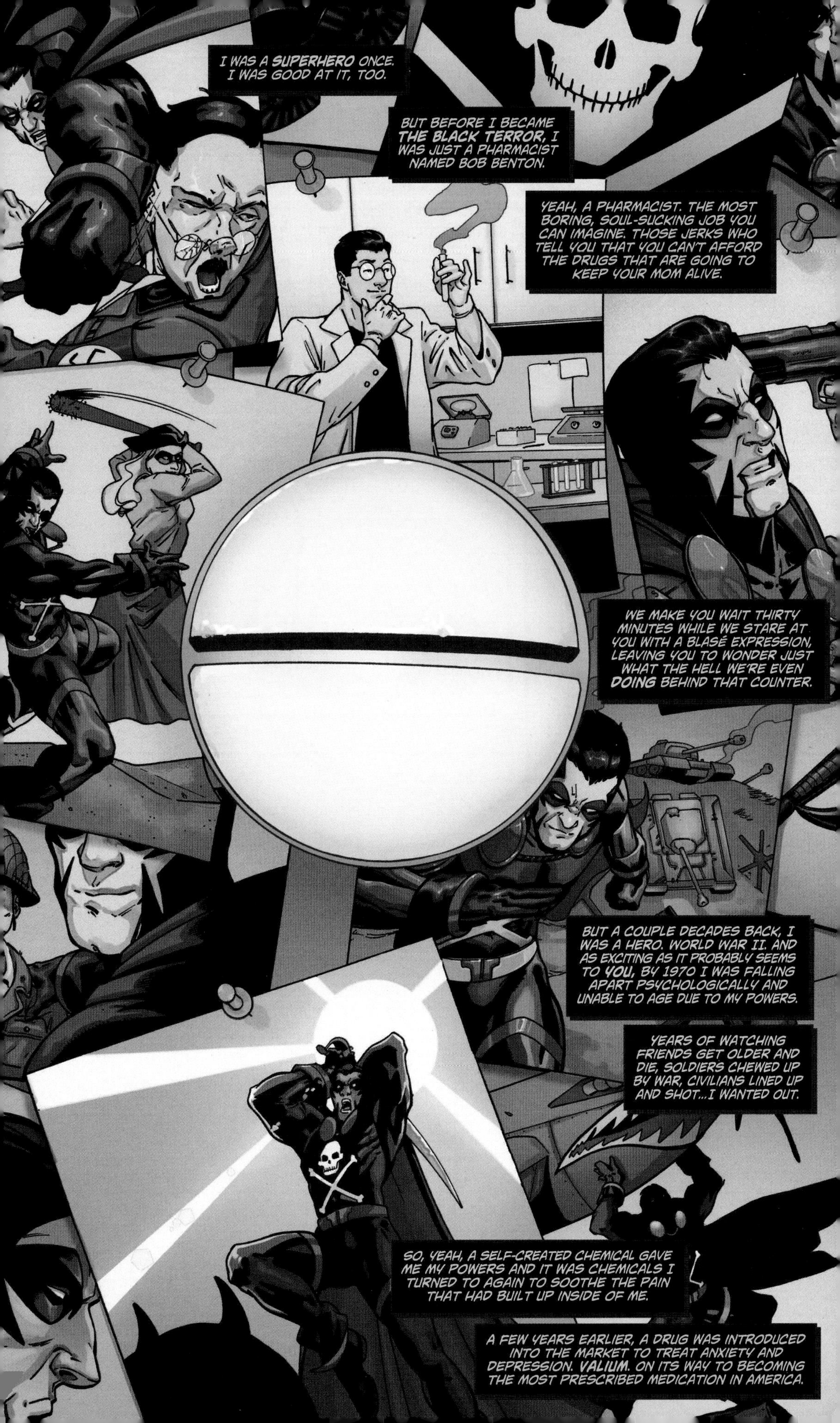
I WAS A SUPERHERO ONCE. I WAS GOOD AT IT, TOO.
BUT BEFORE I BECAME THE BLACK TERROR, I WAS JUST A PHARMACIST NAMED BOB BENTON.
YEAH, A PHARMACIST. THE MOST BORING, SOUL-SUCKING JOB YOU CAN IMAGINE. THOSE JERKS WHO TELL YOU THAT YOU CAN'T AFFORD THE DRUGS THAT ARE GOING TO KEEP YOUR MOM ALIVE.
WE MAKE YOU WAIT THIRTY MINUTES WHILE WE STARE AT YOU WITH A BLASÉ EXPRESSION, LEAVING YOU TO WONDER JUST WHAT THE HELL WE'RE EVEN DOING BEHIND THAT COUNTER.
BUT A COUPLE DECADES BACK, I WAS A HERO. WORLD WAR II. AND AS EXCITING AS IT PROBABLY SEEMS TO YOU, BY 1970 I WAS FALLING APART PSYCHOLOGICALLY AND UNABLE TO AGE DUE TO MY POWERS.
YEARS OF WATCHING FRIENDS GET OLDER AND DIE, SOLDIERS CHEWED UP BY WAR, CIVILIANS LINED UP AND SHOT...I WANTED OUT.
SO, YEAH, A SELF-CREATED CHEMICAL GAVE ME MY POWERS AND IT WAS CHEMICALS I TURNED TO AGAIN TO SOOTHE THE PAIN THAT HAD BUILT UP INSIDE OF ME.
A FEW YEARS EARLIER, A DRUG WAS INTRODUCED INTO THE MARKET TO TREAT ANXIETY AND DEPRESSION. VALIUM. ON ITS WAY TO BECOMING THE MOST PRESCRIBED MEDICATION IN AMERICA.

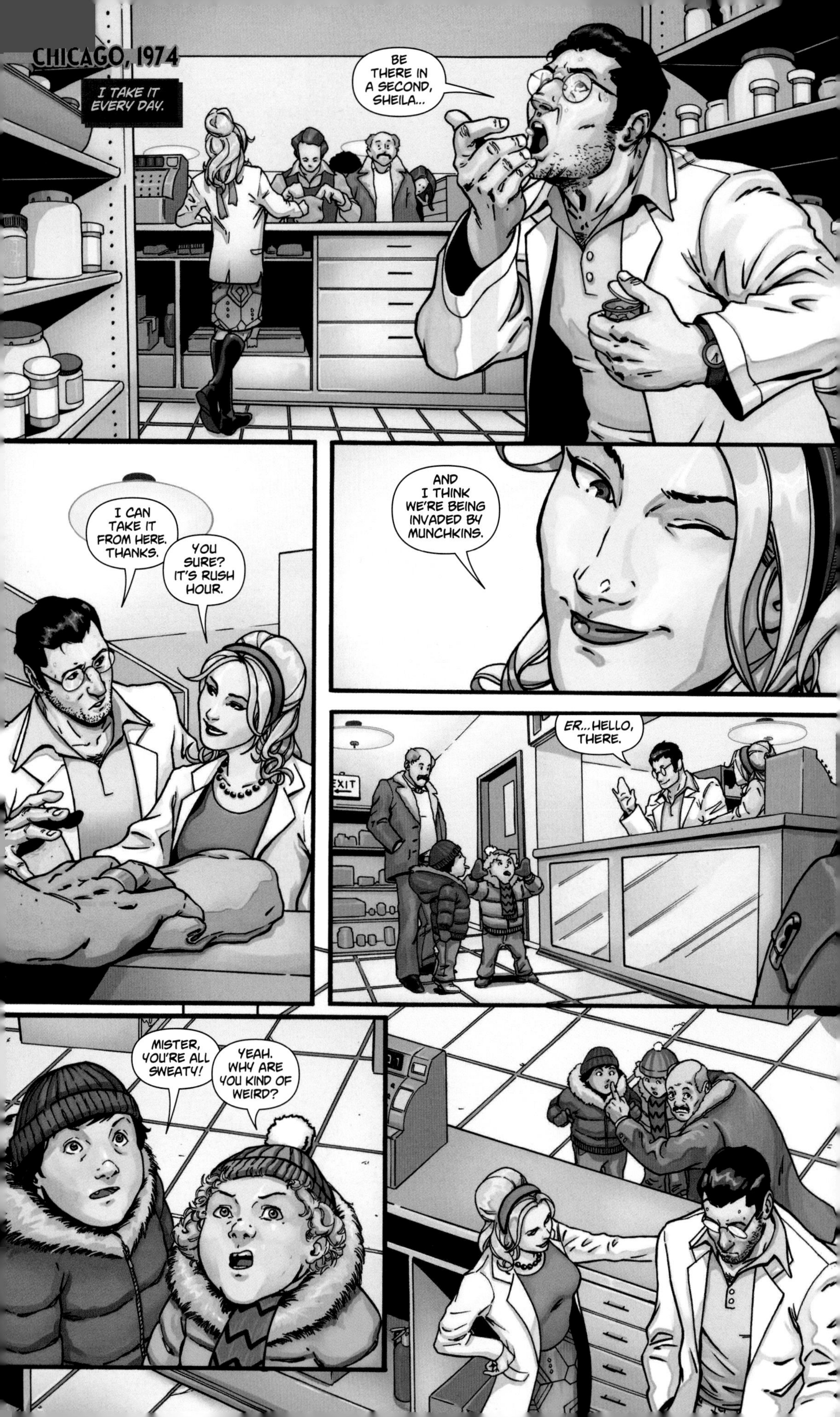
CHICAGO, 1974
I TAKE IT EVERY DAY.
BE THERE IN A SECOND, SHEILA...
I CAN TAKE IT FROM HERE. THANKS.
YOU SURE? IT'S RUSH HOUR.
AND I THINK WE'RE BEING INVADED BY MUNCHKINS.
EXIT
ER... HELLO, THERE.
MISTER, YOU'RE ALL SWEATY!
YEAH. WHY ARE YOU KIND OF WEIRD?

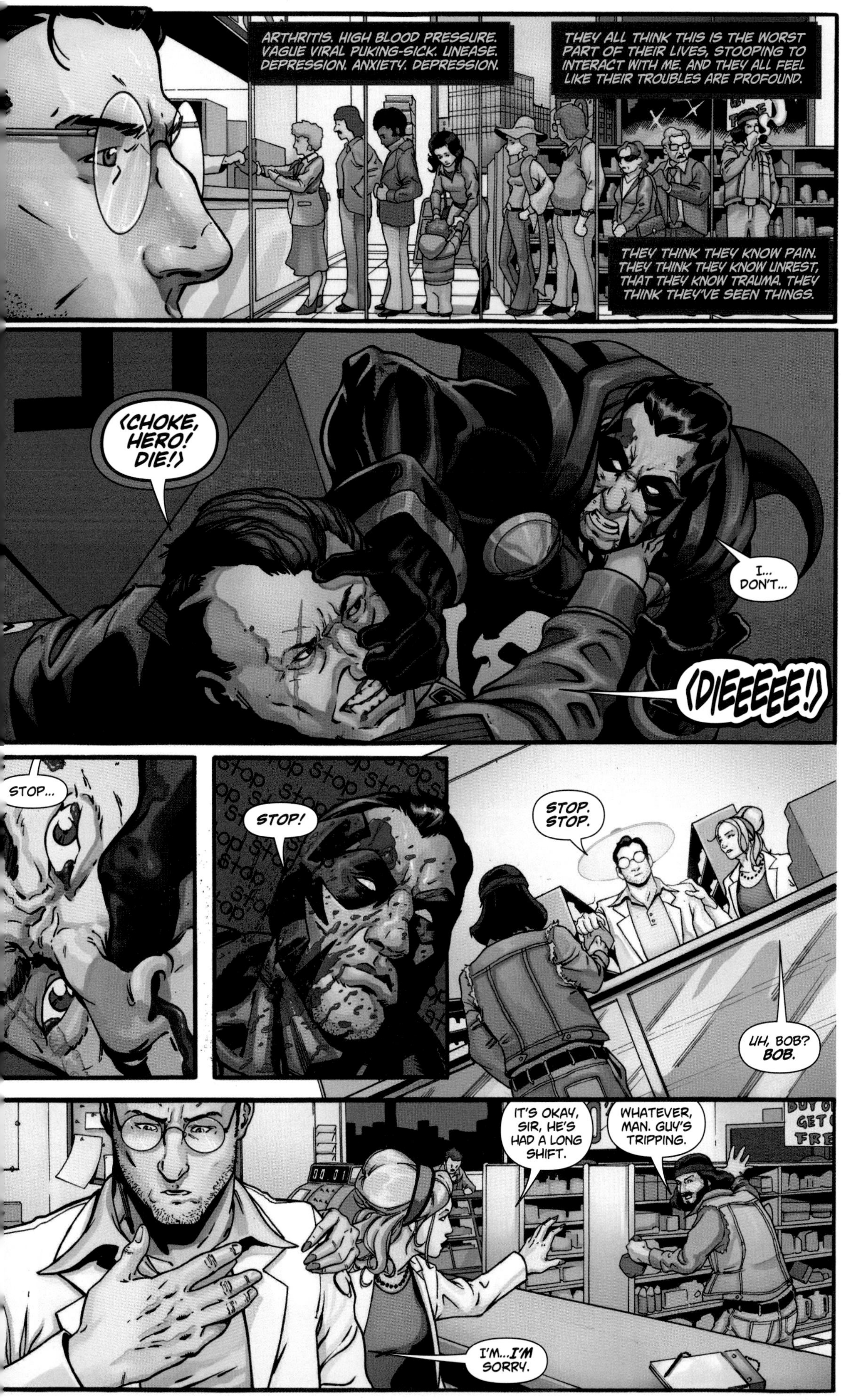
ARTHRITIS. HIGH BLOOD PRESSURE. VAGUE VIRAL PUKING-SICK. UNEASE. DEPRESSION. ANXIETY. DEPRESSION.
THEY ALL THINK THIS IS THE WORST PART OF THEIR LIVES, STOOPING TO INTERACT WITH ME. AND THEY ALL FEEL LIKE THEIR TROUBLES ARE PROFOUND.
THEY THINK THEY KNOW PAIN. THEY THINK THEY KNOW UNREST, THAT THEY KNOW TRAUMA. THEY THINK THEY'VE SEEN THINGS.
⟨CHOKE, HERO! DIE!⟩
I... DON'T...
⟨DIEEEEE!⟩
STOP...
STOP!
STOP. STOP.
UH, BOB? BOB.
IT'S OKAY, SIR, HE'S HAD A LONG SHIFT.
WHATEVER, MAN. GUY'S TRIPPING.
I'M... I'M SORRY.

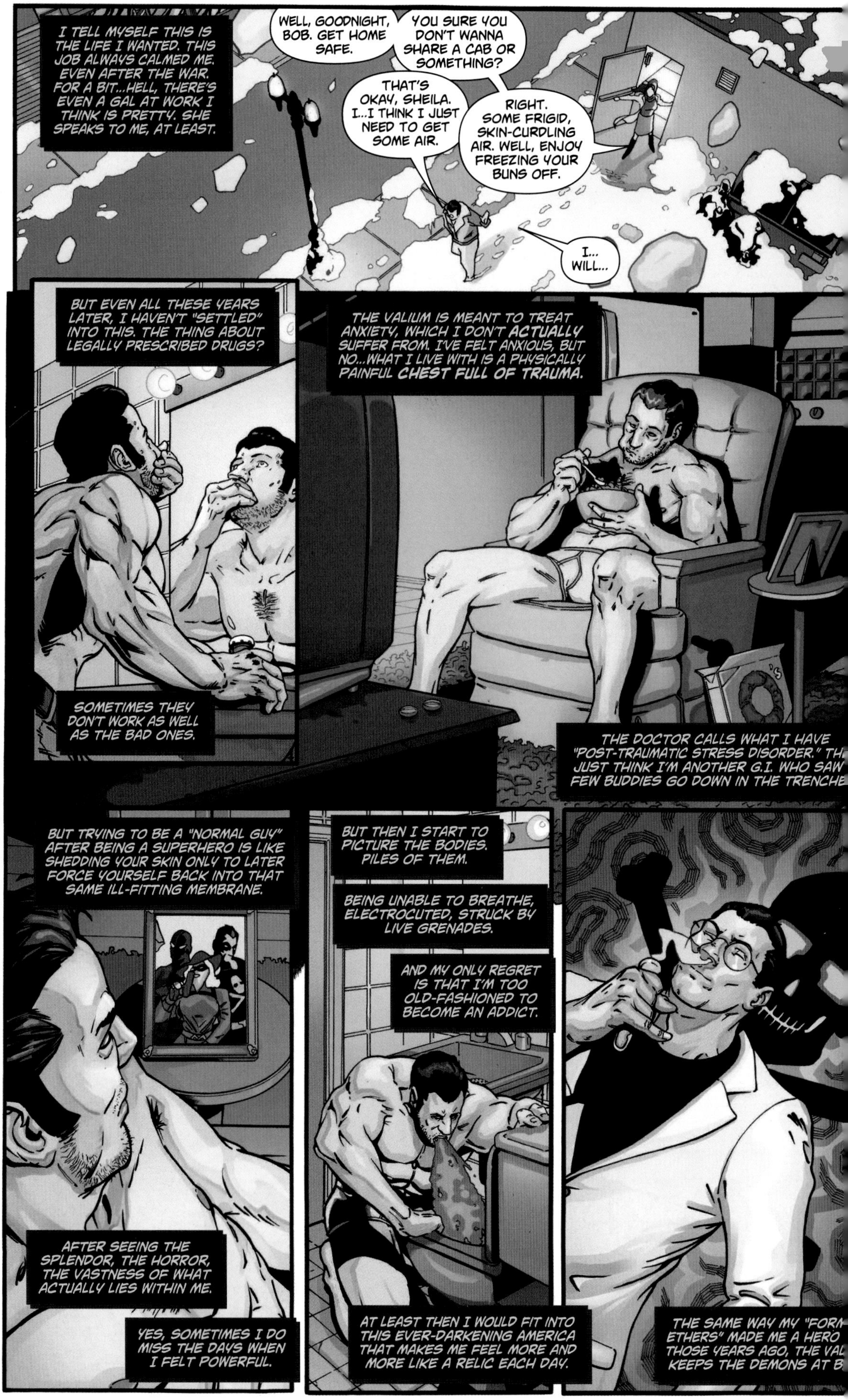

I TELL MYSELF THIS IS THE LIFE I WANTED. THIS JOB ALWAYS CALMED ME. EVEN AFTER THE WAR. FOR A BIT...HELL, THERE'S EVEN A GAL AT WORK I THINK IS PRETTY. SHE SPEAKS TO ME, AT LEAST.
WELL, GOODNIGHT, BOB. GET HOME SAFE.
YOU SURE YOU DON'T WANNA SHARE A CAB OR SOMETHING?
THAT'S OKAY, SHEILA. I...I THINK I JUST NEED TO GET SOME AIR.
RIGHT. SOME FRIGID, SKIN-CURDLING AIR. WELL, ENJOY FREEZING YOUR BUNS OFF.
I... WILL...
BUT EVEN ALL THESE YEARS LATER, I HAVEN'T "SETTLED" INTO THIS. THE THING ABOUT LEGALLY PRESCRIBED DRUGS?
SOMETIMES THEY DON'T WORK AS WELL AS THE BAD ONES.
THE VALIUM IS MEANT TO TREAT ANXIETY, WHICH I DON'T ACTUALLY SUFFER FROM. I'VE FELT ANXIOUS, BUT NO...WHAT I LIVE WITH IS A PHYSICALLY PAINFUL CHEST FULL OF TRAUMA.
THE DOCTOR CALLS WHAT I HAVE "POST-TRAUMATIC STRESS DISORDER." TH JUST THINK I'M ANOTHER G.I. WHO SAW FEW BUDDIES GO DOWN IN THE TRENCHE
BUT TRYING TO BE A "NORMAL GUY" AFTER BEING A SUPERHERO IS LIKE SHEDDING YOUR SKIN ONLY TO LATER FORCE YOURSELF BACK INTO THAT SAME ILL-FITTING MEMBRANE.
AFTER SEEING THE SPLENDOR, THE HORROR, THE VASTNESS OF WHAT ACTUALLY LIES WITHIN ME.
YES, SOMETIMES I DO MISS THE DAYS WHEN I FELT POWERFUL.
BUT THEN I START TO PICTURE THE BODIES. PILES OF THEM.
BEING UNABLE TO BREATHE, ELECTROCUTED, STRUCK BY LIVE GRENADES.
AND MY ONLY REGRET IS THAT I'M TOO OLD-FASHIONED TO BECOME AN ADDICT.
AT LEAST THEN I WOULD FIT INTO THIS EVER-DARKENING AMERICA THAT MAKES ME FEEL MORE AND MORE LIKE A RELIC EACH DAY.
THE SAME WAY MY "FORM ETHERS" MADE ME A HERO THOSE YEARS AGO, THE VAL KEEPS THE DEMONS AT B

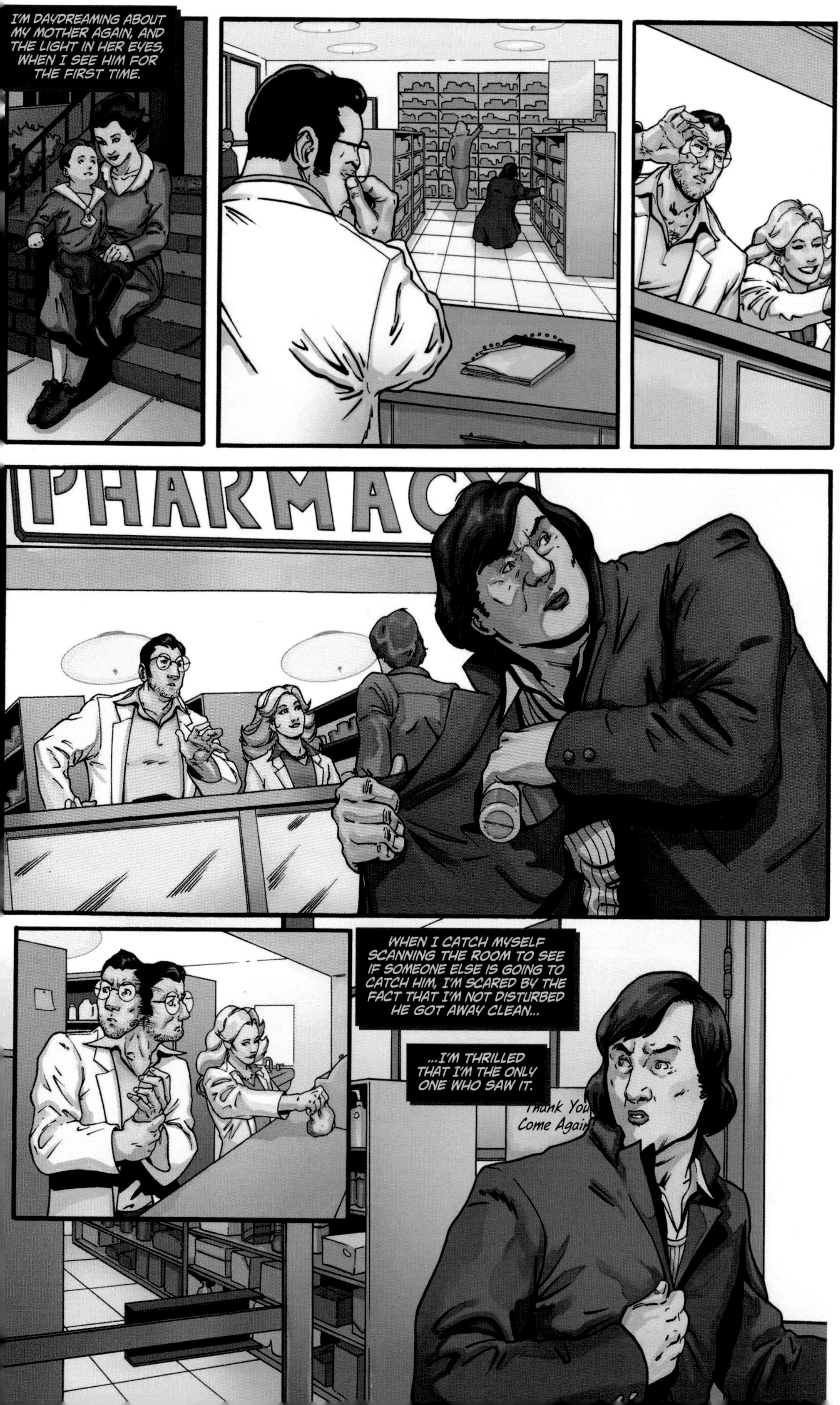
I'M DAYDREAMING ABOUT MY MOTHER AGAIN, AND THE LIGHT IN HER EYES, WHEN I SEE HIM FOR THE FIRST TIME.
PHARMAC
WHEN I CATCH MYSELF SCANNING THE ROOM TO SEE IF SOMEONE ELSE IS GOING TO CATCH HIM, I'M SCARED BY THE FACT THAT I'M NOT DISTURBED HE GOT AWAY CLEAN...
...I'M THRILLED THAT I'M THE ONLY ONE WHO SAW IT.
Thank You
Come Again

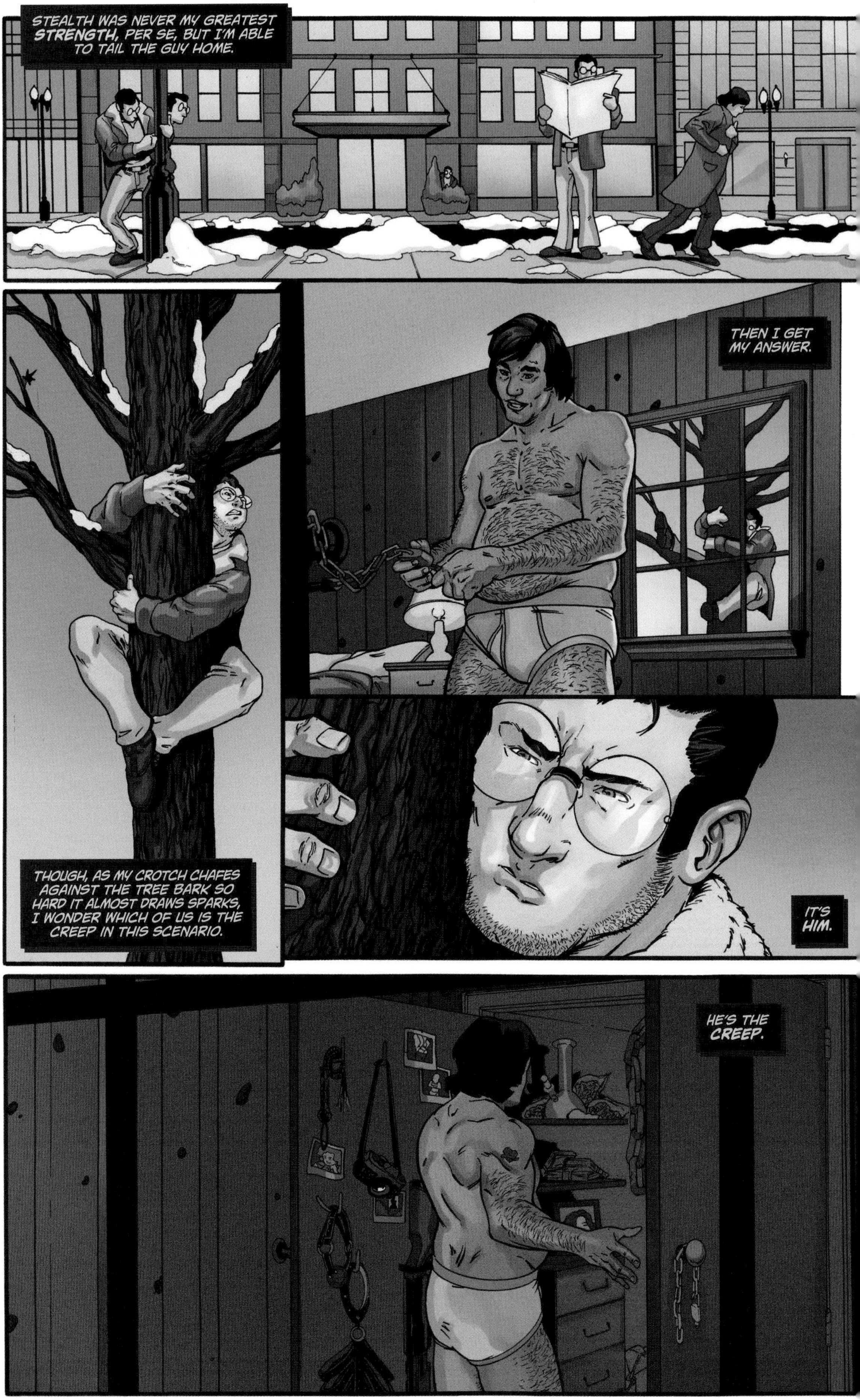
STEALTH WAS NEVER MY GREATEST STRENGTH, PER SE, BUT I'M ABLE TO TAIL THE GUY HOME.
THOUGH, AS MY CROTCH CHAFES AGAINST THE TREE BARK SO HARD IT ALMOST DRAWS SPARKS, I WONDER WHICH OF US IS THE CREEP IN THIS SCENARIO.
THEN I GET MY ANSWER.
IT'S HIM.
HE'S THE CREEP.

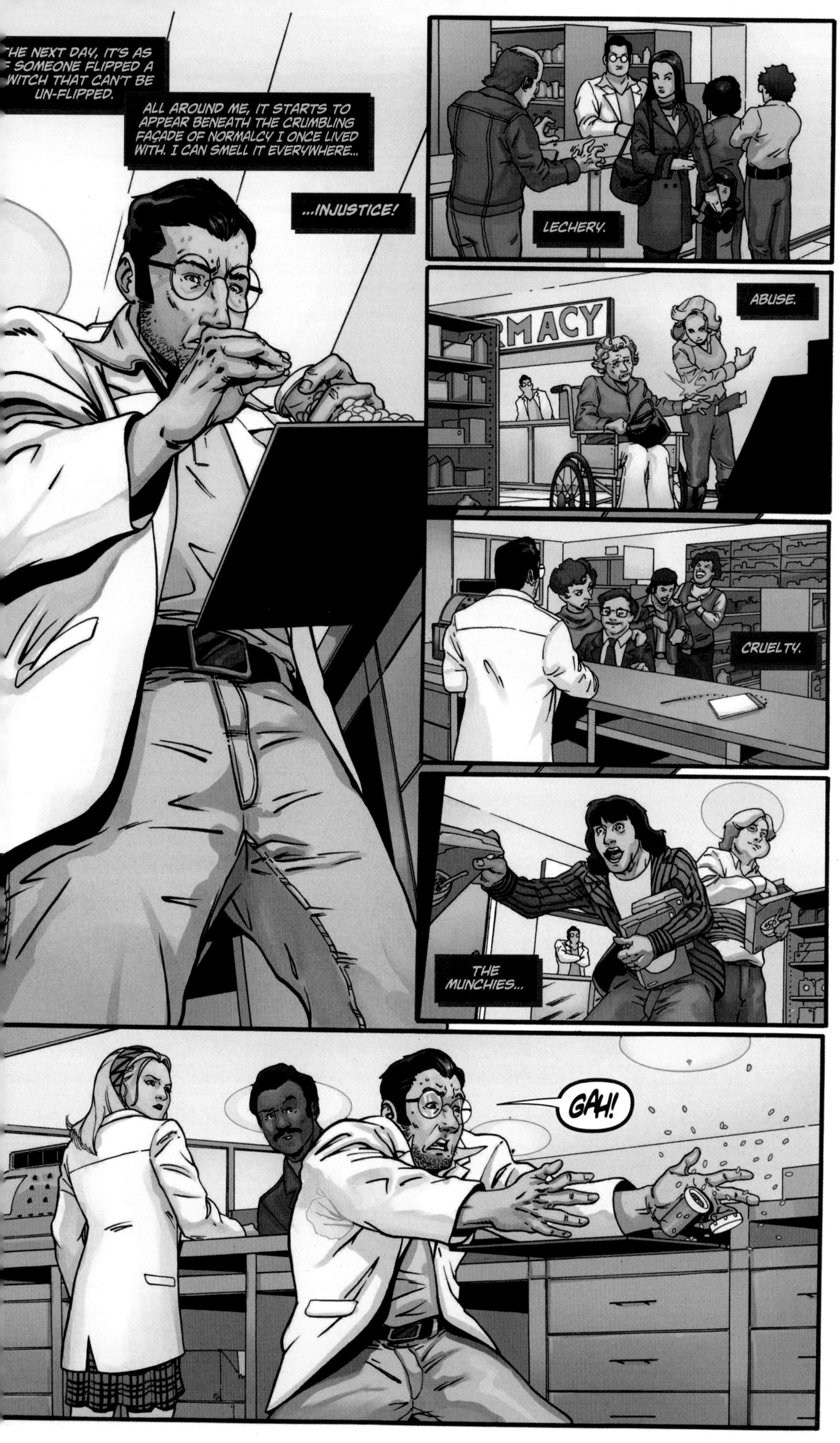
THE NEXT DAY, IT'S AS IF SOMEONE FLIPPED A SWITCH THAT CAN'T BE UN-FLIPPED.
ALL AROUND ME, IT STARTS TO APPEAR BENEATH THE CRUMBLING FAÇADE OF NORMALCY I ONCE LIVED WITH. I CAN SMELL IT EVERYWHERE...
...INJUSTICE!
LECHERY.
RMACY
ABUSE.
CRUELTY.
THE MUNCHIES...
GAH!

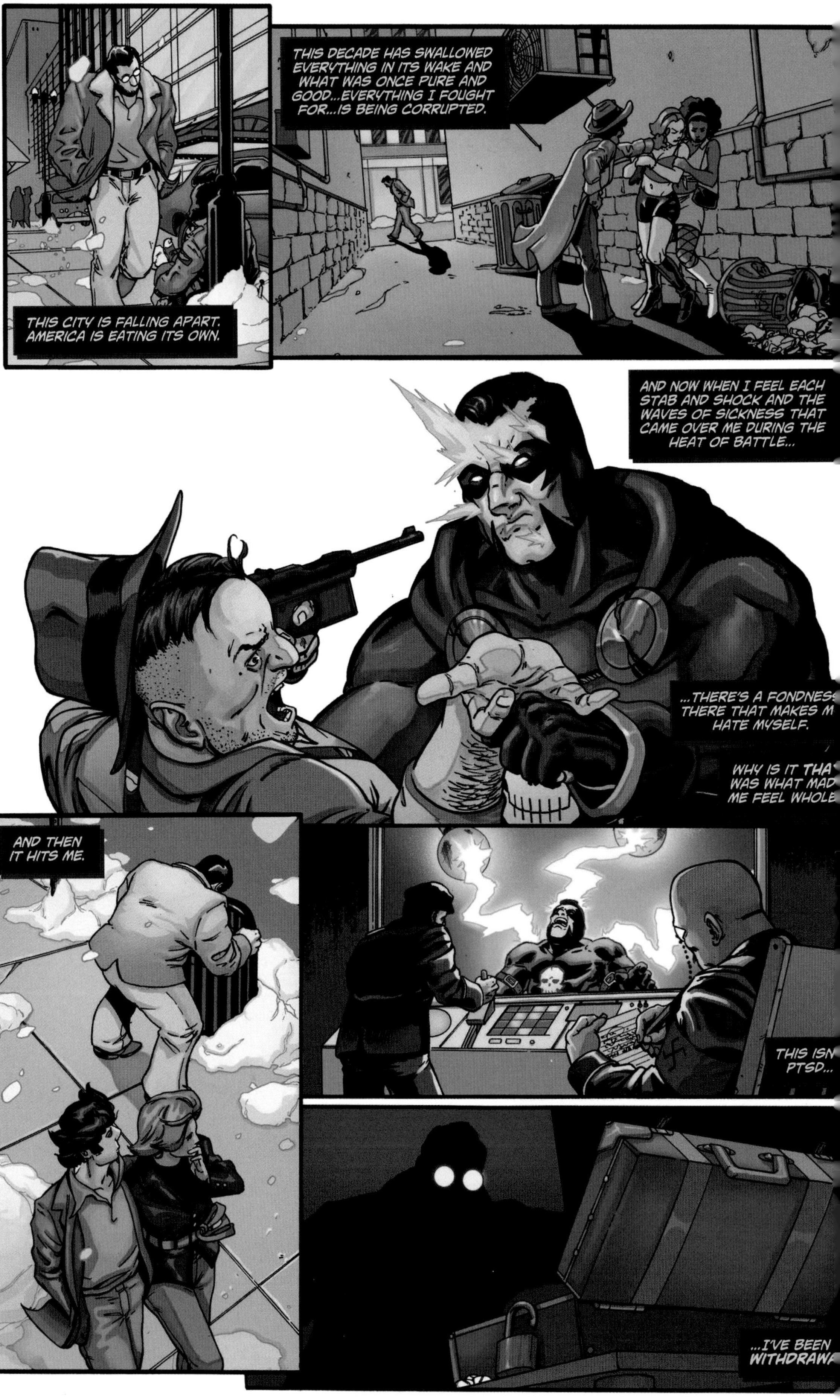

THIS CITY IS FALLING APART. AMERICA IS EATING ITS OWN.
THIS DECADE HAS SWALLOWED EVERYTHING IN ITS WAKE AND WHAT WAS ONCE PURE AND GOOD...EVERYTHING I FOUGHT FOR...IS BEING CORRUPTED.
AND NOW WHEN I FEEL EACH STAB AND SHOCK AND THE WAVES OF SICKNESS THAT CAME OVER ME DURING THE HEAT OF BATTLE...
...THERE'S A FONDNESS THERE THAT MAKES M HATE MYSELF.
WHY IS IT THA WAS WHAT MAD ME FEEL WHOLE
AND THEN IT HITS ME.
THIS ISN PTSD...
...I'VE BEEN WITHDRAWA

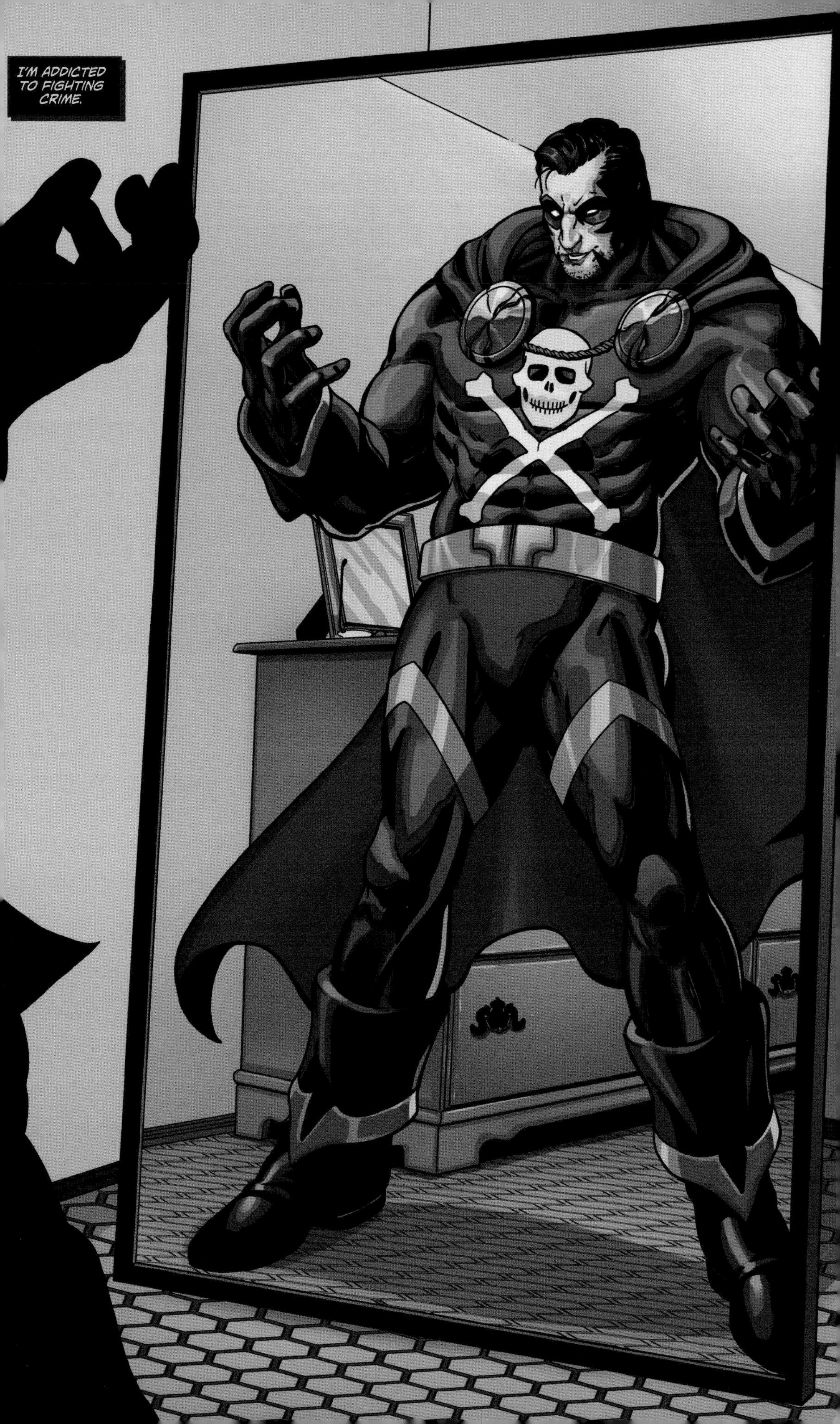
I'M ADDICTED TO FIGHTING CRIME.

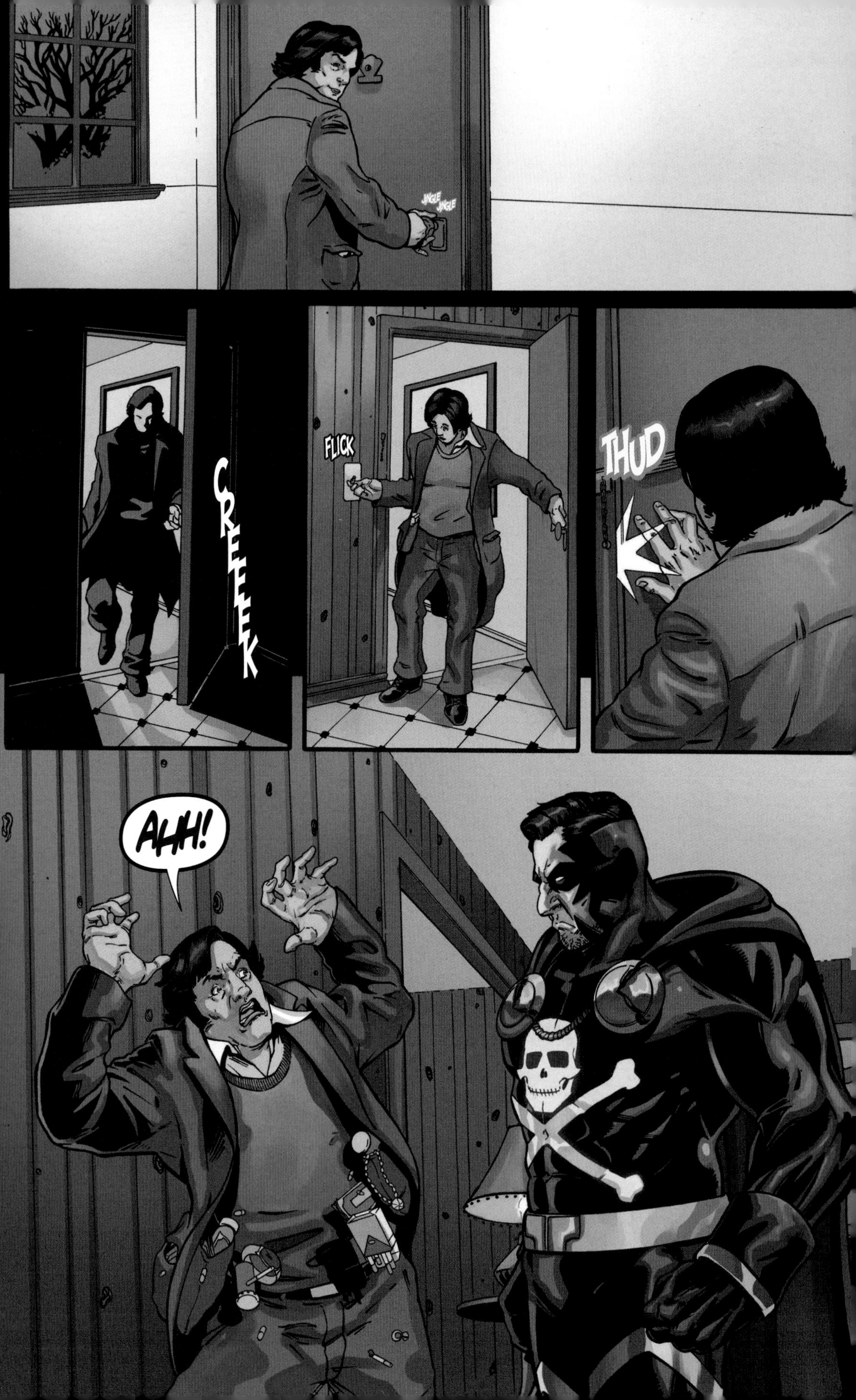
JINGLE JINGLE
CREEEEK
FLICK
THUD
AHH!

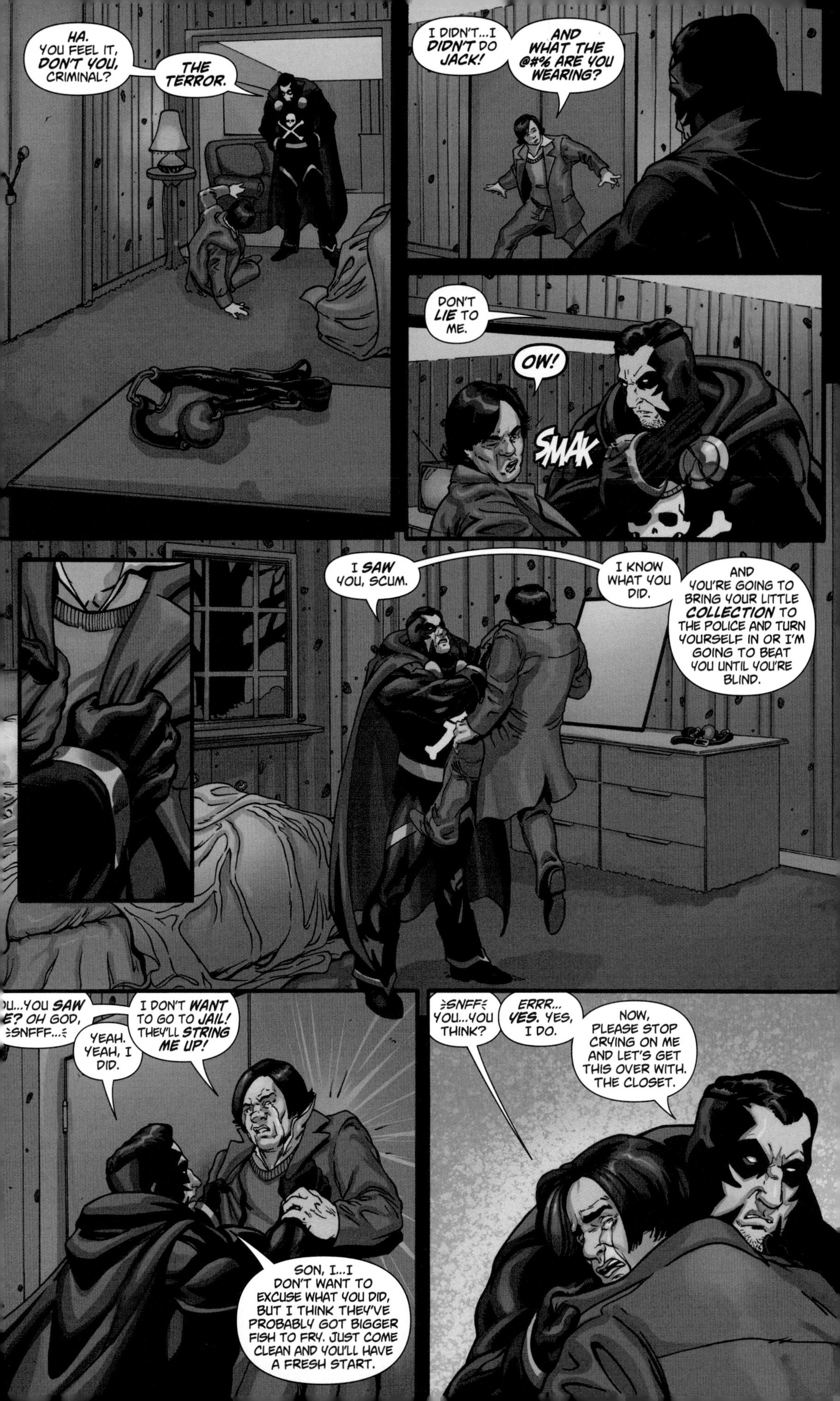

HA. YOU FEEL IT, DON'T YOU, CRIMINAL?
THE TERROR.
I DIDN'T...I DIDN'T DO JACK!
AND WHAT THE @#% ARE YOU WEARING?
DON'T LIE TO ME.
OW!
SMAK
I SAW YOU, SCUM.
I KNOW WHAT YOU DID.
AND YOU'RE GOING TO BRING YOUR LITTLE COLLECTION TO THE POLICE AND TURN YOURSELF IN OR I'M GOING TO BEAT YOU UNTIL YOU'RE BLIND.
YEAH. YEAH, I DID.
I DON'T WANT TO GO TO JAIL! THEY'LL STRING ME UP!
SON, I...I DON'T WANT TO EXCUSE WHAT YOU DID, BUT I THINK THEY'VE PROBABLY GOT BIGGER FISH TO FRY. JUST COME CLEAN AND YOU'LL HAVE A FRESH START.
YOU...YOU THINK?
ERRR... YES. YES, I DO.
NOW, PLEASE STOP CRYING ON ME AND LET'S GET THIS OVER WITH. THE CLOSET.

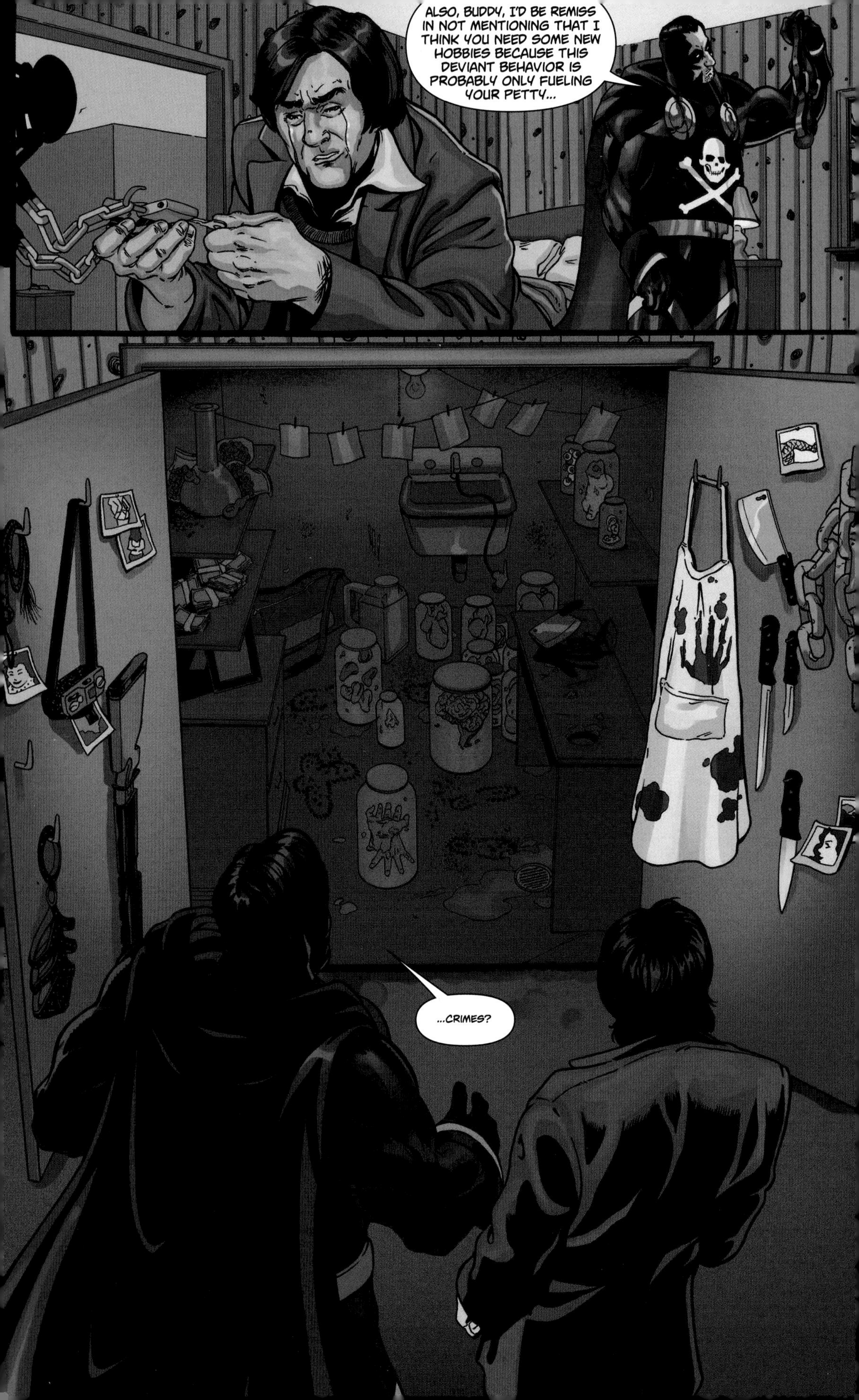
ALSO, BUDDY, I'D BE REMISS IN NOT MENTIONING THAT I THINK YOU NEED SOME NEW HOBBIES BECAUSE THIS DEVIANT BEHAVIOR IS PROBABLY ONLY FUELING YOUR PETTY...
...CRIMES?

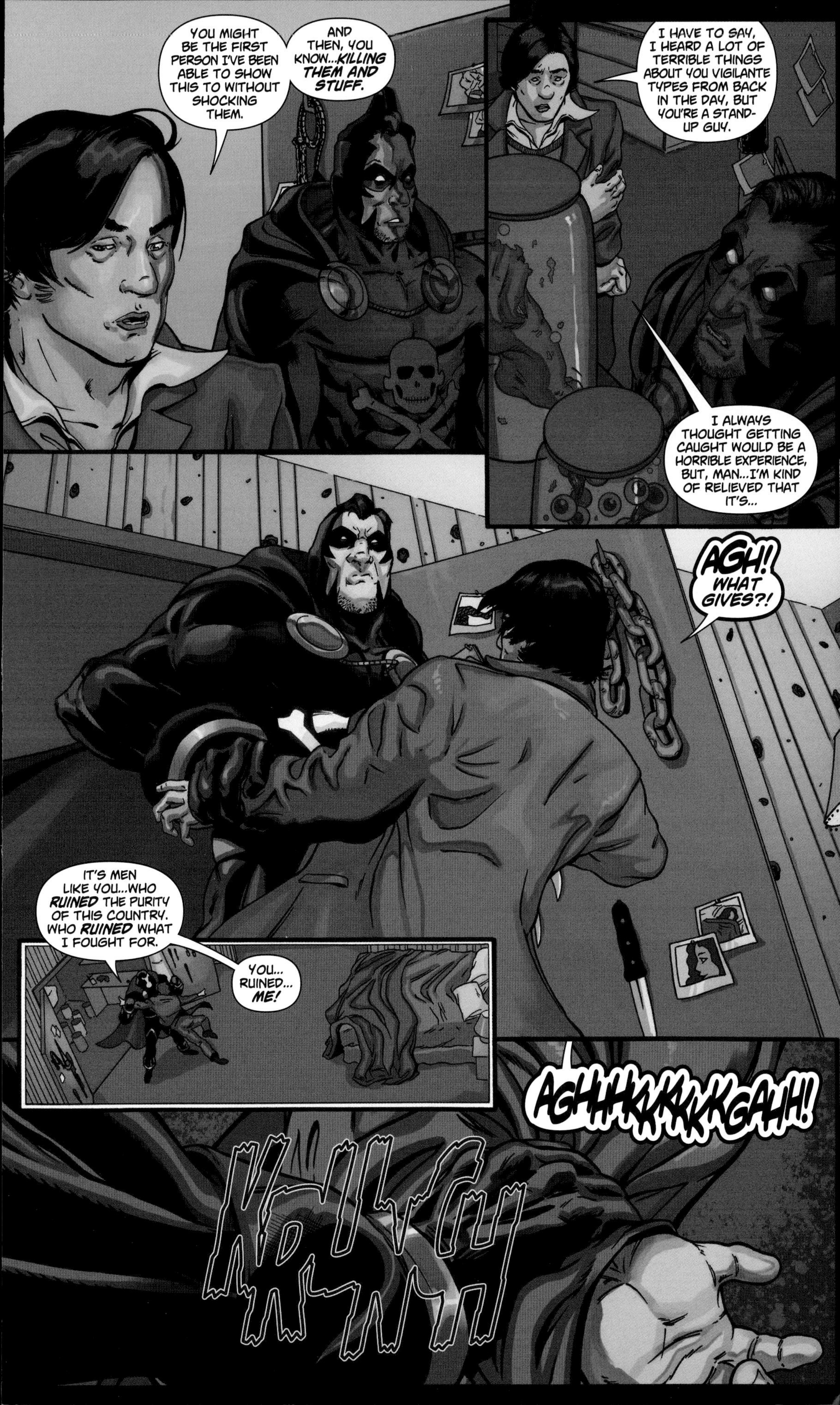
YOU MIGHT BE THE FIRST PERSON I'VE BEEN ABLE TO SHOW THIS TO WITHOUT SHOCKING THEM.
AND THEN, YOU KNOW...KILLING THEM AND STUFF.
I HAVE TO SAY, I HEARD A LOT OF TERRIBLE THINGS ABOUT YOU VIGILANTE TYPES FROM BACK IN THE DAY, BUT YOU'RE A STAND-UP GUY.
I ALWAYS THOUGHT GETTING CAUGHT WOULD BE A HORRIBLE EXPERIENCE, BUT, MAN...I'M KIND OF RELIEVED THAT IT'S...
AGH! WHAT GIVES?!
IT'S MEN LIKE YOU...WHO RUINED THE PURITY OF THIS COUNTRY. WHO RUINED WHAT I FOUGHT FOR.
YOU... RUINED... ME!
AGHHHKKKKKGAHH!

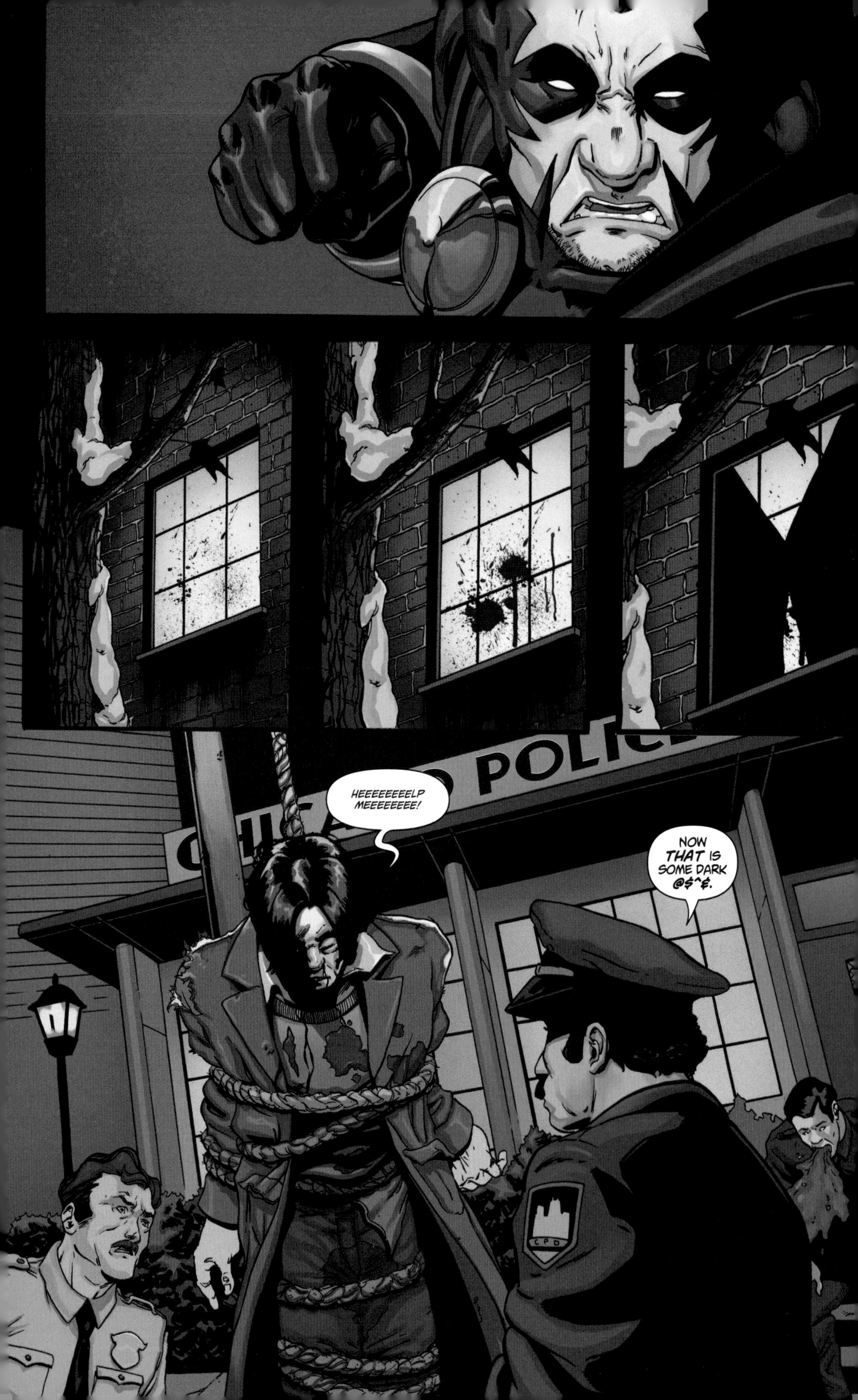
HEEEEEEEELP MEEEEEEEE!
NOW THAT IS SOME DARK @$^&.
POLIC

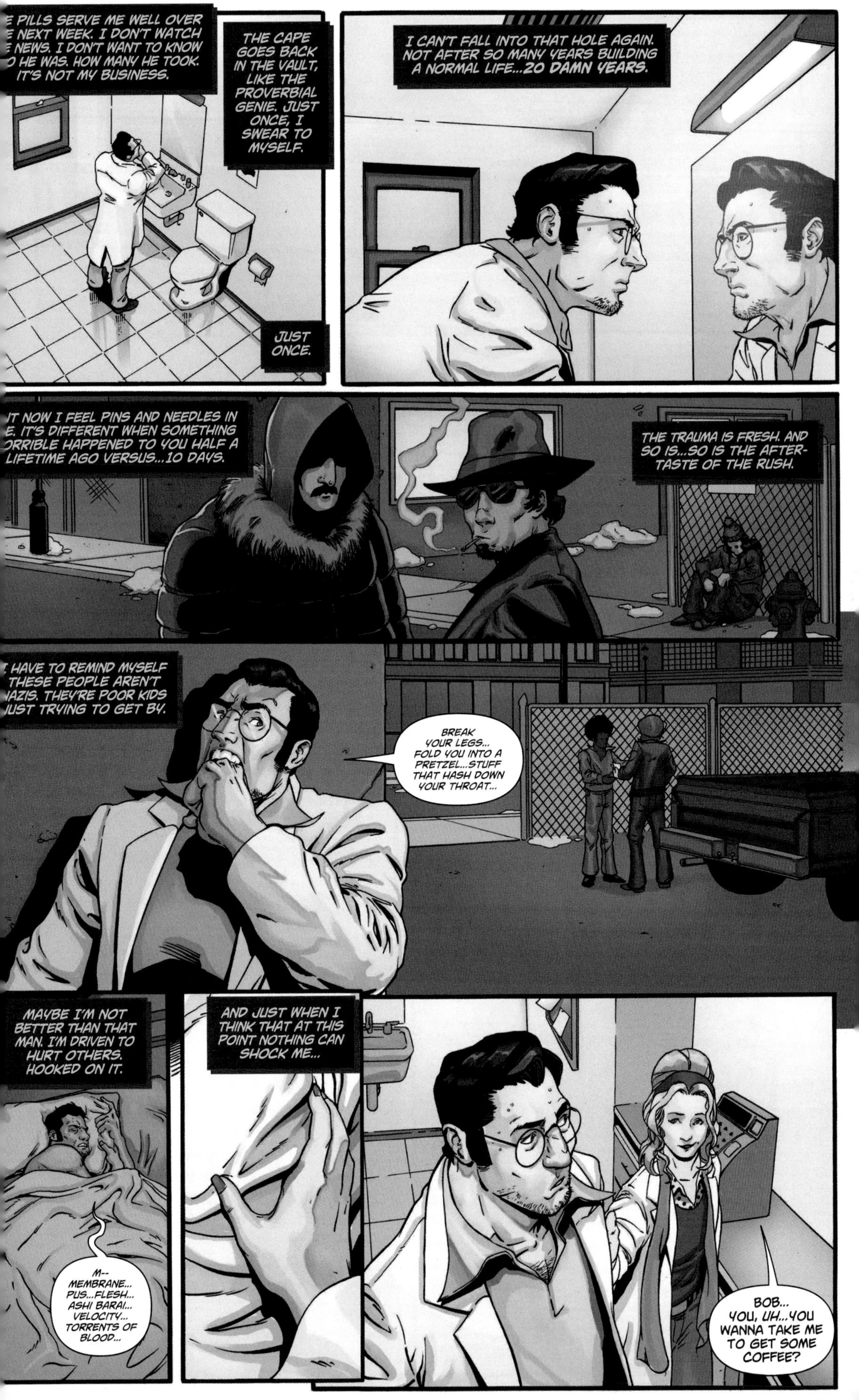

E PILLS SERVE ME WELL OVER E NEXT WEEK. I DON'T WATCH E NEWS. I DON'T WANT TO KNOW O HE WAS. HOW MANY HE TOOK. IT'S NOT MY BUSINESS.
THE CAPE GOES BACK IN THE VAULT, LIKE THE PROVERBIAL GENIE. JUST ONCE, I SWEAR TO MYSELF.
JUST ONCE.
I CAN'T FALL INTO THAT HOLE AGAIN. NOT AFTER SO MANY YEARS BUILDING A NORMAL LIFE...20 DAMN YEARS.
IT NOW I FEEL PINS AND NEEDLES IN E. IT'S DIFFERENT WHEN SOMETHING ORRIBLE HAPPENED TO YOU HALF A LIFETIME AGO VERSUS...10 DAYS.
THE TRAUMA IS FRESH. AND SO IS...SO IS THE AFTER-TASTE OF THE RUSH.
HAVE TO REMIND MYSELF THESE PEOPLE AREN'T NAZIS. THEY'RE POOR KIDS JUST TRYING TO GET BY.
BREAK YOUR LEGS... FOLD YOU INTO A PRETZEL...STUFF THAT HASH DOWN YOUR THROAT...
MAYBE I'M NOT BETTER THAN THAT MAN. I'M DRIVEN TO HURT OTHERS. HOOKED ON IT.
M-- MEMBRANE... PUS...FLESH... ASHI BARAI... VELOCITY... TORRENTS OF BLOOD...
AND JUST WHEN I THINK THAT AT THIS POINT NOTHING CAN SHOCK ME...
BOB... YOU, UH...YOU WANNA TAKE ME TO GET SOME COFFEE?

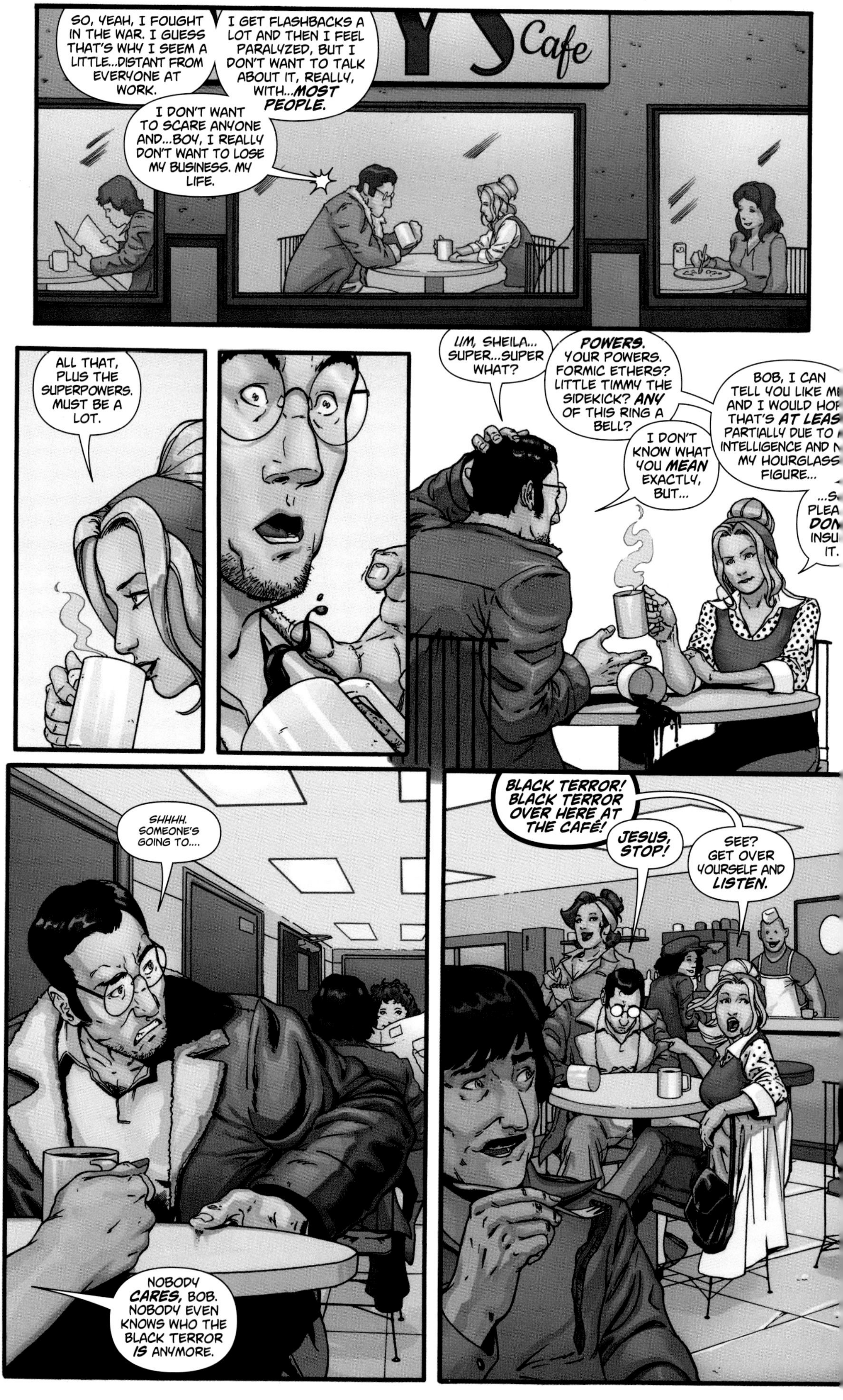

Cafe
SO, YEAH, I FOUGHT IN THE WAR. I GUESS THAT'S WHY I SEEM A LITTLE...DISTANT FROM EVERYONE AT WORK.
I GET FLASHBACKS A LOT AND THEN I FEEL PARALYZED, BUT I DON'T WANT TO TALK ABOUT IT, REALLY, WITH...MOST PEOPLE.
I DON'T WANT TO SCARE ANYONE AND...BOY, I REALLY DON'T WANT TO LOSE MY BUSINESS. MY LIFE.
ALL THAT, PLUS THE SUPERPOWERS. MUST BE A LOT.
UM, SHEILA... SUPER...SUPER WHAT?
POWERS. YOUR POWERS. FORMIC ETHERS? LITTLE TIMMY THE SIDEKICK? ANY OF THIS RING A BELL?
I DON'T KNOW WHAT YOU MEAN EXACTLY, BUT...
SHHHH. SOMEONE'S GOING TO....
NOBODY CARES, BOB. NOBODY EVEN KNOWS WHO THE BLACK TERROR IS ANYMORE.
BLACK TERROR! BLACK TERROR OVER HERE AT THE CAFÉ!
JESUS, STOP!
SEE? GET OVER YOURSELF AND LISTEN.

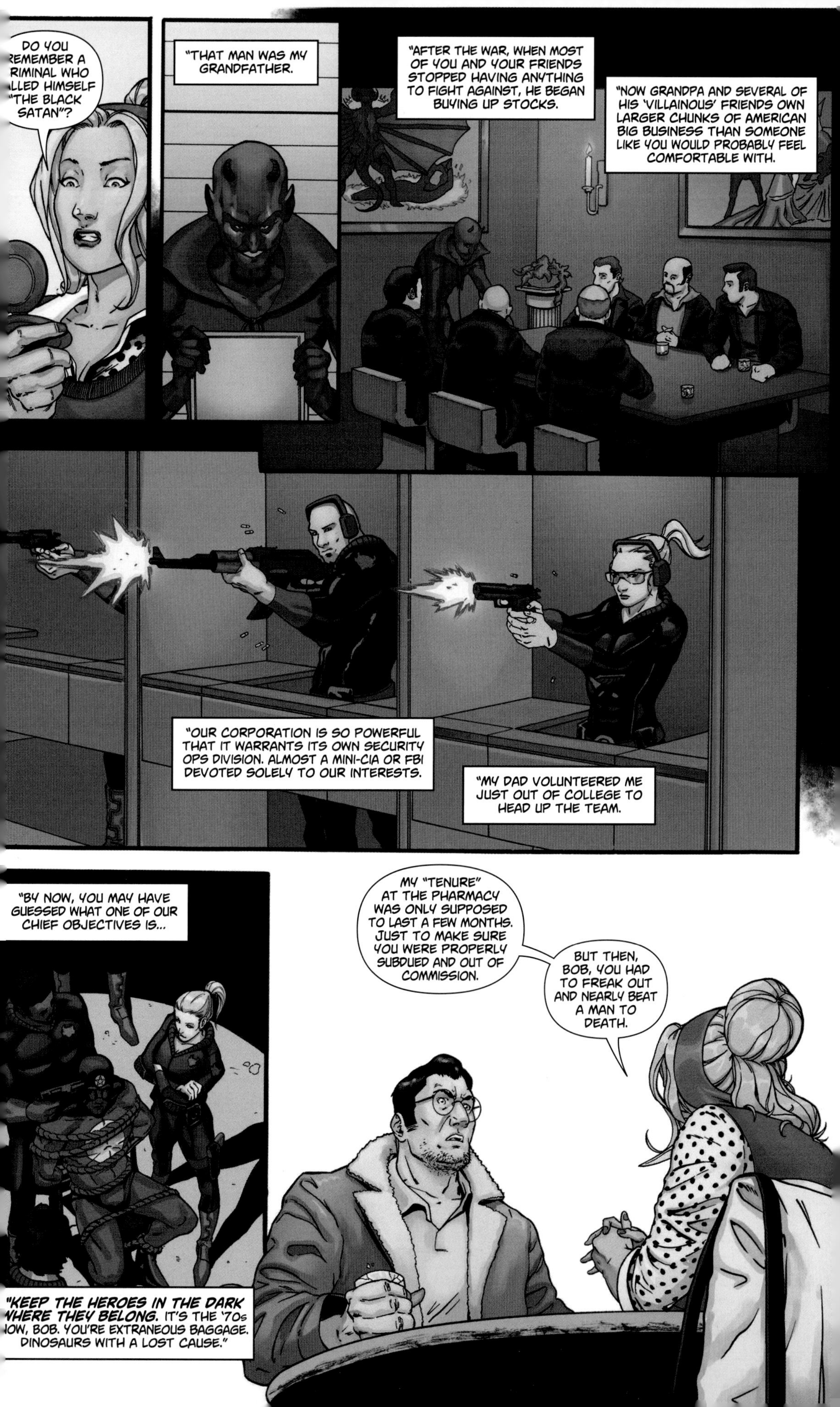

DO YOU REMEMBER A CRIMINAL WHO CALLED HIMSELF "THE BLACK SATAN"?
"THAT MAN WAS MY GRANDFATHER.
"AFTER THE WAR, WHEN MOST OF YOU AND YOUR FRIENDS STOPPED HAVING ANYTHING TO FIGHT AGAINST, HE BEGAN BUYING UP STOCKS.
"NOW GRANDPA AND SEVERAL OF HIS 'VILLAINOUS' FRIENDS OWN LARGER CHUNKS OF AMERICAN BIG BUSINESS THAN SOMEONE LIKE YOU WOULD PROBABLY FEEL COMFORTABLE WITH.
"OUR CORPORATION IS SO POWERFUL THAT IT WARRANTS ITS OWN SECURITY OPS DIVISION. ALMOST A MINI-CIA OR FBI DEVOTED SOLELY TO OUR INTERESTS.
"MY DAD VOLUNTEERED ME JUST OUT OF COLLEGE TO HEAD UP THE TEAM.
"BY NOW, YOU MAY HAVE GUESSED WHAT ONE OF OUR CHIEF OBJECTIVES IS...
"KEEP THE HEROES IN THE DARK WHERE THEY BELONG. IT'S THE '70s NOW, BOB. YOU'RE EXTRANEOUS BAGGAGE. DINOSAURS WITH A LOST CAUSE."
MY "TENURE" AT THE PHARMACY WAS ONLY SUPPOSED TO LAST A FEW MONTHS. JUST TO MAKE SURE YOU WERE PROPERLY SUBDUED AND OUT OF COMMISSION.
BUT THEN, BOB, YOU HAD TO FREAK OUT AND NEARLY BEAT A MAN TO DEATH.

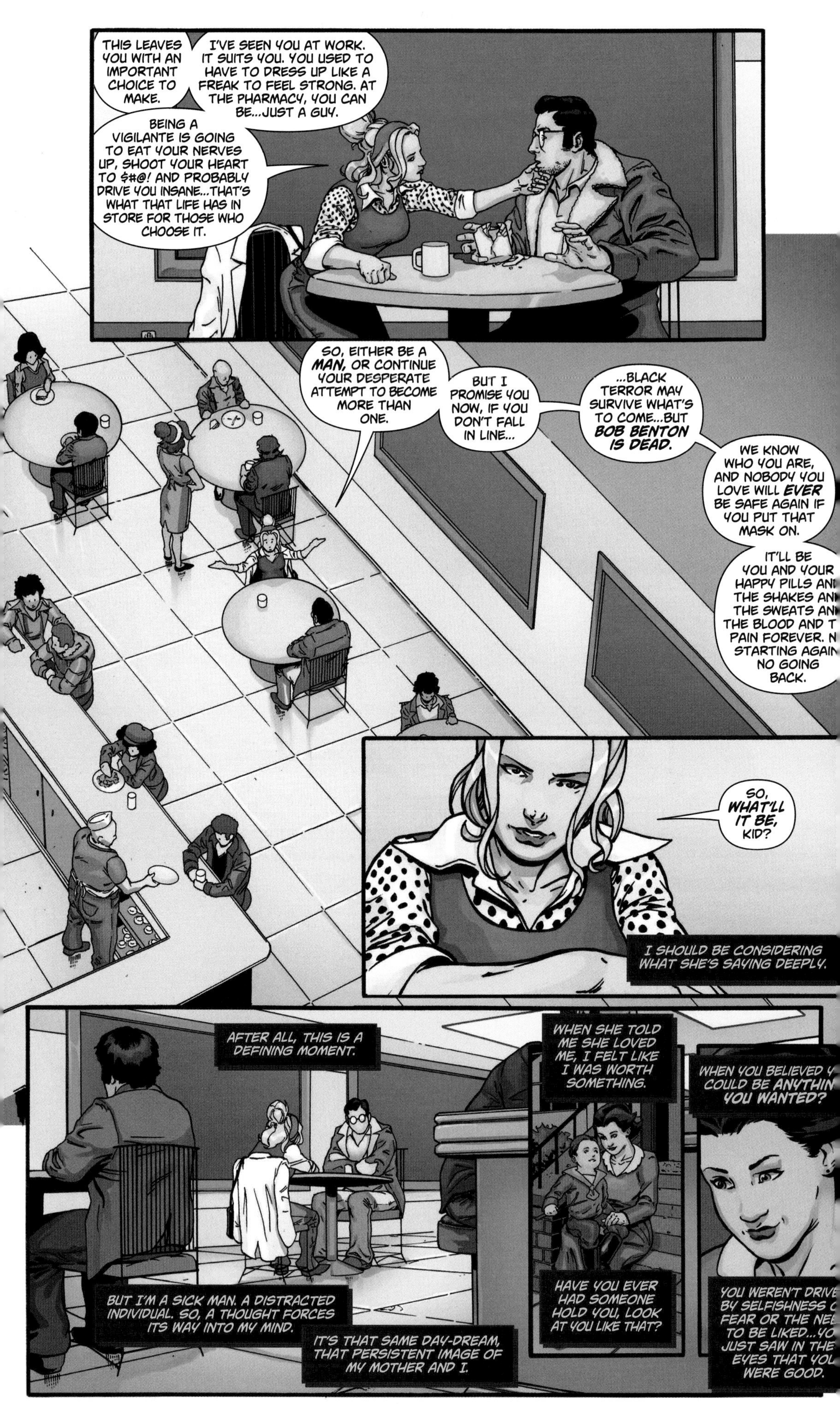

THIS LEAVES YOU WITH AN IMPORTANT CHOICE TO MAKE.
I'VE SEEN YOU AT WORK. IT SUITS YOU. YOU USED TO HAVE TO DRESS UP LIKE A FREAK TO FEEL STRONG. AT THE PHARMACY, YOU CAN BE...JUST A GUY.
BEING A VIGILANTE IS GOING TO EAT YOUR NERVES UP, SHOOT YOUR HEART TO $#@! AND PROBABLY DRIVE YOU INSANE...THAT'S WHAT THAT LIFE HAS IN STORE FOR THOSE WHO CHOOSE IT.
SO, EITHER BE A MAN, OR CONTINUE YOUR DESPERATE ATTEMPT TO BECOME MORE THAN ONE.
BUT I PROMISE YOU NOW, IF YOU DON'T FALL IN LINE...
...BLACK TERROR MAY SURVIVE WHAT'S TO COME...BUT BOB BENTON IS DEAD.
WE KNOW WHO YOU ARE, AND NOBODY YOU LOVE WILL EVER BE SAFE AGAIN IF YOU PUT THAT MASK ON.
IT'LL BE YOU AND YOUR HAPPY PILLS AN THE SHAKES AN THE SWEATS AN THE BLOOD AND T PAIN FOREVER. N STARTING AGAIN NO GOING BACK.
SO, WHAT'LL IT BE, KID?
I SHOULD BE CONSIDERING WHAT SHE'S SAYING DEEPLY.
AFTER ALL, THIS IS A DEFINING MOMENT.
BUT I'M A SICK MAN. A DISTRACTED INDIVIDUAL. SO, A THOUGHT FORCES ITS WAY INTO MY MIND.
IT'S THAT SAME DAY-DREAM, THAT PERSISTENT IMAGE OF MY MOTHER AND I.
WHEN SHE TOLD ME SHE LOVED ME, I FELT LIKE I WAS WORTH SOMETHING.
HAVE YOU EVER HAD SOMEONE HOLD YOU, LOOK AT YOU LIKE THAT?
WHEN YOU BELIEVED Y COULD BE ANYTHIN YOU WANTED?
YOU WEREN'T DRIVE BY SELFISHNESS FEAR OR THE NE TO BE LIKED...YO JUST SAW IN THE EYES THAT YOU WERE GOOD.

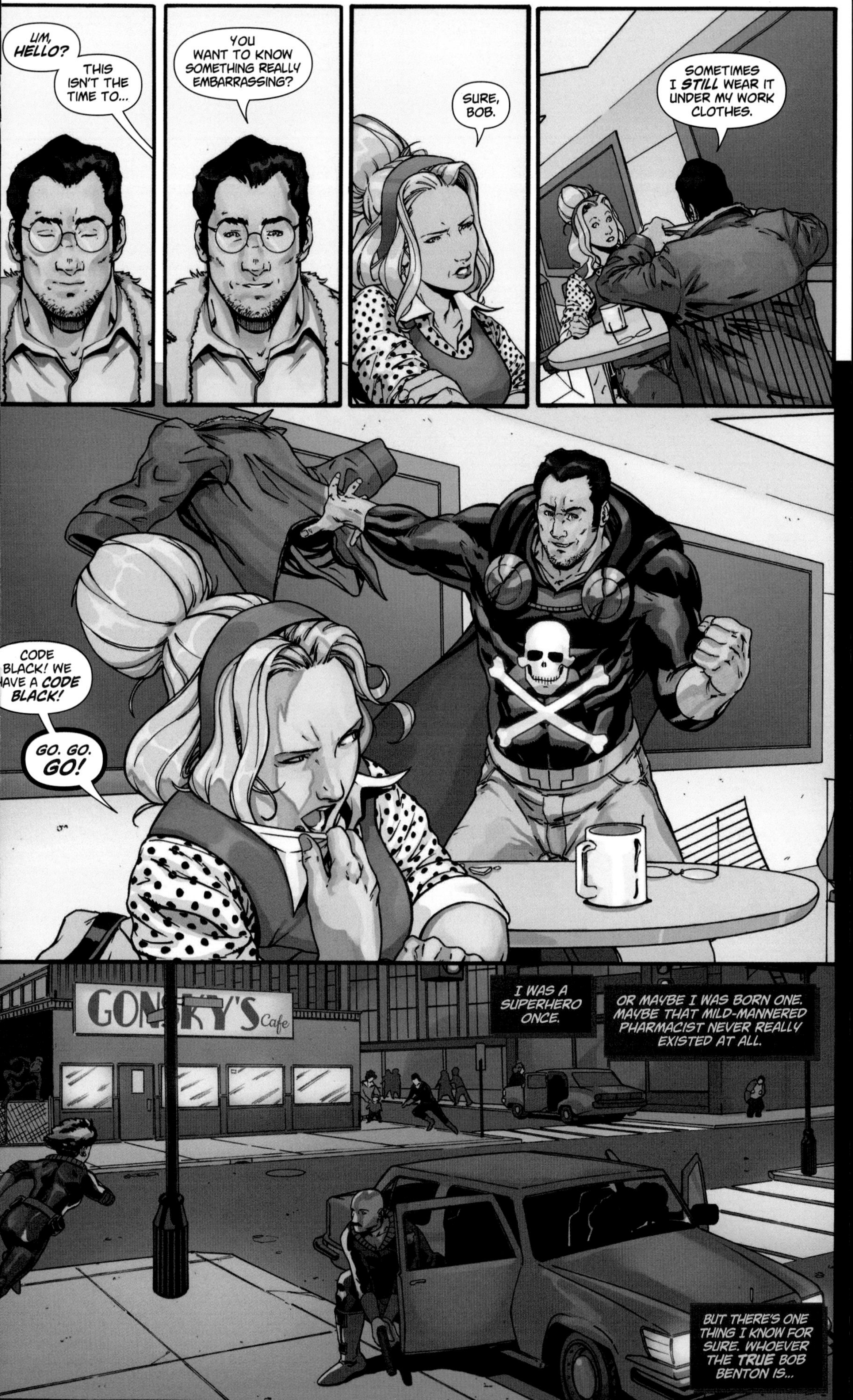
UM, HELLO?
THIS ISN'T THE TIME TO...
YOU WANT TO KNOW SOMETHING REALLY EMBARRASSING?
SURE, BOB.
SOMETIMES I STILL WEAR IT UNDER MY WORK CLOTHES.
CODE BLACK! WE HAVE A CODE BLACK!
GO. GO. GO!
GONSKY'S Cafe
I WAS A SUPERHERO ONCE.
OR MAYBE I WAS BORN ONE. MAYBE THAT MILD-MANNERED PHARMACIST NEVER REALLY EXISTED AT ALL.
BUT THERE'S ONE THING I KNOW FOR SURE. WHOEVER THE TRUE BOB BENTON IS...

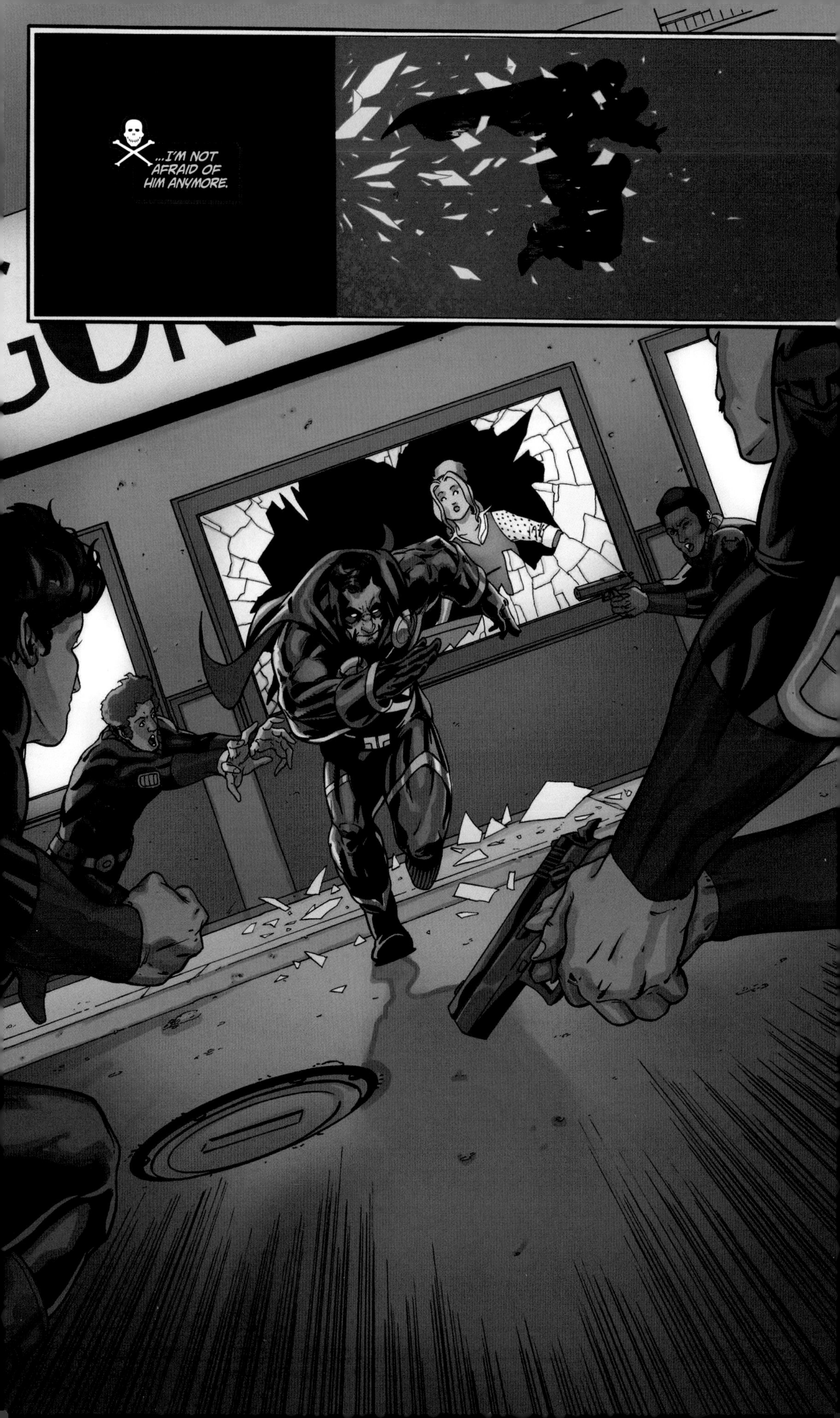
...I'M NOT AFRAID OF HIM ANYMORE.

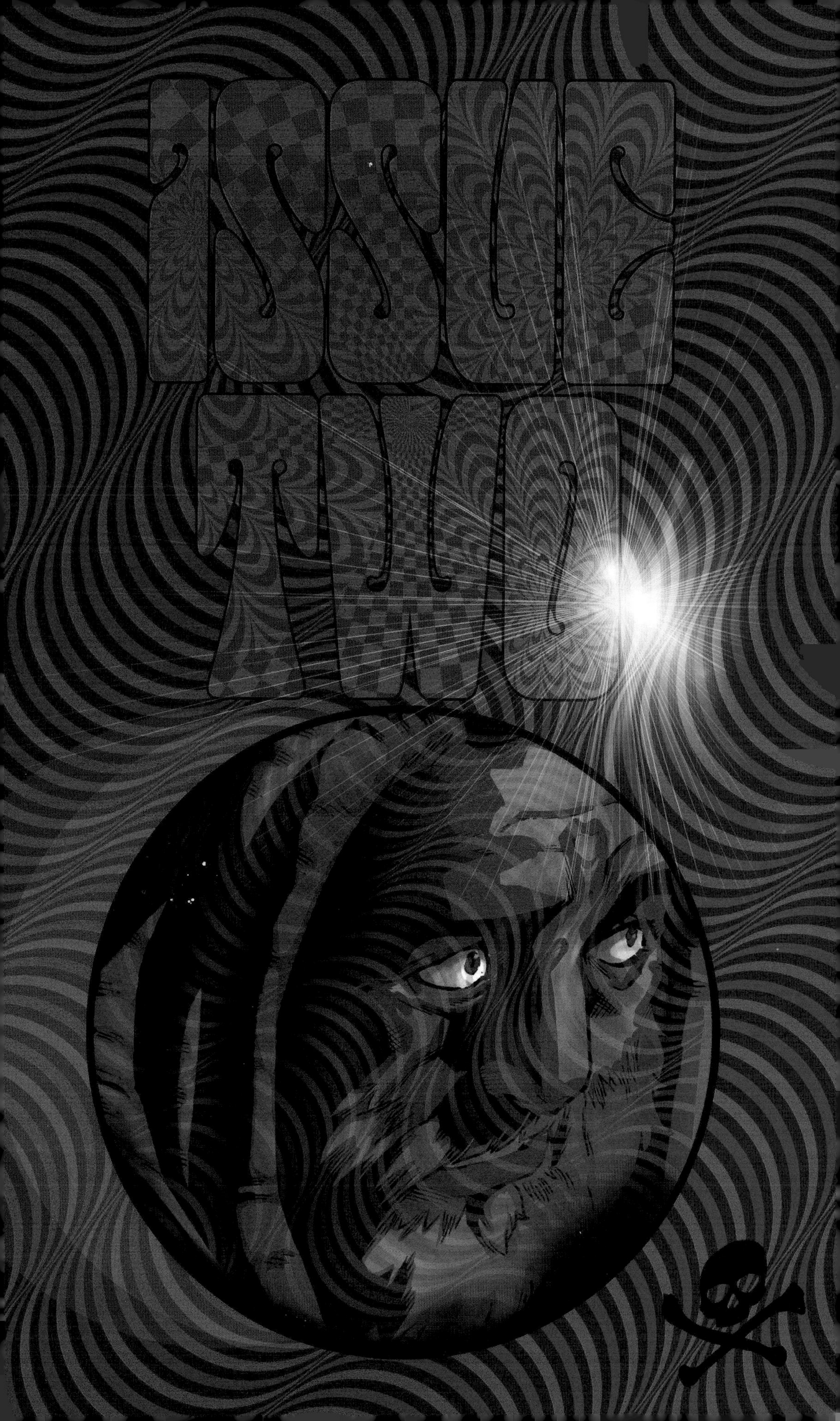
ISSUE
TWO

ISSUE 2
COVER ART BY RAHZZAH

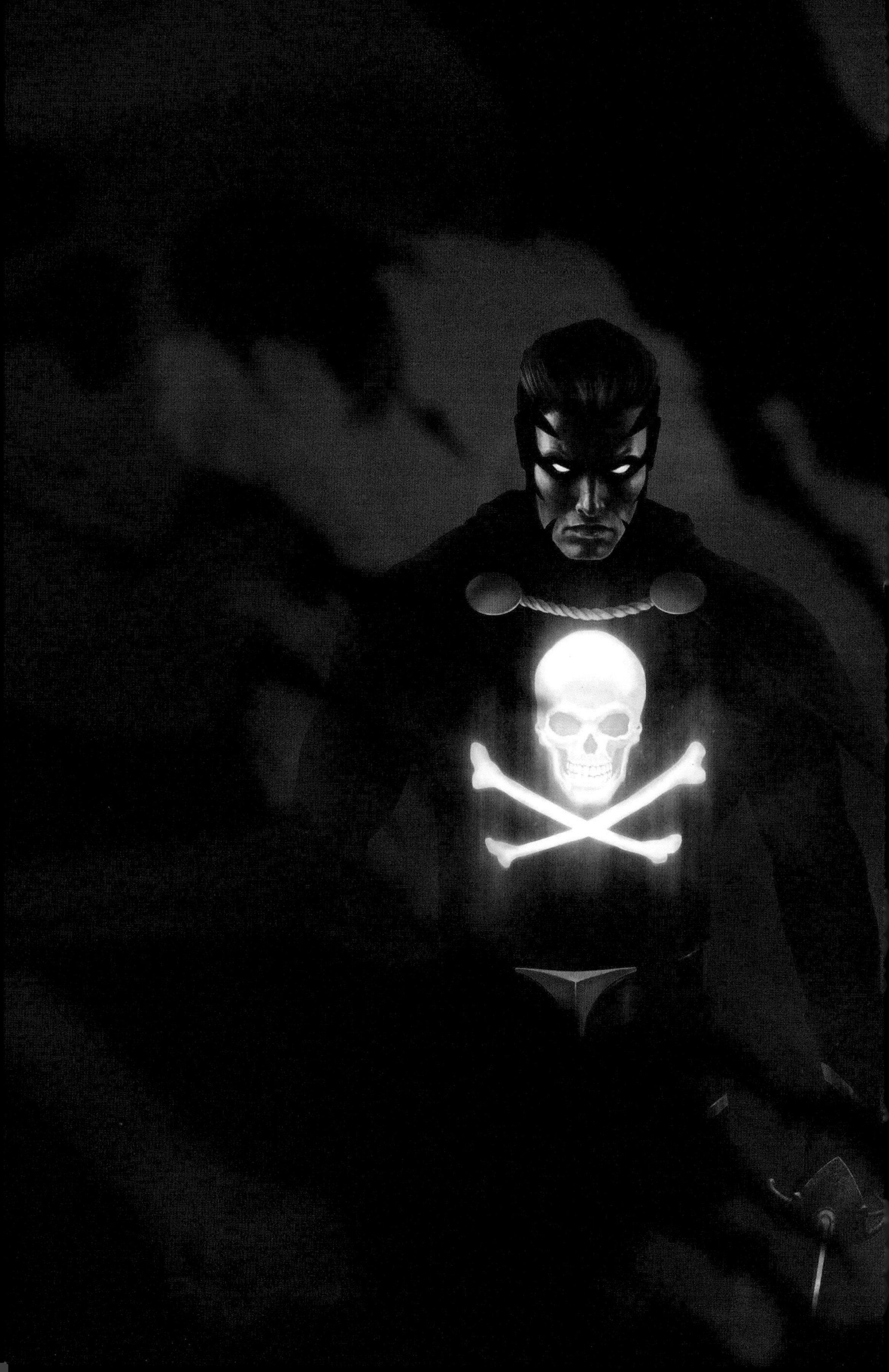

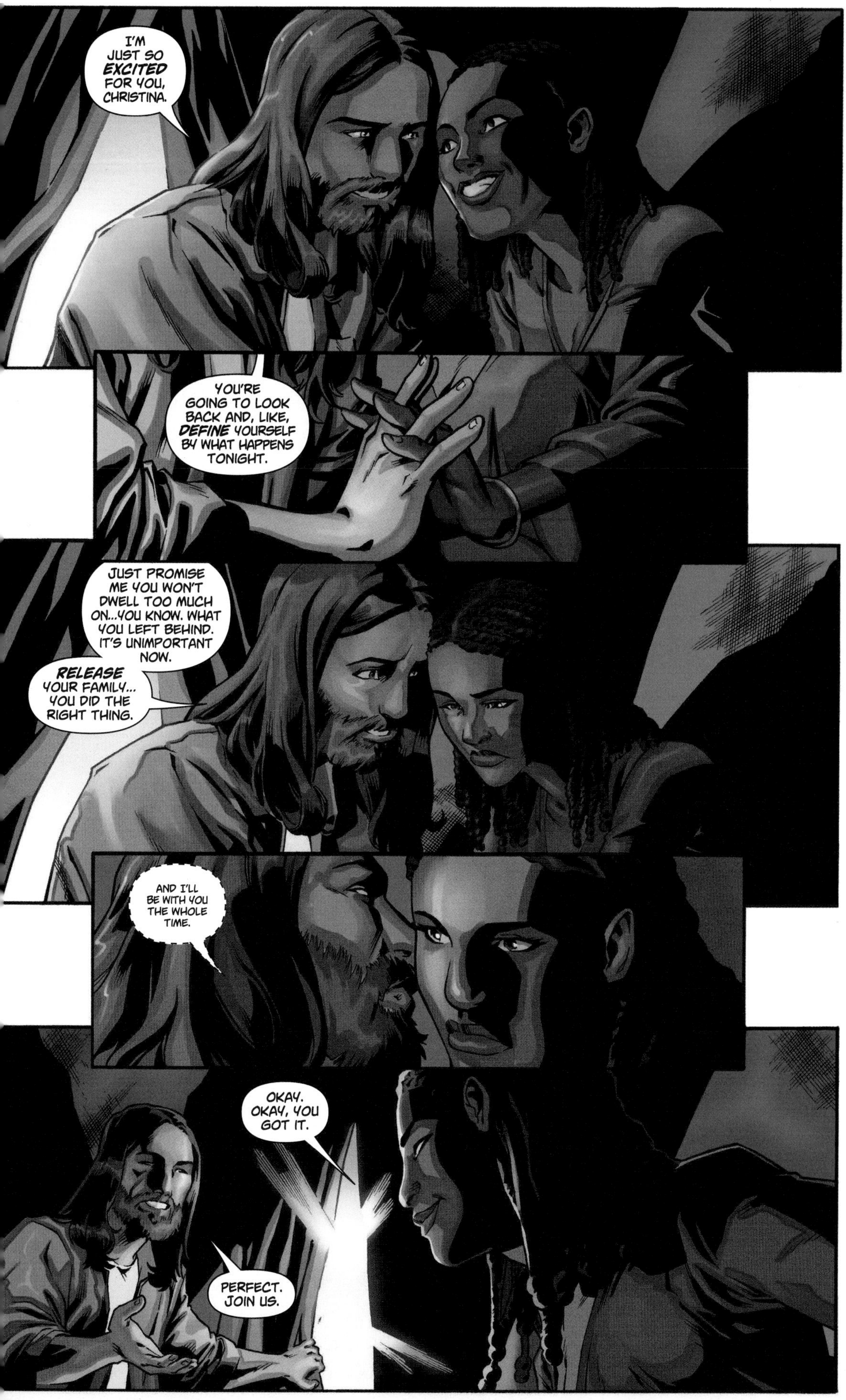
I'M JUST SO EXCITED FOR YOU, CHRISTINA.
YOU'RE GOING TO LOOK BACK AND, LIKE, DEFINE YOURSELF BY WHAT HAPPENS TONIGHT.
JUST PROMISE ME YOU WON'T DWELL TOO MUCH ON...YOU KNOW. WHAT YOU LEFT BEHIND. IT'S UNIMPORTANT NOW.
RELEASE YOUR FAMILY... YOU DID THE RIGHT THING.
AND I'LL BE WITH YOU THE WHOLE TIME.
OKAY. OKAY, YOU GOT IT.
PERFECT. JOIN US.

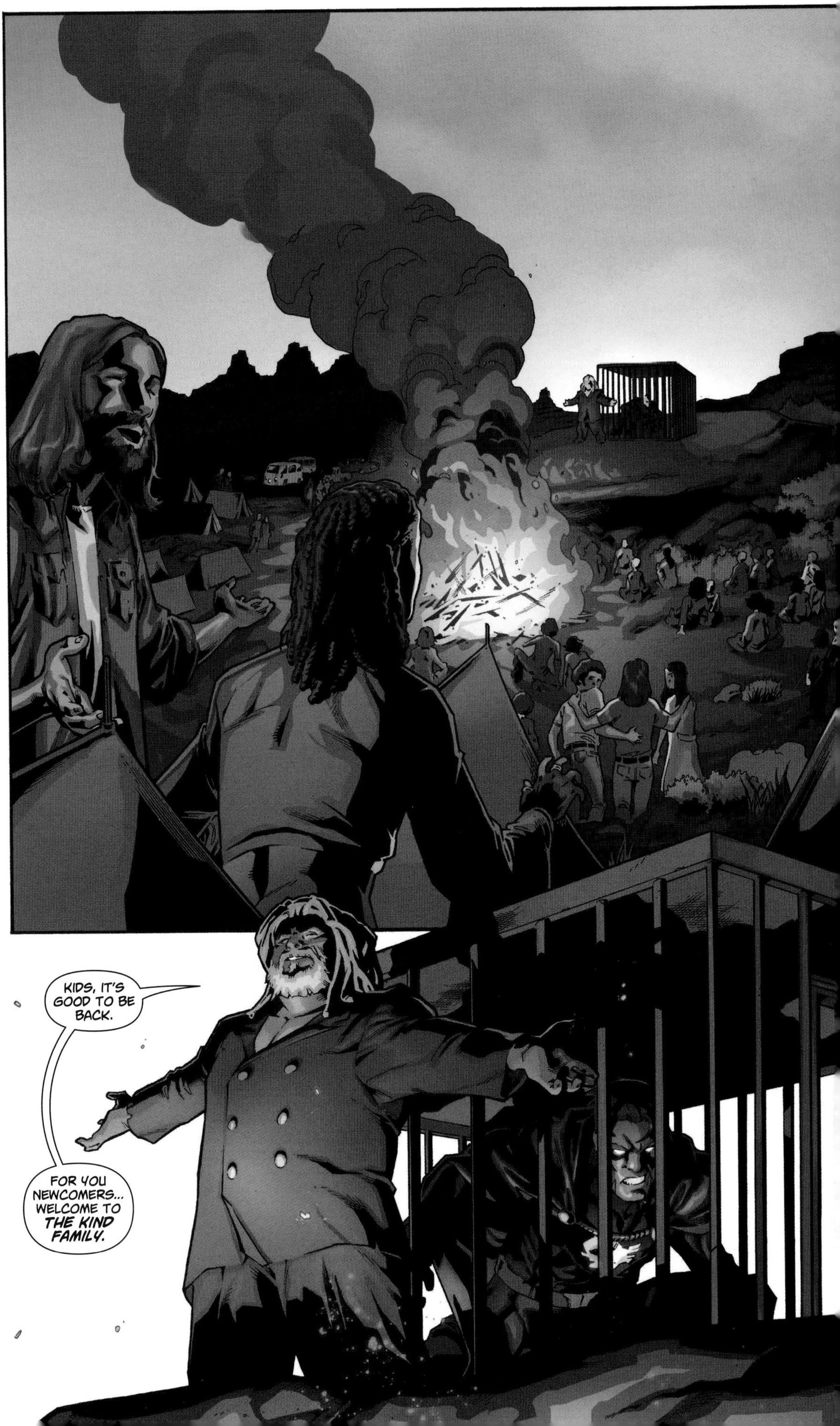
KIDS, IT'S GOOD TO BE BACK.
FOR YOU NEWCOMERS... WELCOME TO THE KIND FAMILY.

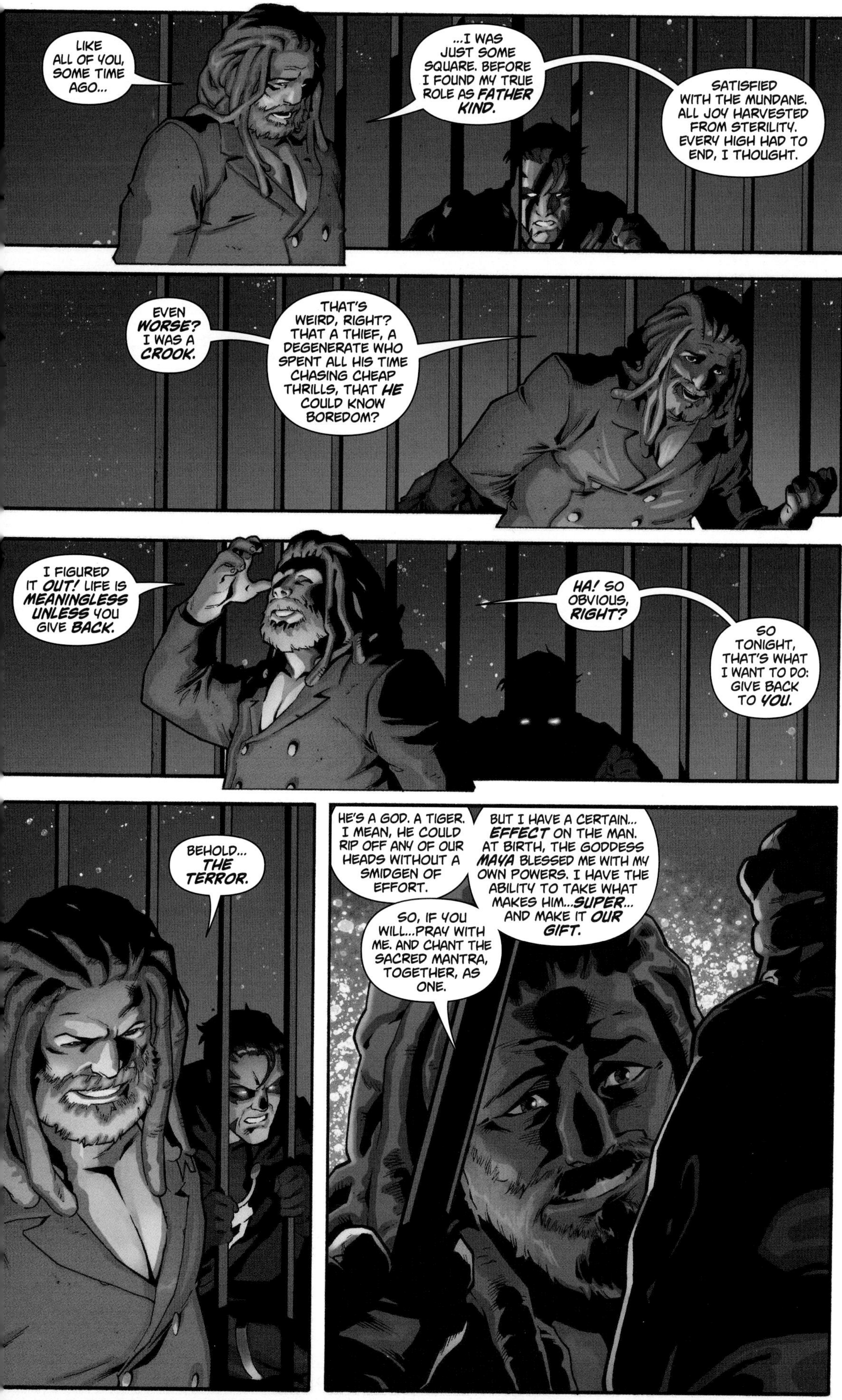
LIKE ALL OF YOU, SOME TIME AGO...
...I WAS JUST SOME SQUARE. BEFORE I FOUND MY TRUE ROLE AS FATHER KIND.
SATISFIED WITH THE MUNDANE. ALL JOY HARVESTED FROM STERILITY. EVERY HIGH HAD TO END, I THOUGHT.
EVEN WORSE? I WAS A CROOK.
THAT'S WEIRD, RIGHT? THAT A THIEF, A DEGENERATE WHO SPENT ALL HIS TIME CHASING CHEAP THRILLS, THAT HE COULD KNOW BOREDOM?
I FIGURED IT OUT! LIFE IS MEANINGLESS UNLESS YOU GIVE BACK.
HA! SO OBVIOUS, RIGHT?
SO TONIGHT, THAT'S WHAT I WANT TO DO: GIVE BACK TO YOU.
BEHOLD... THE TERROR.
HE'S A GOD. A TIGER. I MEAN, HE COULD RIP OFF ANY OF OUR HEADS WITHOUT A SMIDGEN OF EFFORT.
BUT I HAVE A CERTAIN... EFFECT ON THE MAN. AT BIRTH, THE GODDESS MAYA BLESSED ME WITH MY OWN POWERS. I HAVE THE ABILITY TO TAKE WHAT MAKES HIM...SUPER... AND MAKE IT OUR GIFT.
SO, IF YOU WILL...PRAY WITH ME. AND CHANT THE SACRED MANTRA, TOGETHER, AS ONE.

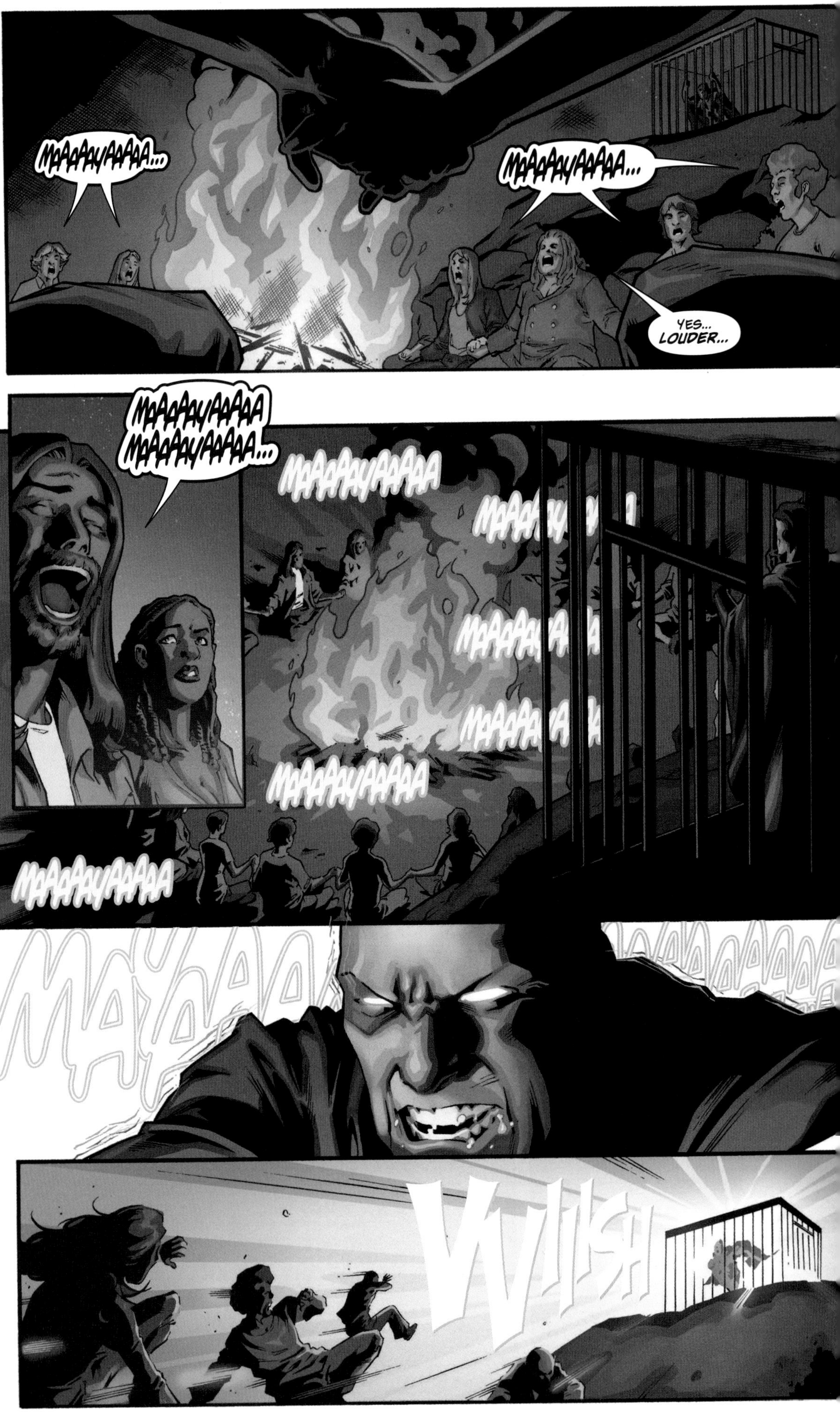
MAAAAAYAAAAA...
MAAAAAYAAAAA...
YES... LOUDER...
MAAAAAYAAAAA
MAAAAAYAAAAA...
MAAAAAYAAAAA
MAAAAAYAAAAA
MAAAAAYAAAAA
WHSH

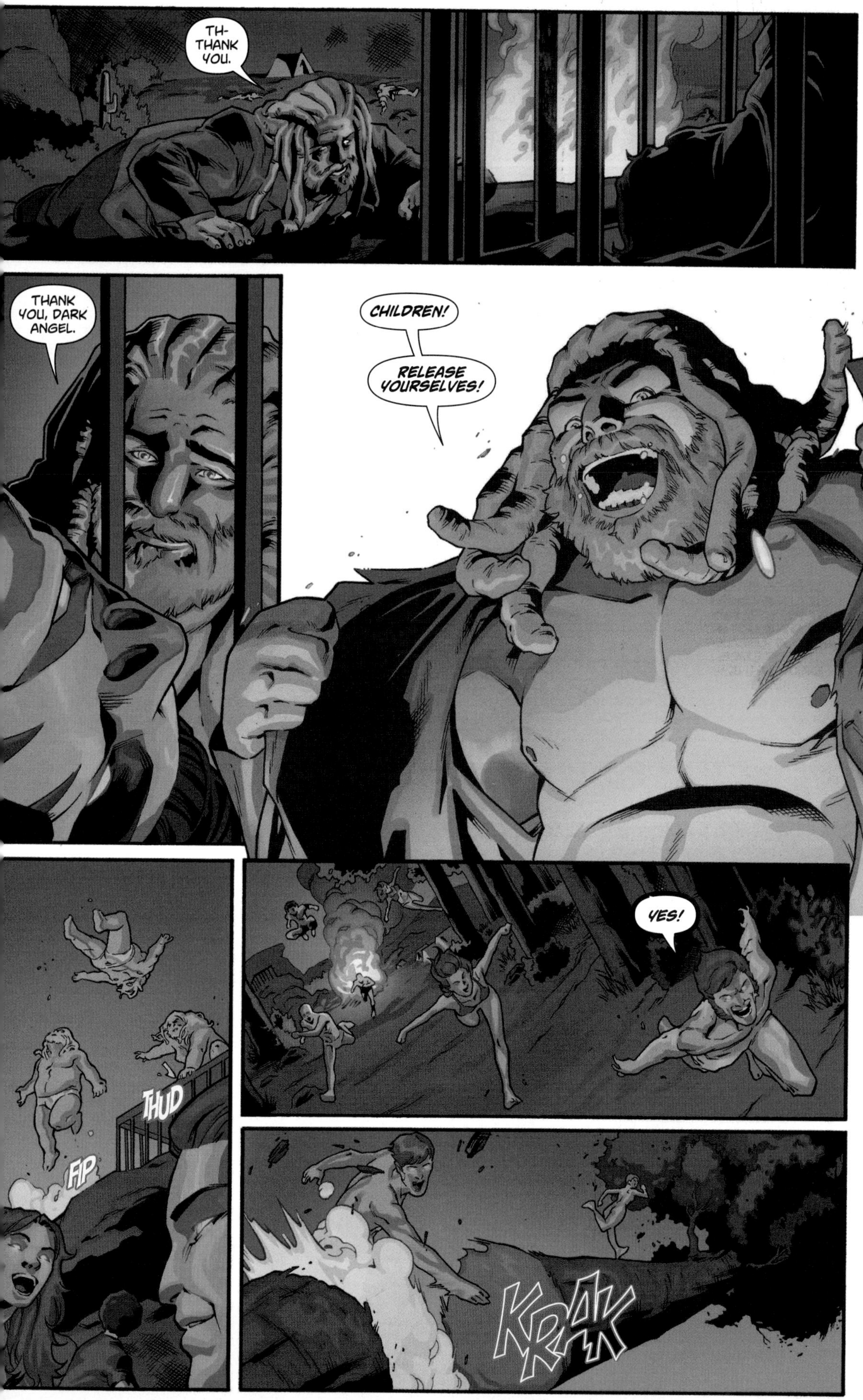
TH-
THANK
YOU.
THANK
YOU, DARK
ANGEL.
CHILDREN!
RELEASE
YOURSELVES!
THUD
FIP
YES!
KRAK

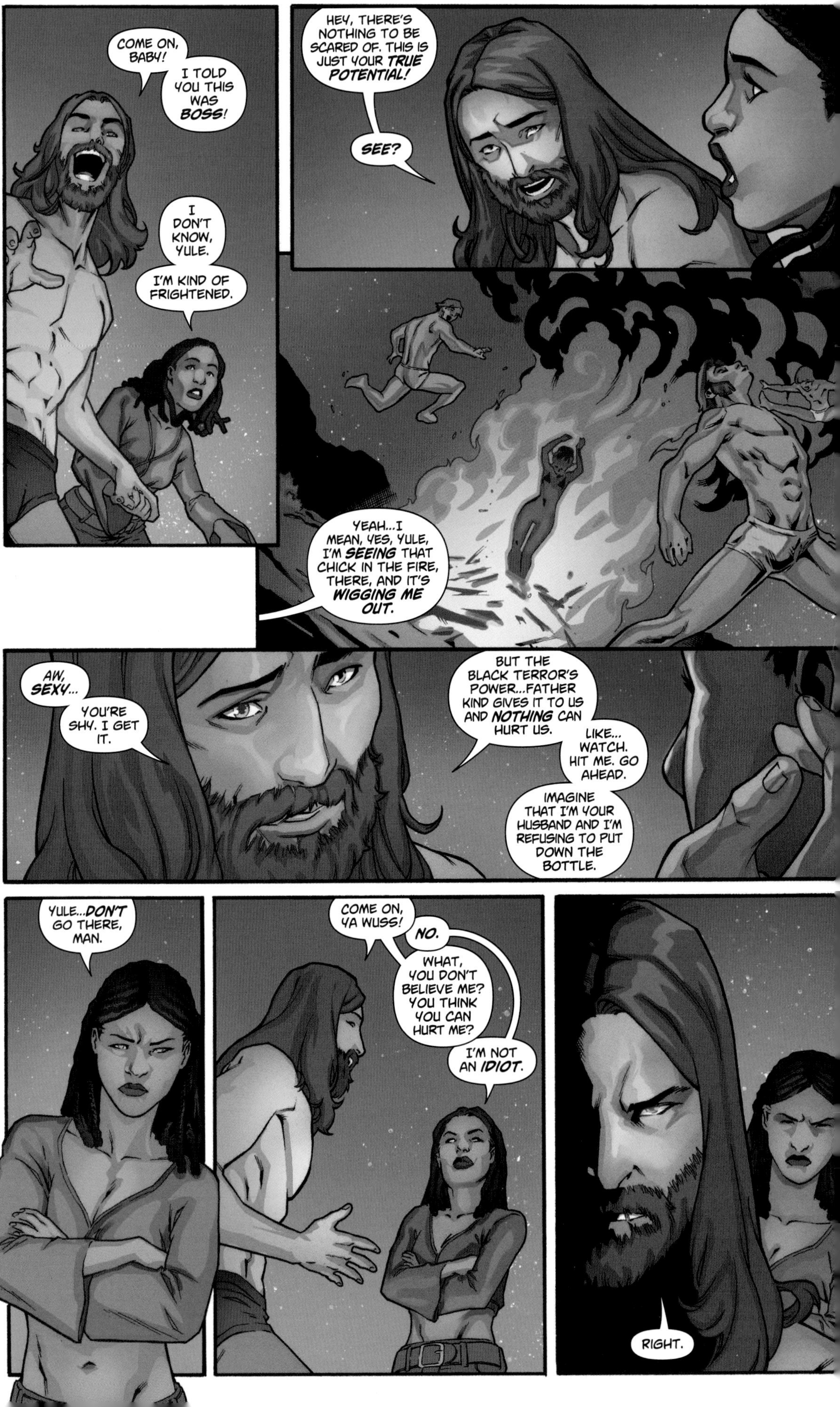
COME ON, BABY!
I TOLD YOU THIS WAS **BOSS**!
I DON'T KNOW, YULE.
I'M KIND OF FRIGHTENED.
HEY, THERE'S NOTHING TO BE SCARED OF. THIS IS JUST YOUR **TRUE POTENTIAL**!
SEE?
YEAH...I MEAN, YES, YULE, I'M **SEEING** THAT CHICK IN THE FIRE, THERE, AND IT'S **WIGGING ME OUT**.
AW, **SEXY**...
YOU'RE SHY. I GET IT.
BUT THE BLACK TERROR'S POWER...FATHER KIND GIVES IT TO US AND **NOTHING** CAN HURT US.
LIKE... WATCH. HIT ME. GO AHEAD.
IMAGINE THAT I'M YOUR HUSBAND AND I'M REFUSING TO PUT DOWN THE BOTTLE.
YULE...**DON'T** GO THERE, MAN.
COME ON, YA WUSS!
NO.
WHAT, YOU DON'T BELIEVE ME? YOU THINK YOU CAN HURT ME?
I'M NOT AN **IDIOT**.
RIGHT.

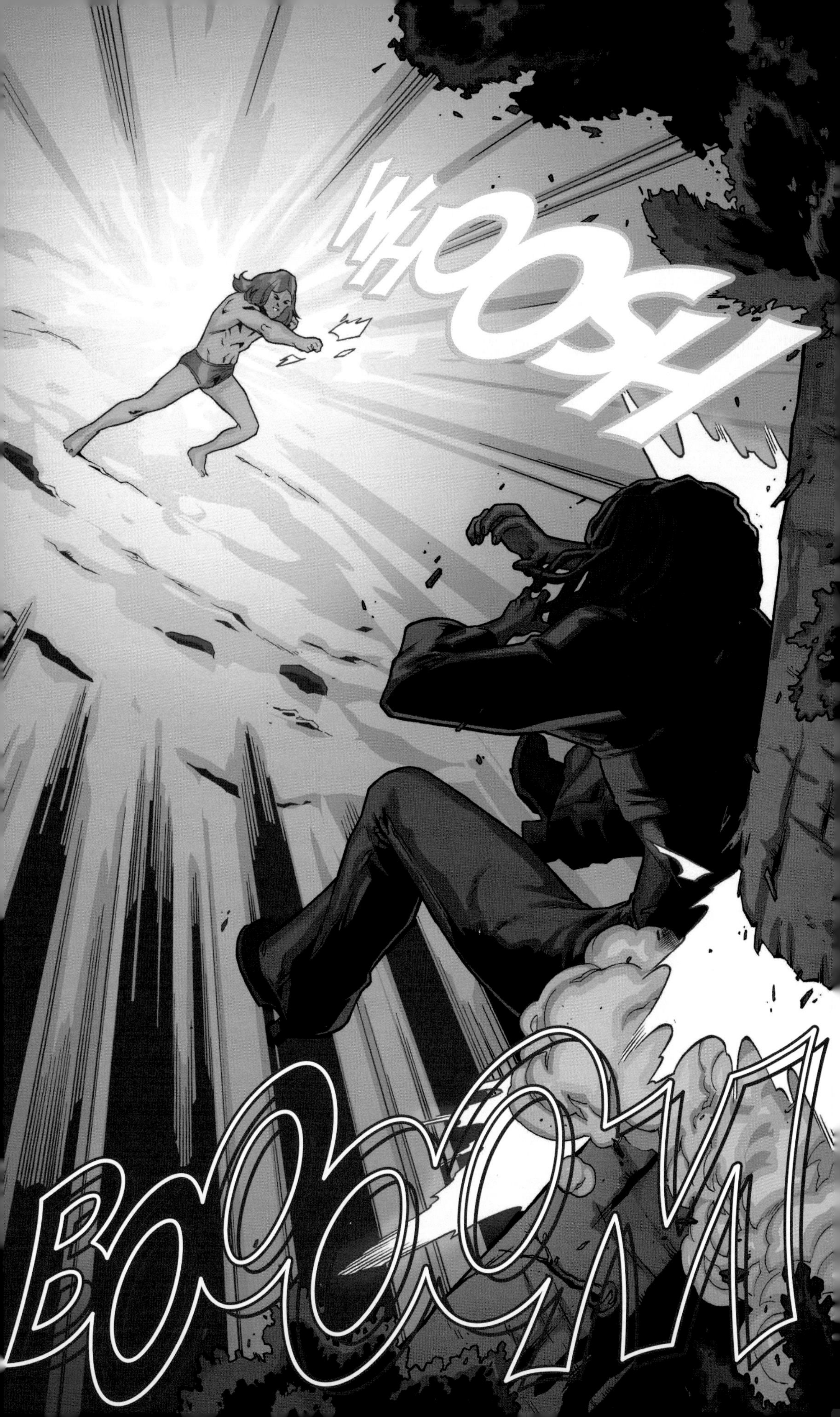
WHOOSH
BOOOOM

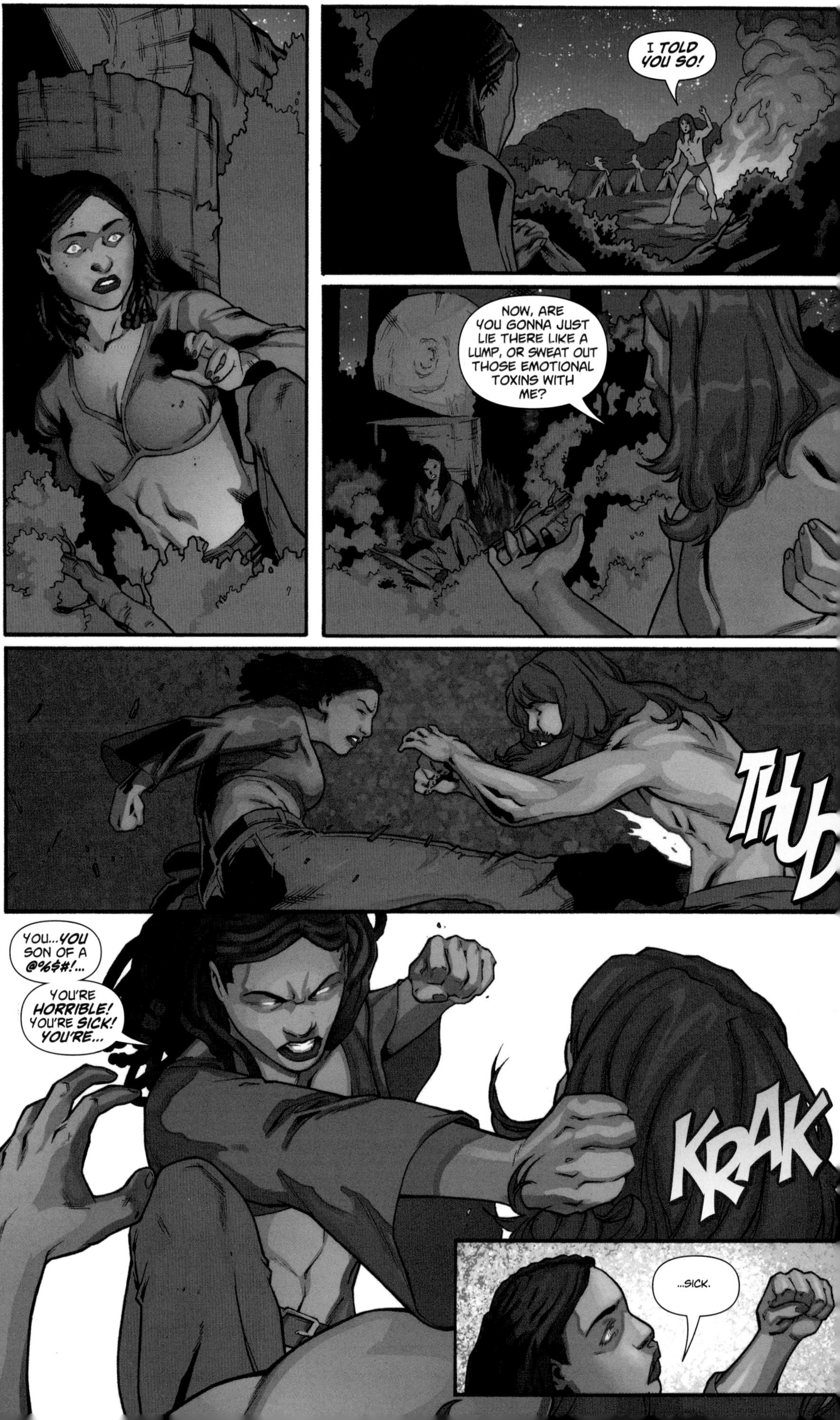
I TOLD YOU SO!
NOW, ARE YOU GONNA JUST LIE THERE LIKE A LUMP, OR SWEAT OUT THOSE EMOTIONAL TOXINS WITH ME?
THUD
YOU...YOU SON OF A @%$#!...
YOU'RE HORRIBLE! YOU'RE SICK! YOU'RE...
KRAK
...SICK.

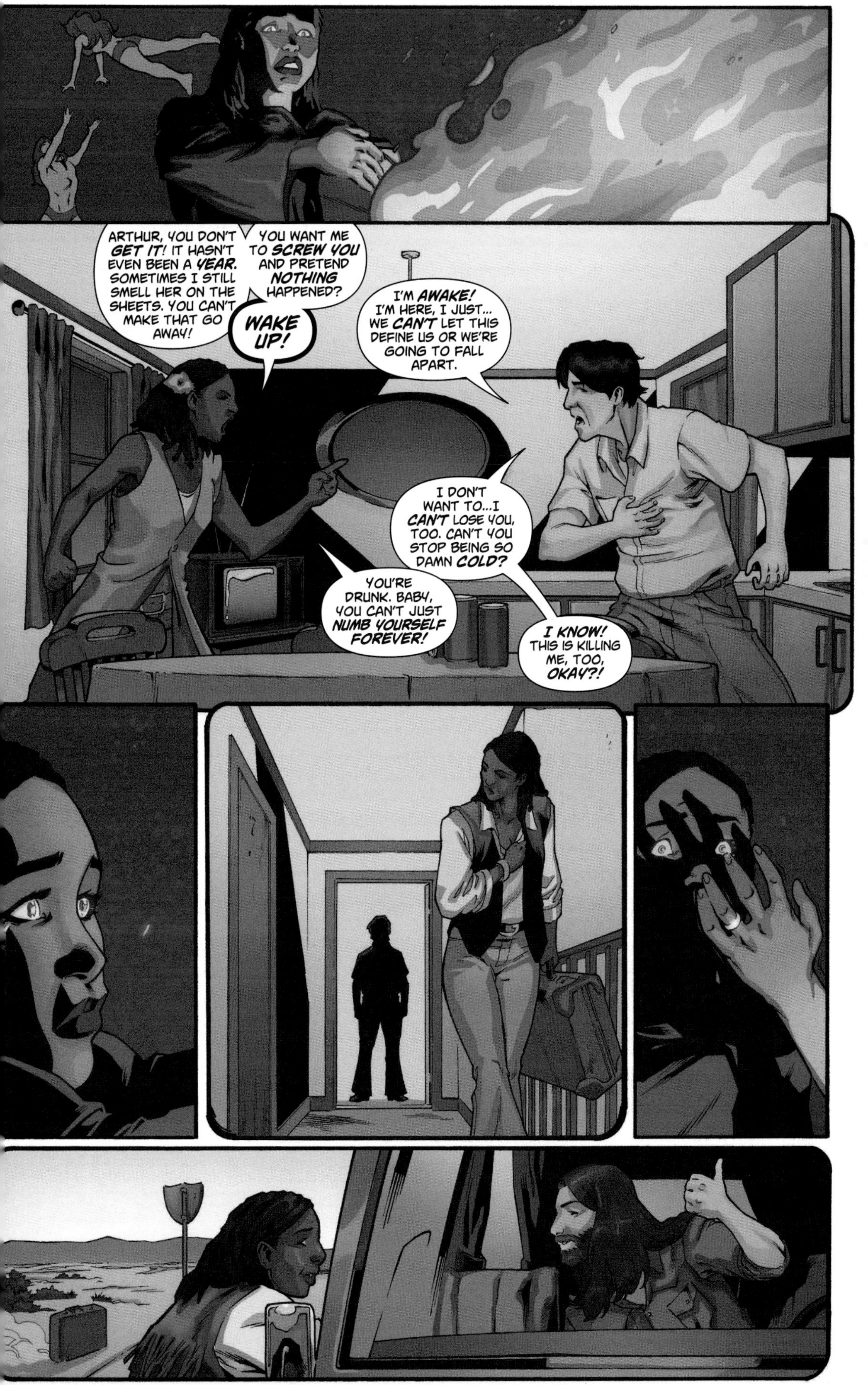
ARTHUR, YOU DON'T GET IT! IT HASN'T EVEN BEEN A YEAR. SOMETIMES I STILL SMELL HER ON THE SHEETS. YOU CAN'T MAKE THAT GO AWAY!
YOU WANT ME TO SCREW YOU AND PRETEND NOTHING HAPPENED?
WAKE UP!
I'M AWAKE! I'M HERE, I JUST... WE CAN'T LET THIS DEFINE US OR WE'RE GOING TO FALL APART.
I DON'T WANT TO...I CAN'T LOSE YOU, TOO. CAN'T YOU STOP BEING SO DAMN COLD?
YOU'RE DRUNK. BABY, YOU CAN'T JUST NUMB YOURSELF FOREVER!
I KNOW! THIS IS KILLING ME, TOO, OKAY?!

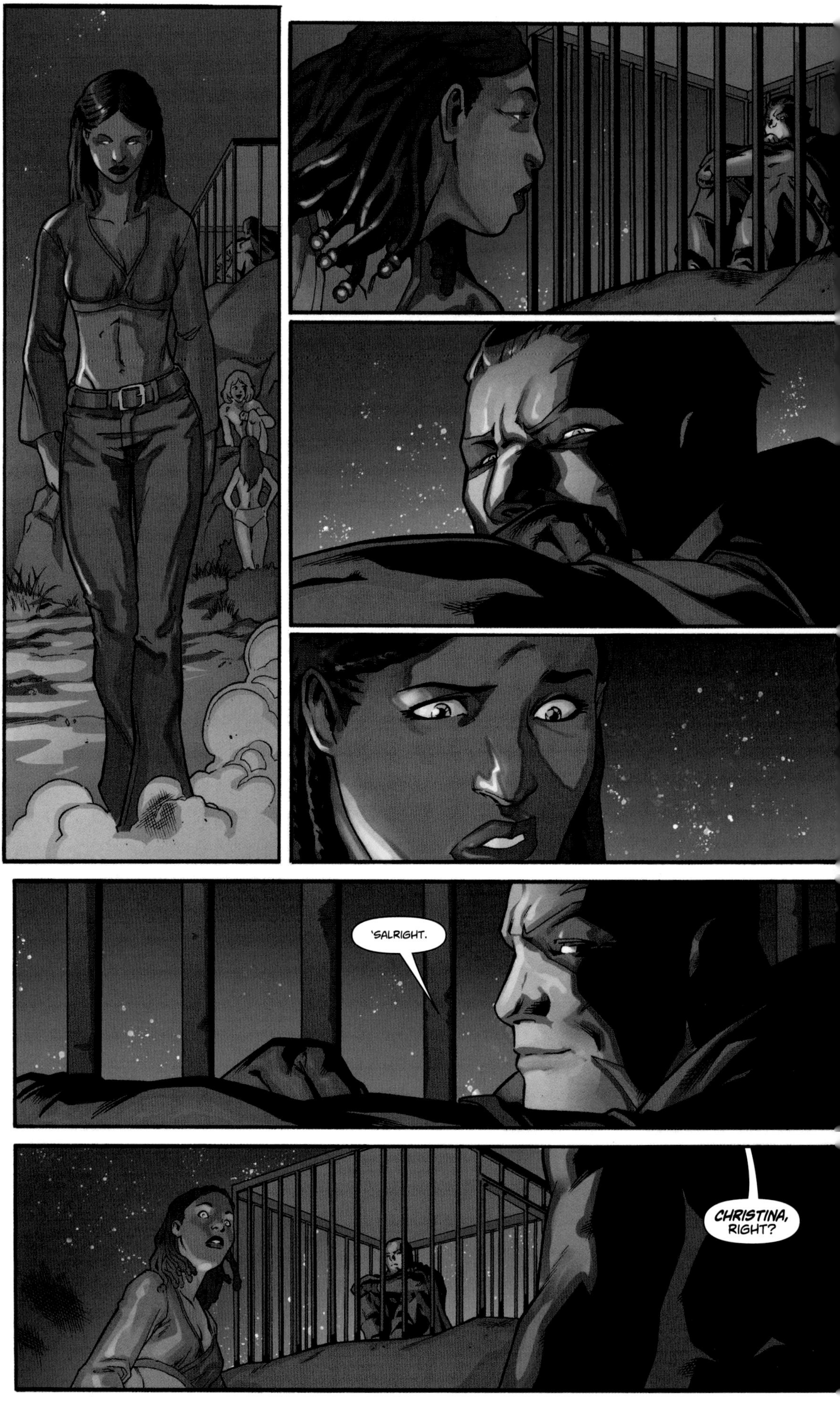
'SALRIGHT.
CHRISTINA, RIGHT?

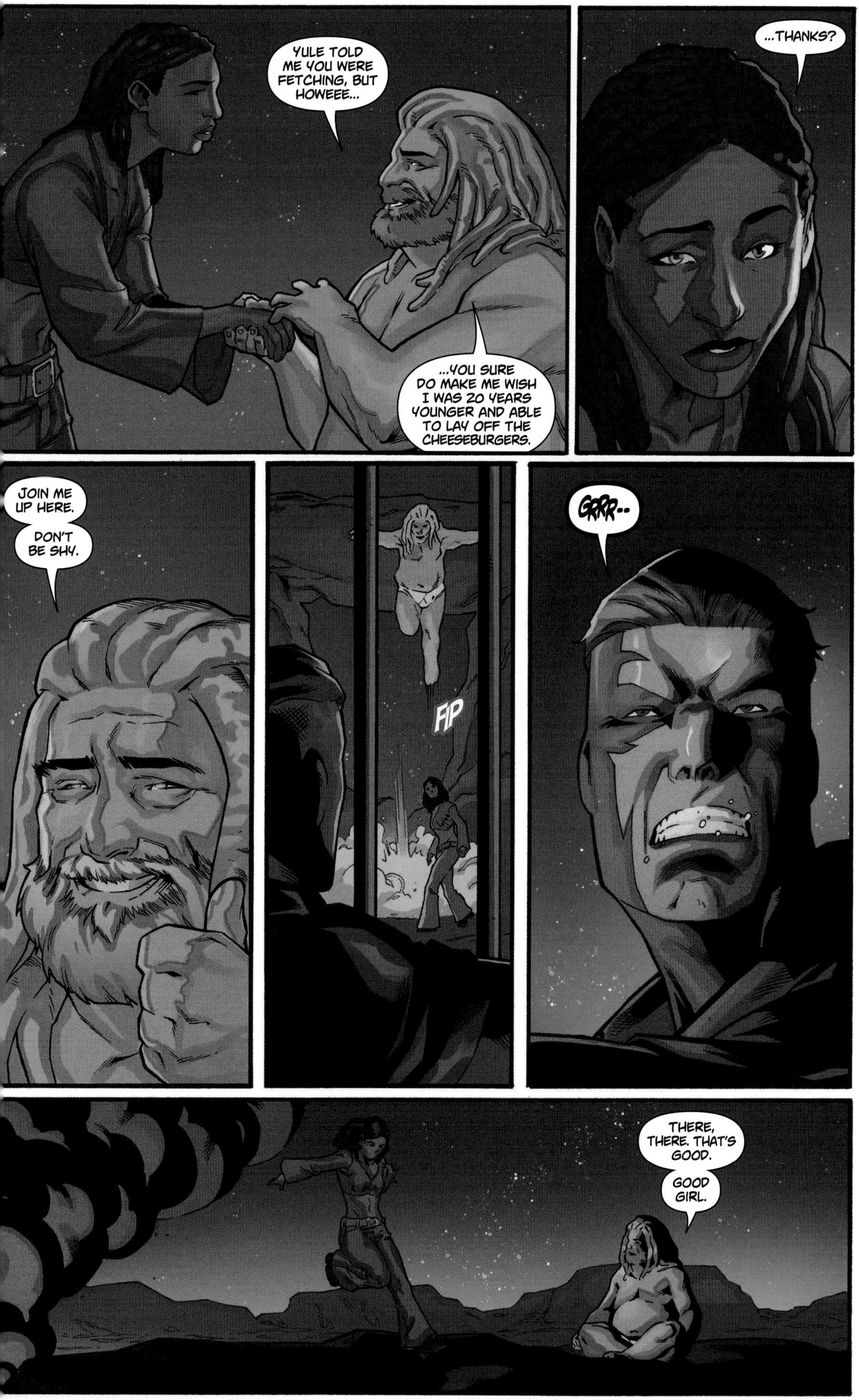
YULE TOLD ME YOU WERE FETCHING, BUT HOWEEE...
...YOU SURE DO MAKE ME WISH I WAS 20 YEARS YOUNGER AND ABLE TO LAY OFF THE CHEESEBURGERS.
...THANKS?
JOIN ME UP HERE.
DON'T BE SHY.
FIP
GRRR..
THERE, THERE. THAT'S GOOD.
GOOD GIRL.

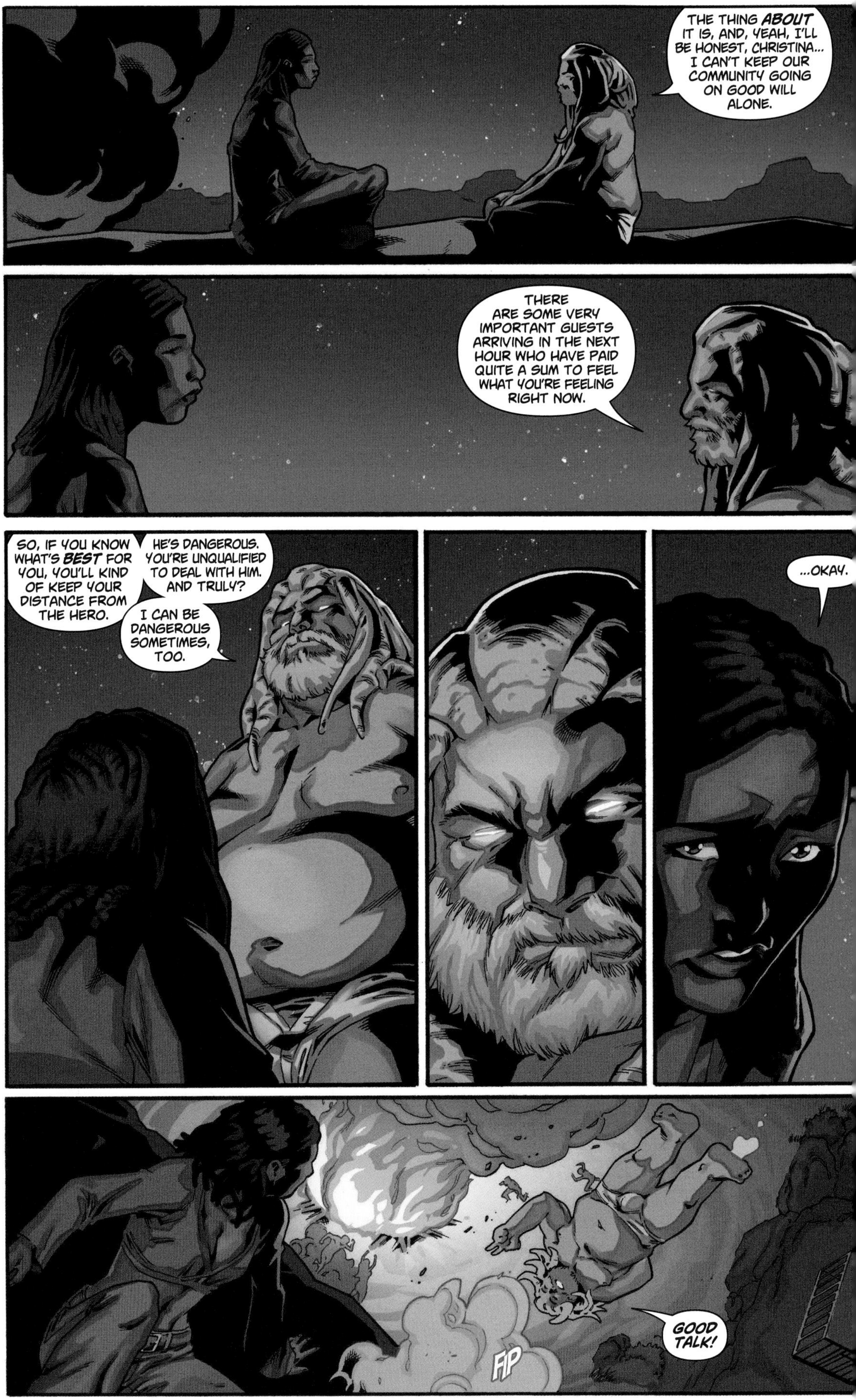

THE THING ABOUT IT IS, AND, YEAH, I'LL BE HONEST, CHRISTINA... I CAN'T KEEP OUR COMMUNITY GOING ON GOOD WILL ALONE.
THERE ARE SOME VERY IMPORTANT GUESTS ARRIVING IN THE NEXT HOUR WHO HAVE PAID QUITE A SUM TO FEEL WHAT YOU'RE FEELING RIGHT NOW.
SO, IF YOU KNOW WHAT'S BEST FOR YOU, YOU'LL KIND OF KEEP YOUR DISTANCE FROM THE HERO.
HE'S DANGEROUS. YOU'RE UNQUALIFIED TO DEAL WITH HIM. AND TRULY?
I CAN BE DANGEROUS SOMETIMES, TOO.
...OKAY.
GOOD TALK!
FIP

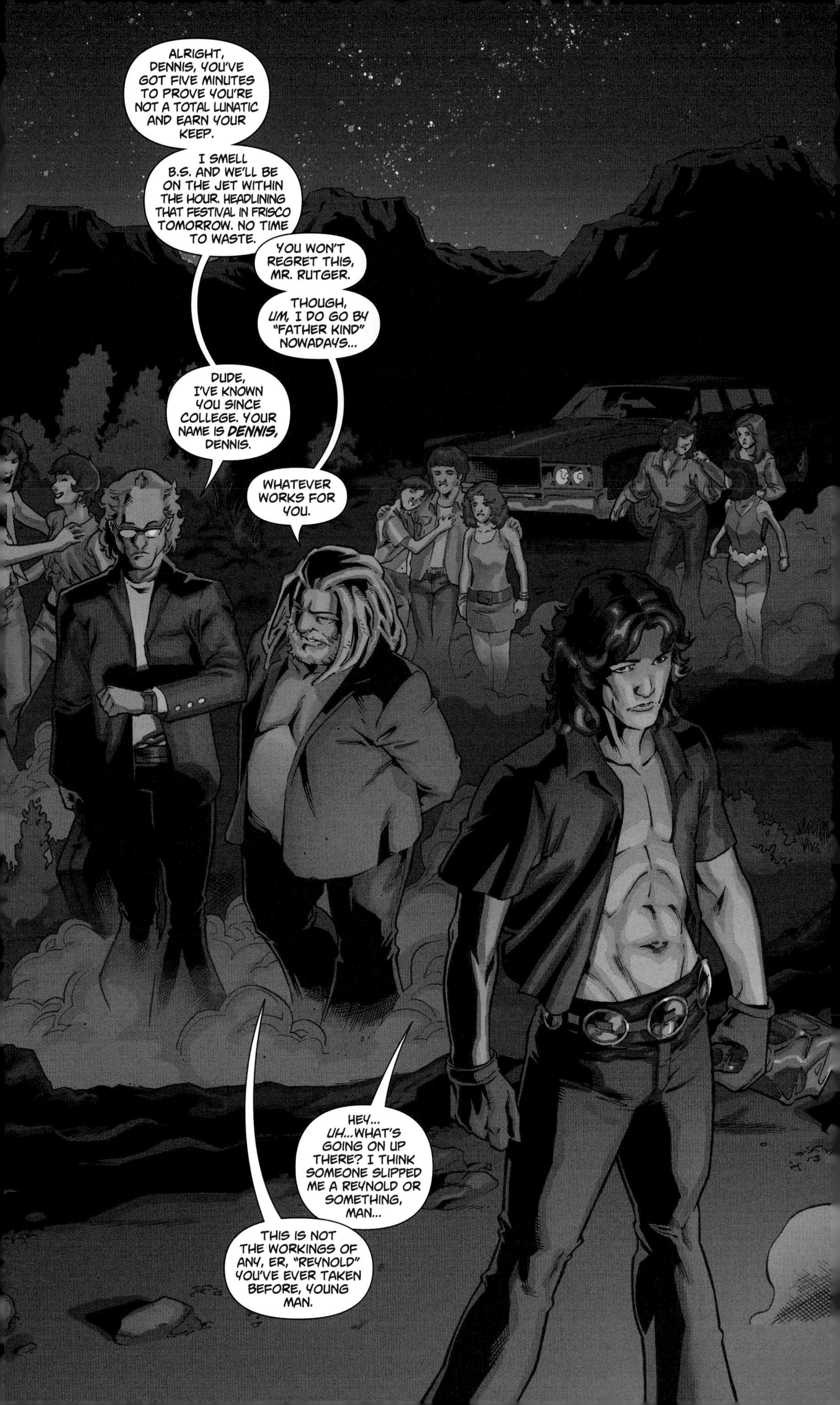
ALRIGHT, DENNIS, YOU'VE GOT FIVE MINUTES TO PROVE YOU'RE NOT A TOTAL LUNATIC AND EARN YOUR KEEP.
I SMELL B.S. AND WE'LL BE ON THE JET WITHIN THE HOUR. HEADLINING THAT FESTIVAL IN FRISCO TOMORROW. NO TIME TO WASTE.
YOU WON'T REGRET THIS, MR. RUTGER.
THOUGH, UM, I DO GO BY "FATHER KIND" NOWADAYS...
DUDE, I'VE KNOWN YOU SINCE COLLEGE. YOUR NAME IS DENNIS, DENNIS.
WHATEVER WORKS FOR YOU.
HEY... UH...WHAT'S GOING ON UP THERE? I THINK SOMEONE SLIPPED ME A REYNOLD OR SOMETHING, MAN...
THIS IS NOT THE WORKINGS OF ANY, ER, "REYNOLD" YOU'VE EVER TAKEN BEFORE, YOUNG MAN.

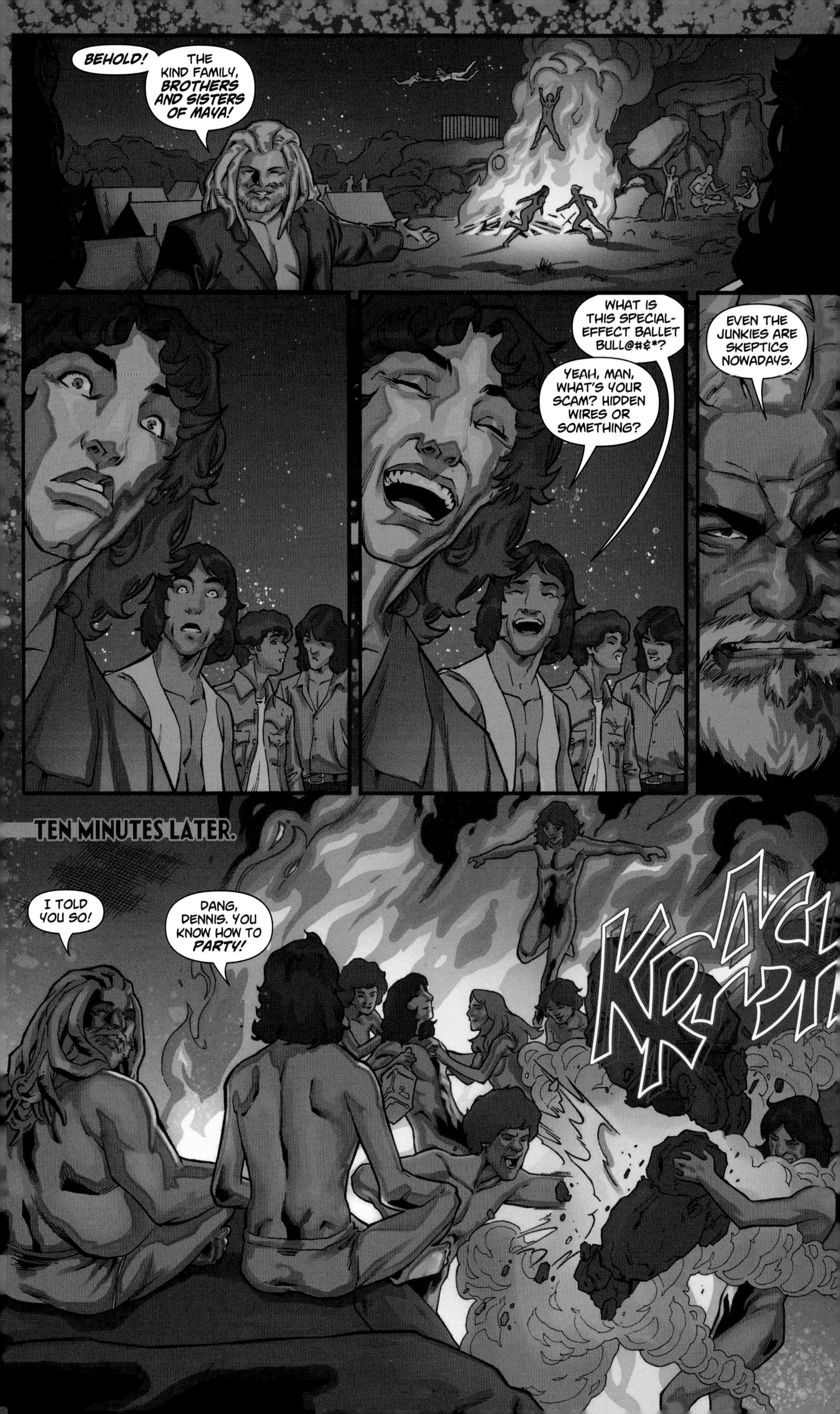
BEHOLD!
THE KIND FAMILY, BROTHERS AND SISTERS OF MAYA!
WHAT IS THIS SPECIAL-EFFECT BALLET BULL@#$*?
YEAH, MAN, WHAT'S YOUR SCAM? HIDDEN WIRES OR SOMETHING?
EVEN THE JUNKIES ARE SKEPTICS NOWADAYS.
TEN MINUTES LATER.
I TOLD YOU SO!
DANG, DENNIS. YOU KNOW HOW TO PARTY!

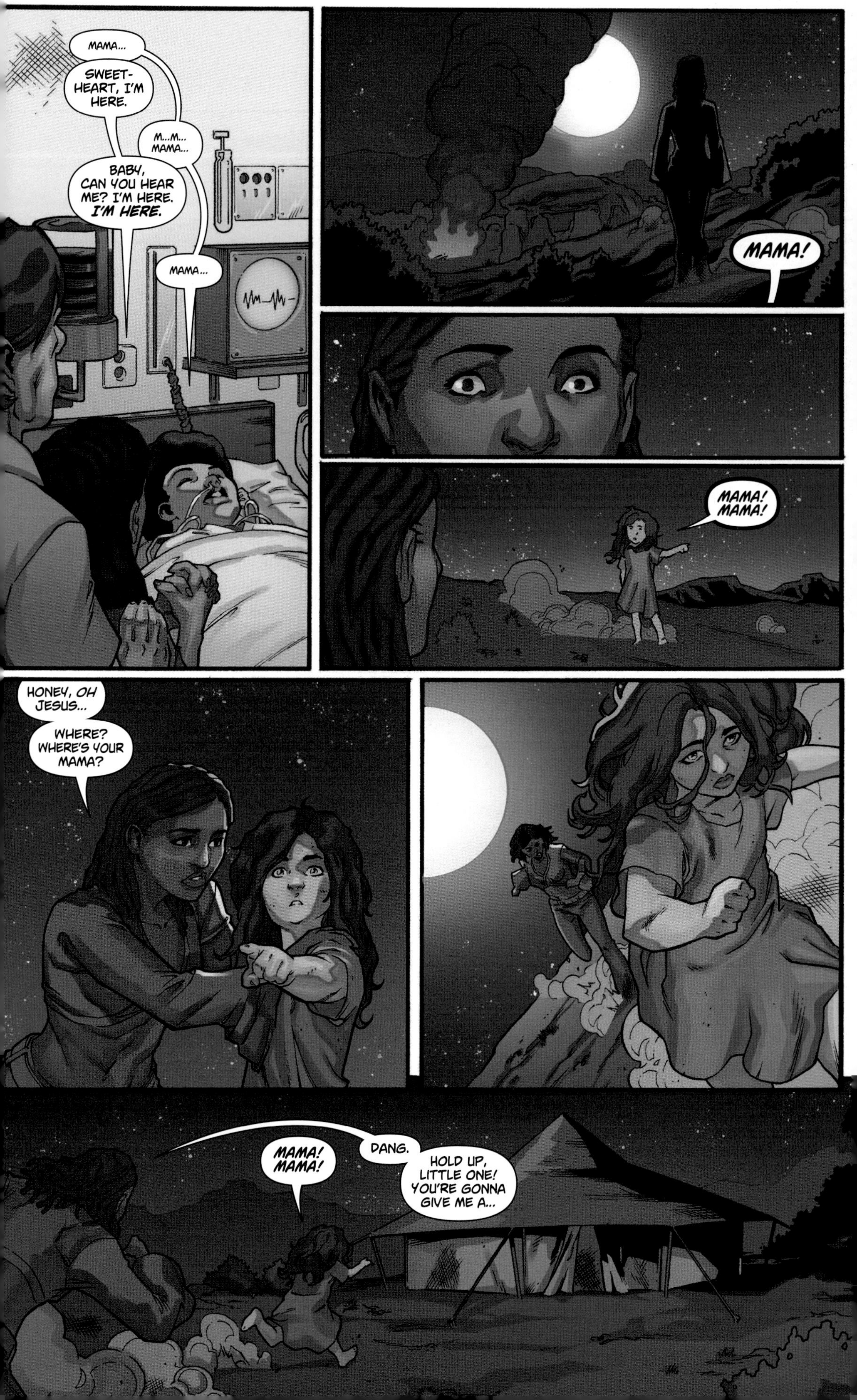
MAMA...
SWEET-HEART, I'M HERE.
M...M... MAMA...
BABY, CAN YOU HEAR ME? I'M HERE. *I'M HERE.*
MAMA...
MAMA!
MAMA! MAMA!
HONEY, OH JESUS...
WHERE? WHERE'S YOUR MAMA?
MAMA! MAMA!
DANG.
HOLD UP, LITTLE ONE! YOU'RE GONNA GIVE ME A...

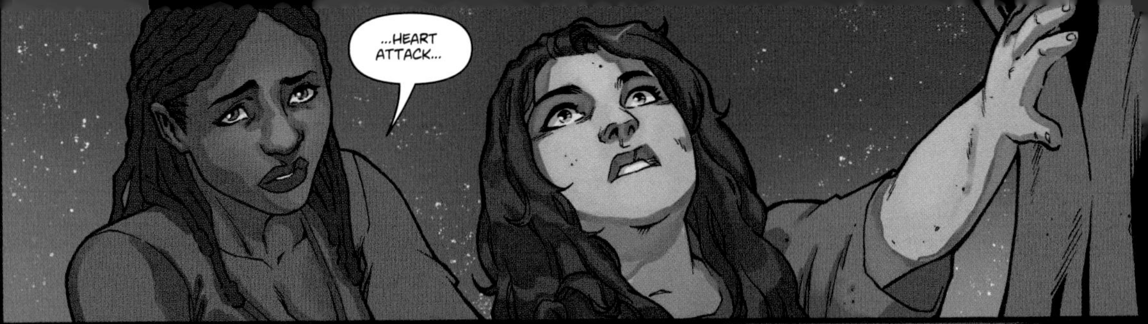
...HEART
ATTACK...

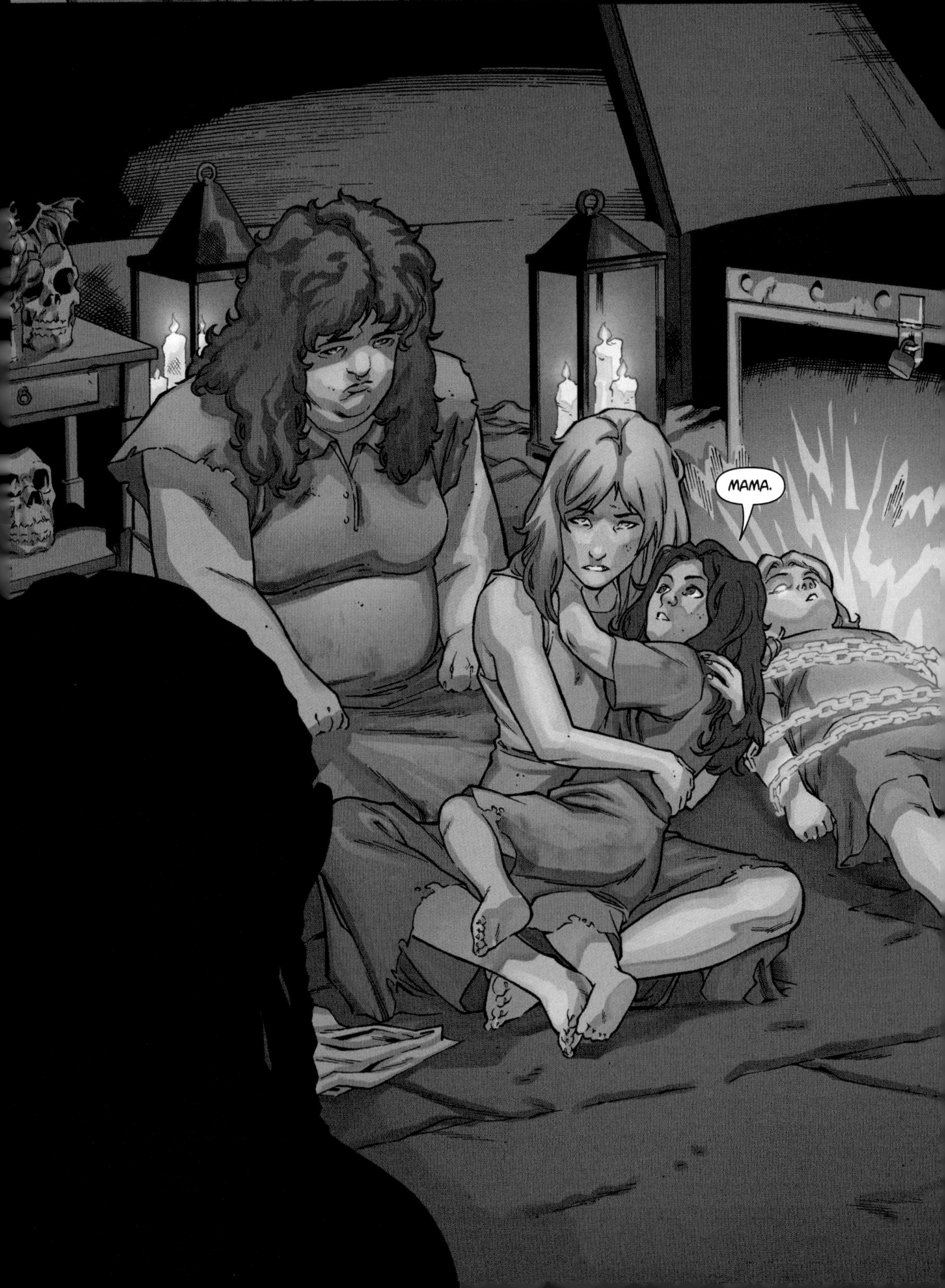
MAMA.

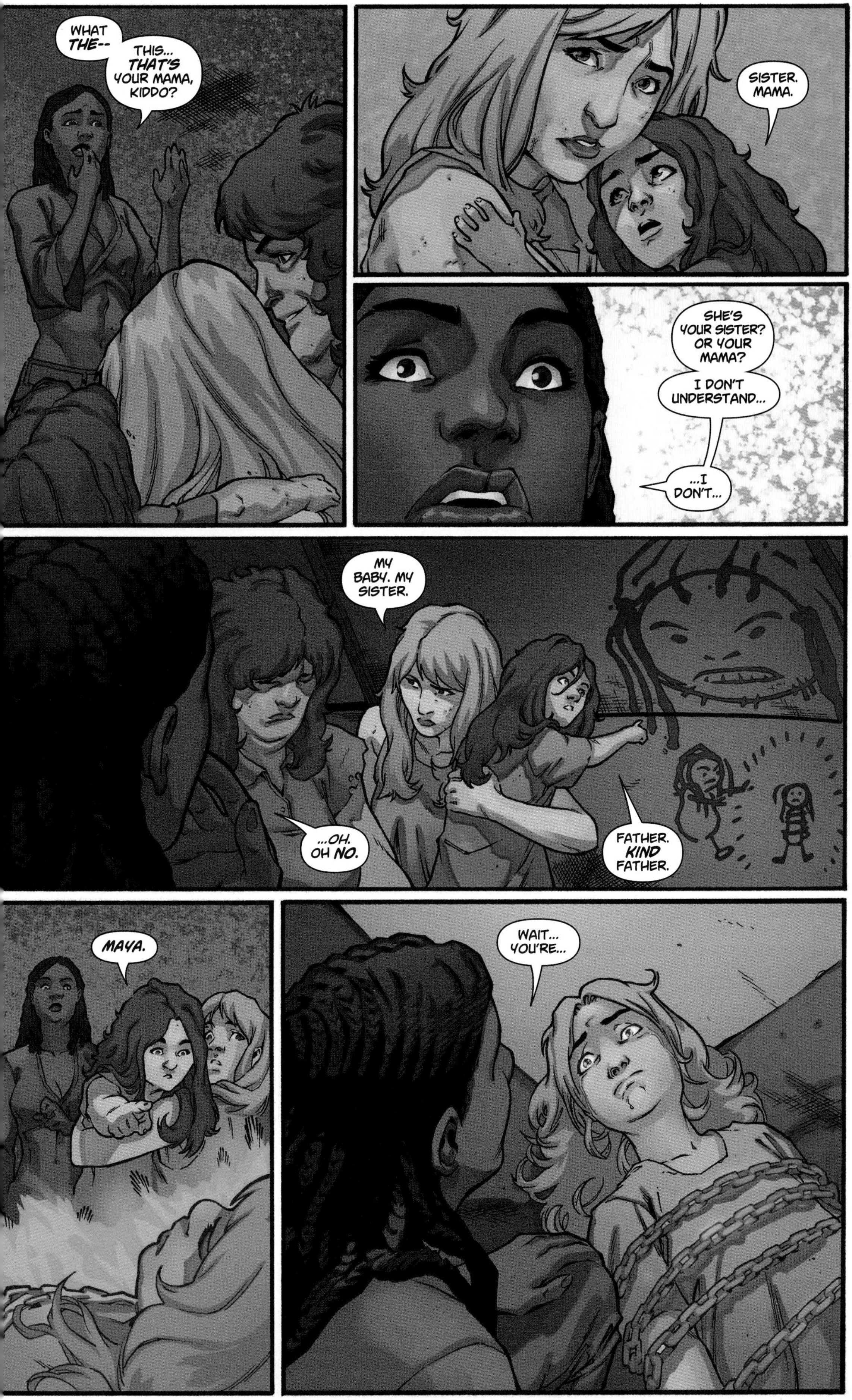
WHAT THE--
THIS... THAT'S YOUR MAMA, KIDDO?
SISTER. MAMA.
SHE'S YOUR SISTER? OR YOUR MAMA?
I DON'T UNDERSTAND...
...I DON'T...
MY BABY. MY SISTER.
...OH. OH NO.
FATHER. KIND FATHER.
MAYA.
WAIT... YOU'RE...

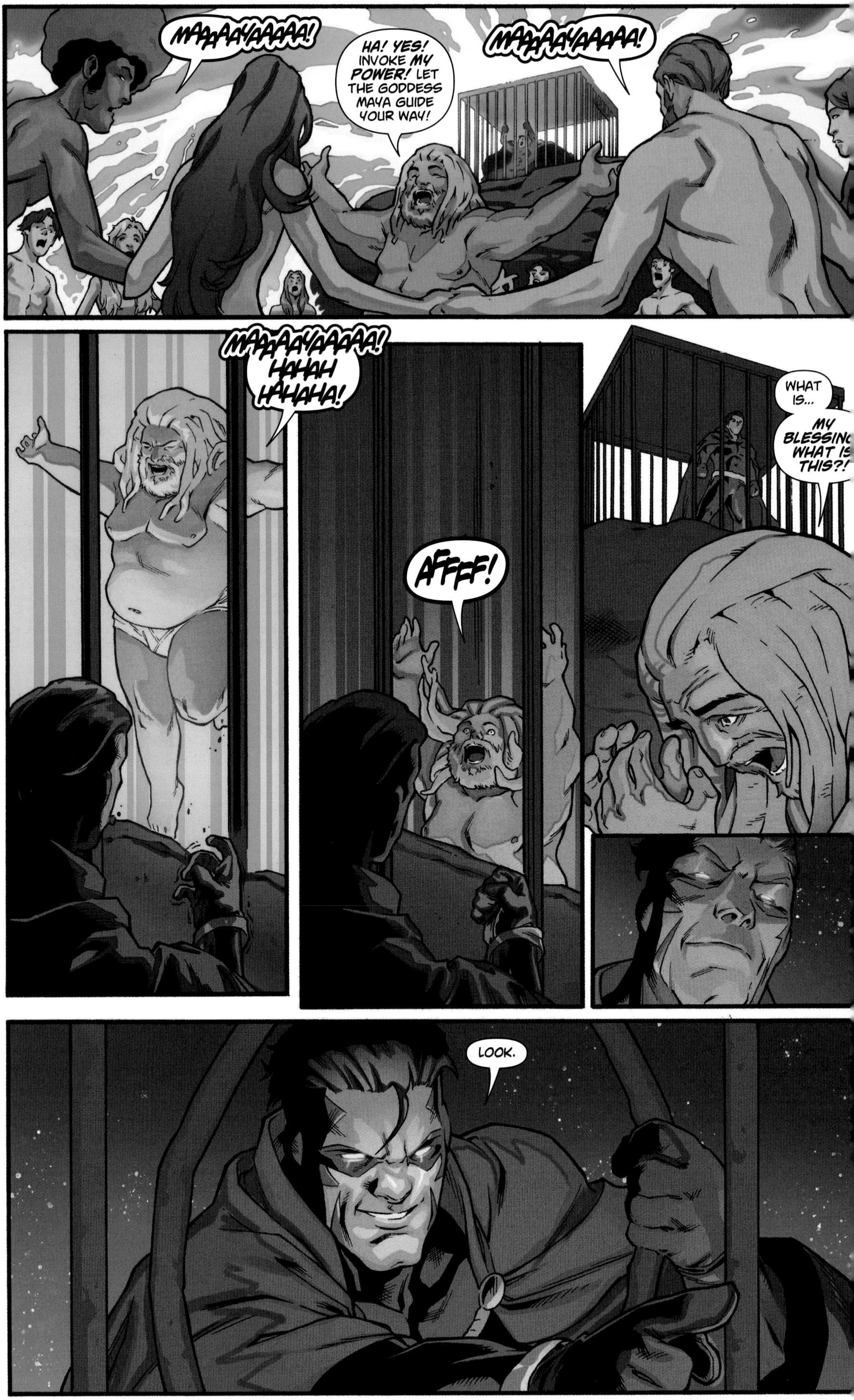
MAAAAAYAAAAA!
HA! YES! INVOKE MY POWER! LET THE GODDESS MAYA GUIDE YOUR WAY!
MAAAAAYAAAAA!
MAAAAAYAAAAA! HAHAH HAHAHA!
AFFFF!
WHAT IS...
MY BLESSING WHAT IS THIS?!
LOOK.

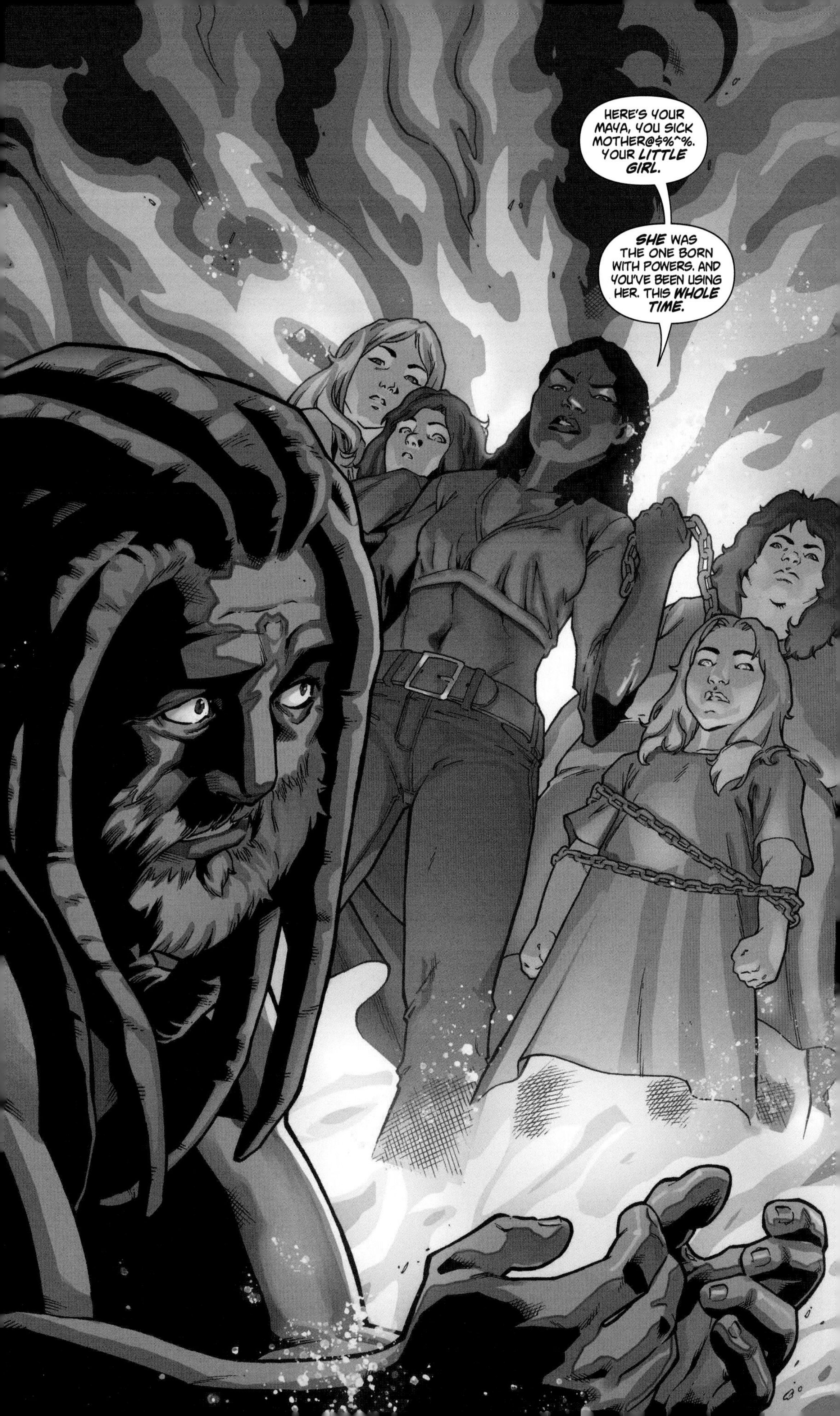
HERE'S YOUR MAYA, YOU SICK MOTHER@$%^%. YOUR LITTLE GIRL.
SHE WAS THE ONE BORN WITH POWERS. AND YOU'VE BEEN USING HER. THIS WHOLE TIME.

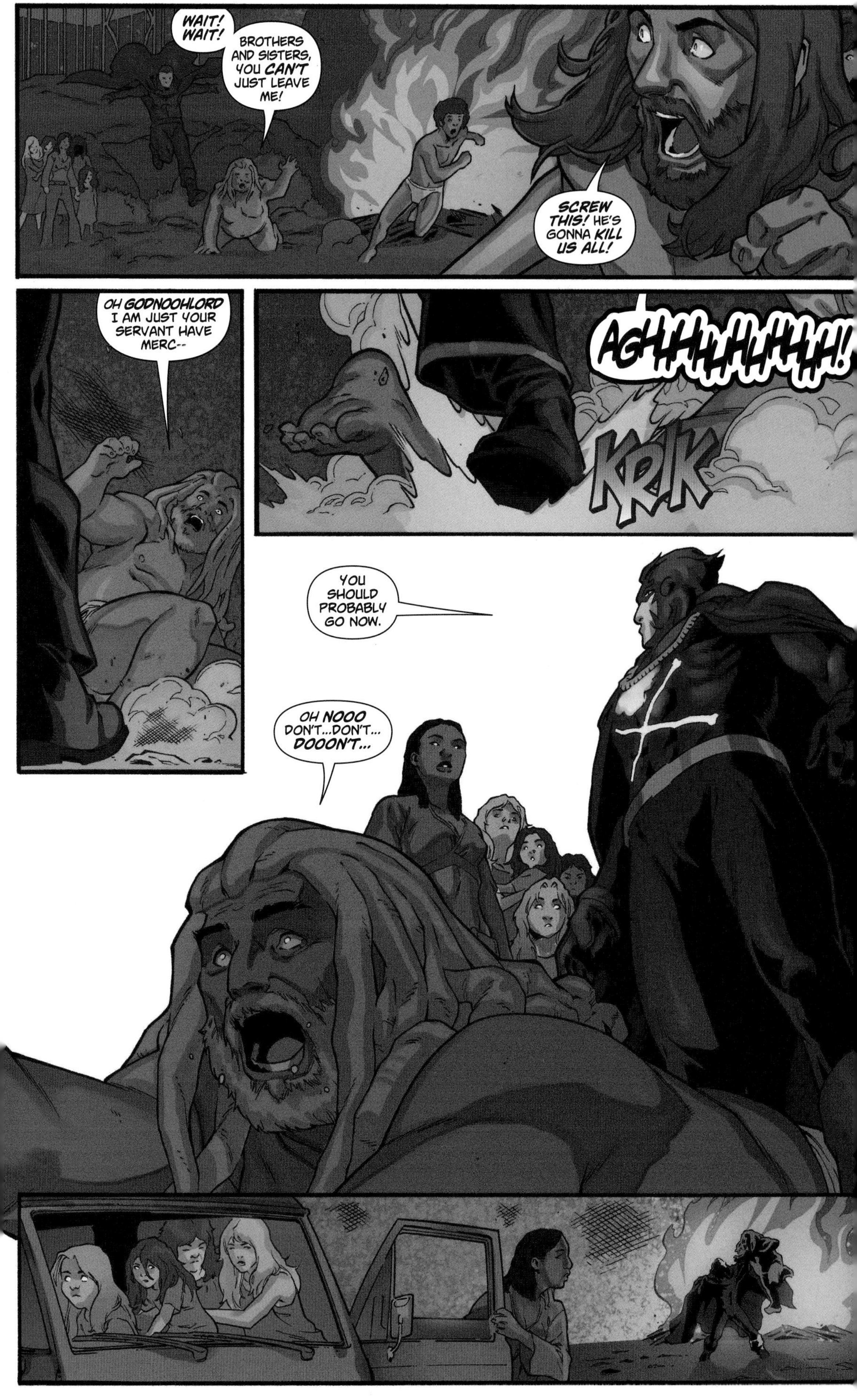
WAIT! WAIT!
BROTHERS AND SISTERS, YOU CAN'T JUST LEAVE ME!
SCREW THIS! HE'S GONNA KILL US ALL!
OH GODNOOHLORD I AM JUST YOUR SERVANT HAVE MERC--
AGHHHHHHHHHH!
KRIK
YOU SHOULD PROBABLY GO NOW.
OH NOOO DON'T...DON'T... DOOON'T...

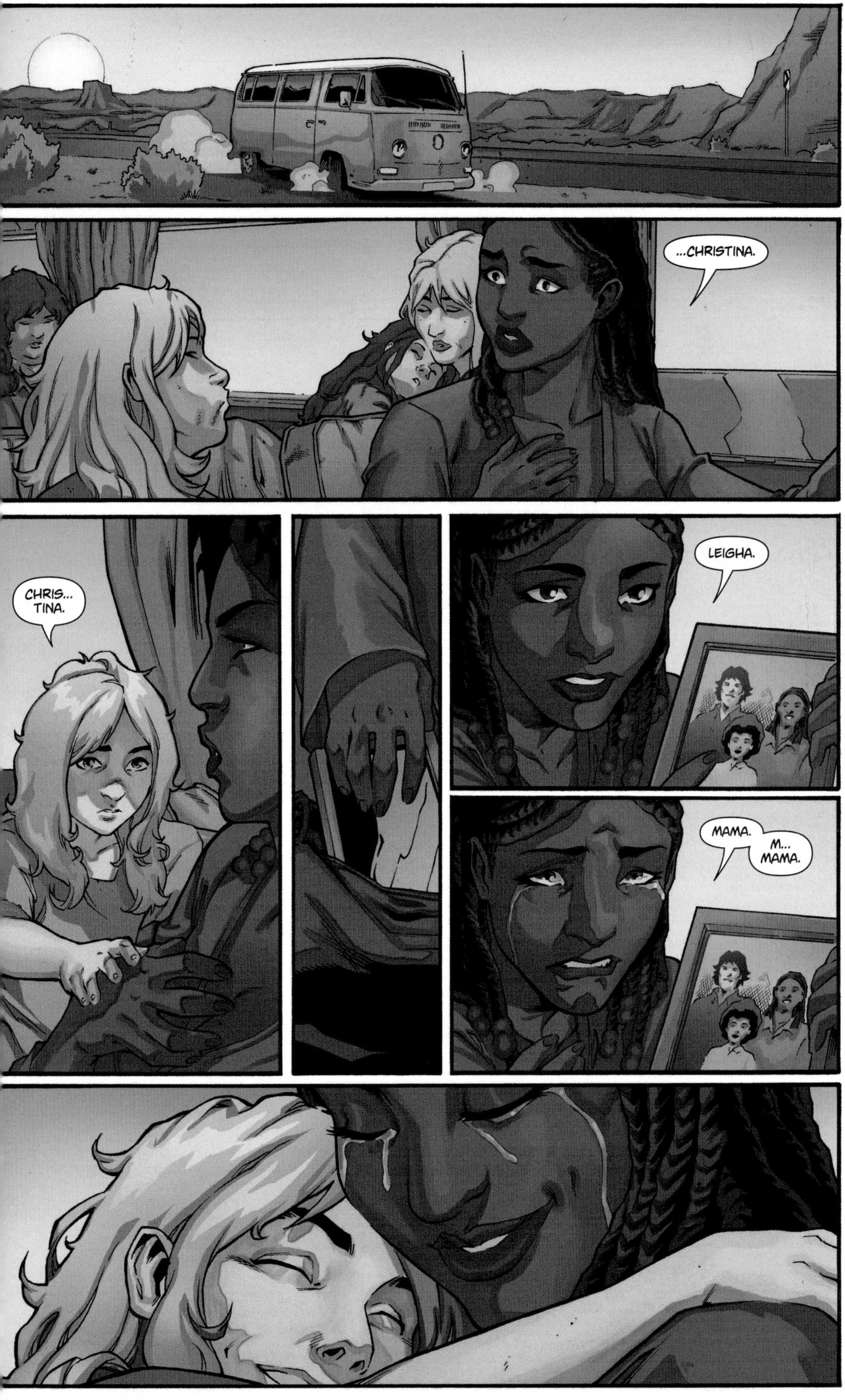
...CHRISTINA.
CHRIS... TINA.
LEIGHA.
MAMA.
M... MAMA.

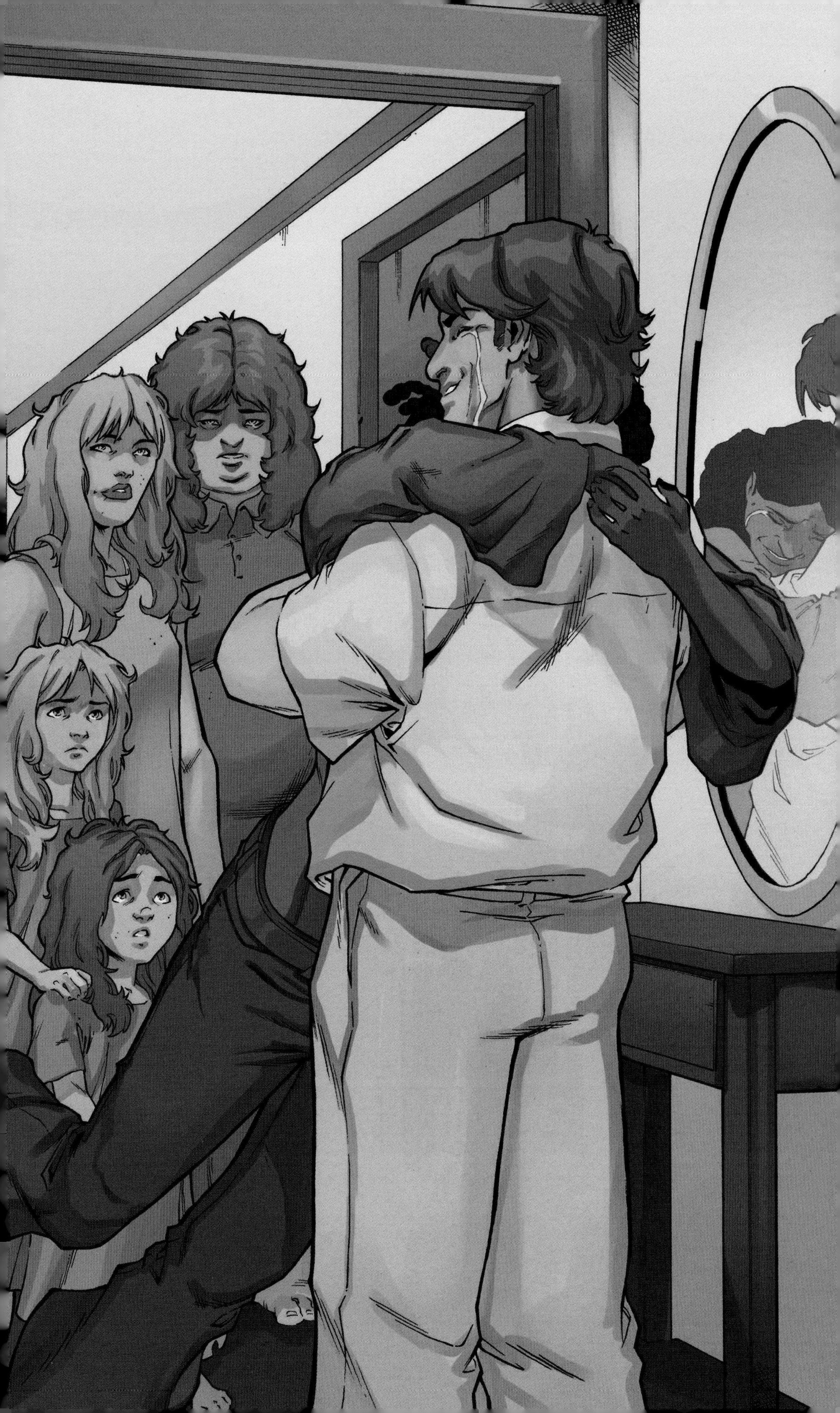

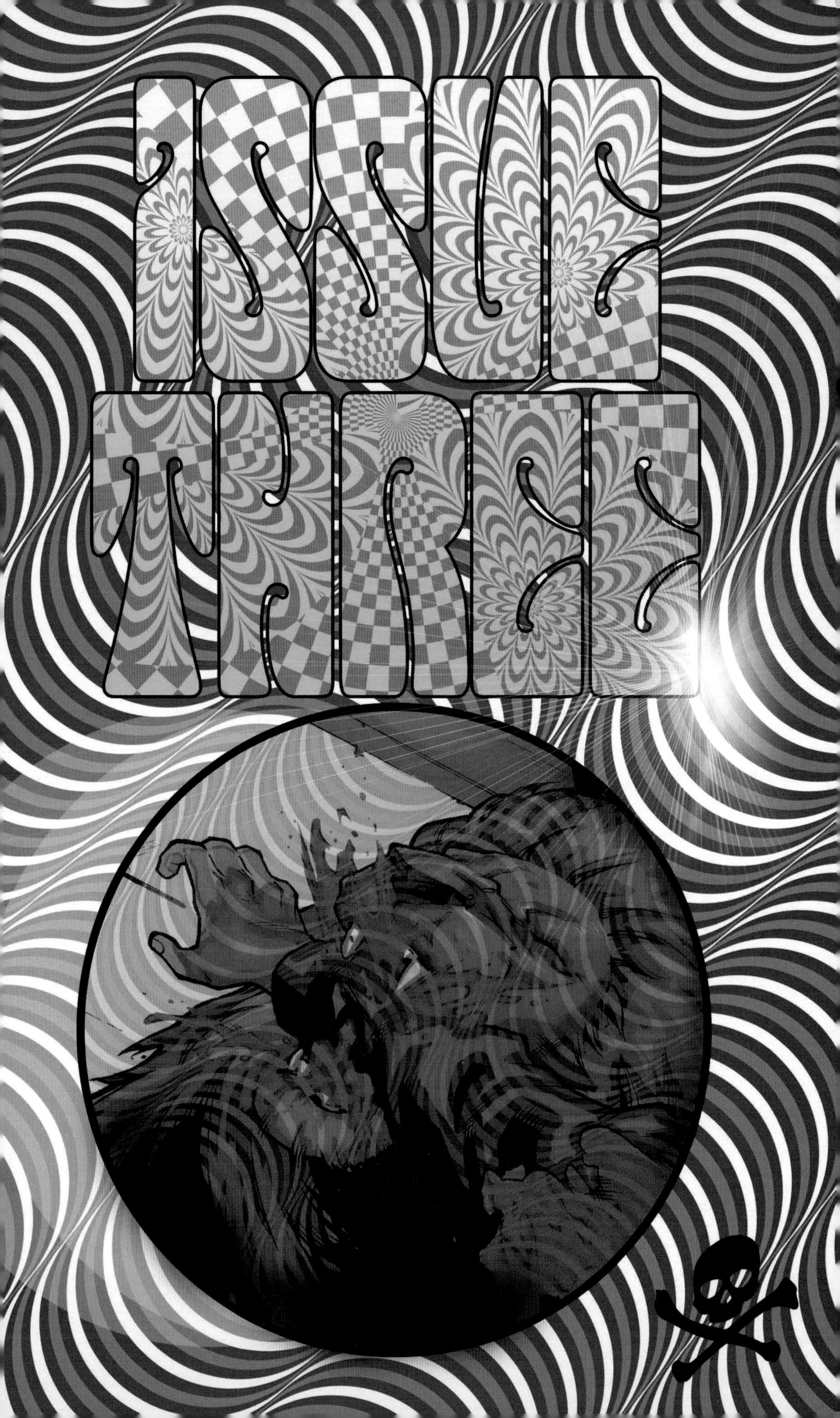
ISSUE
THREE

ISSUE 3
COVER ART BY RAHZZAH

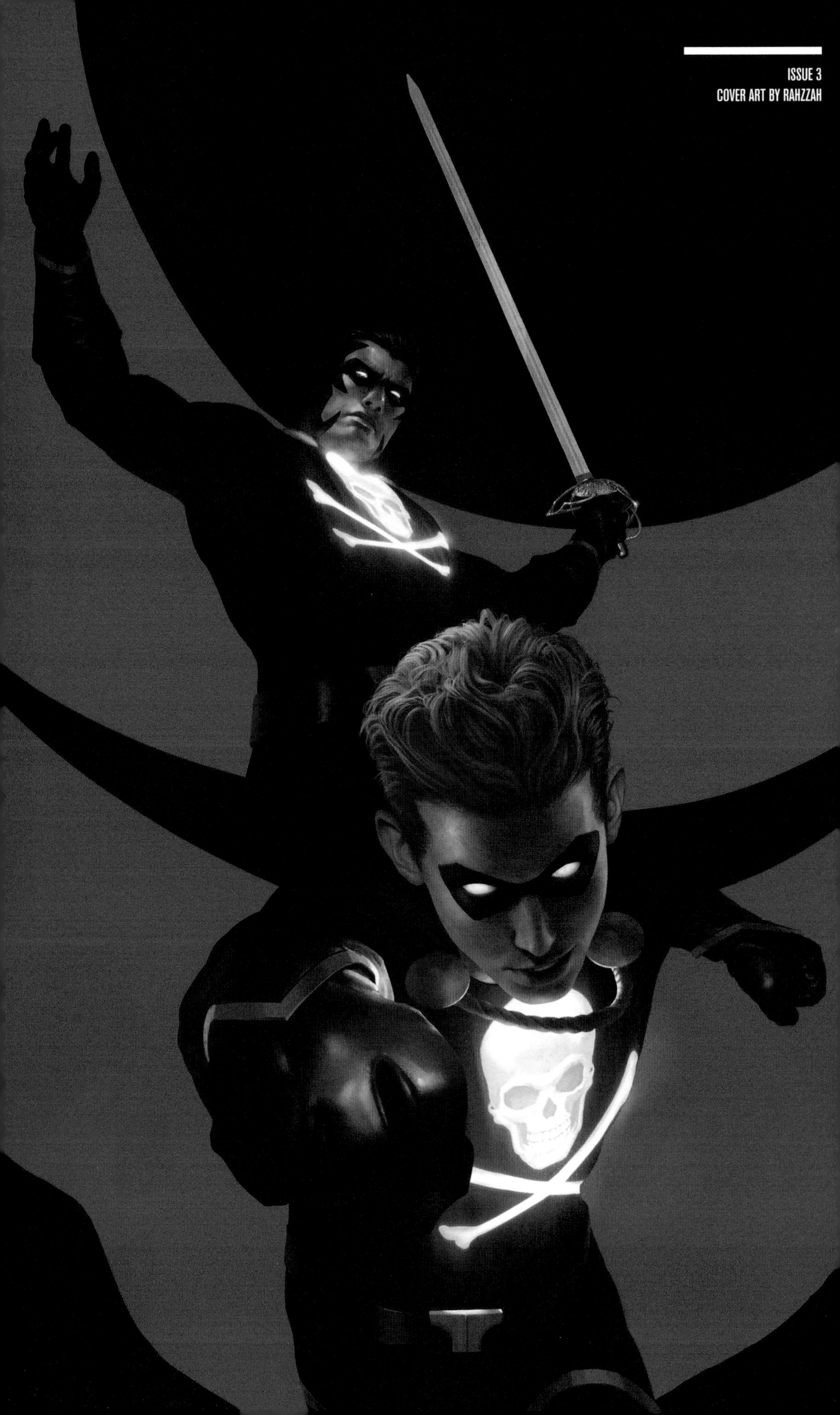

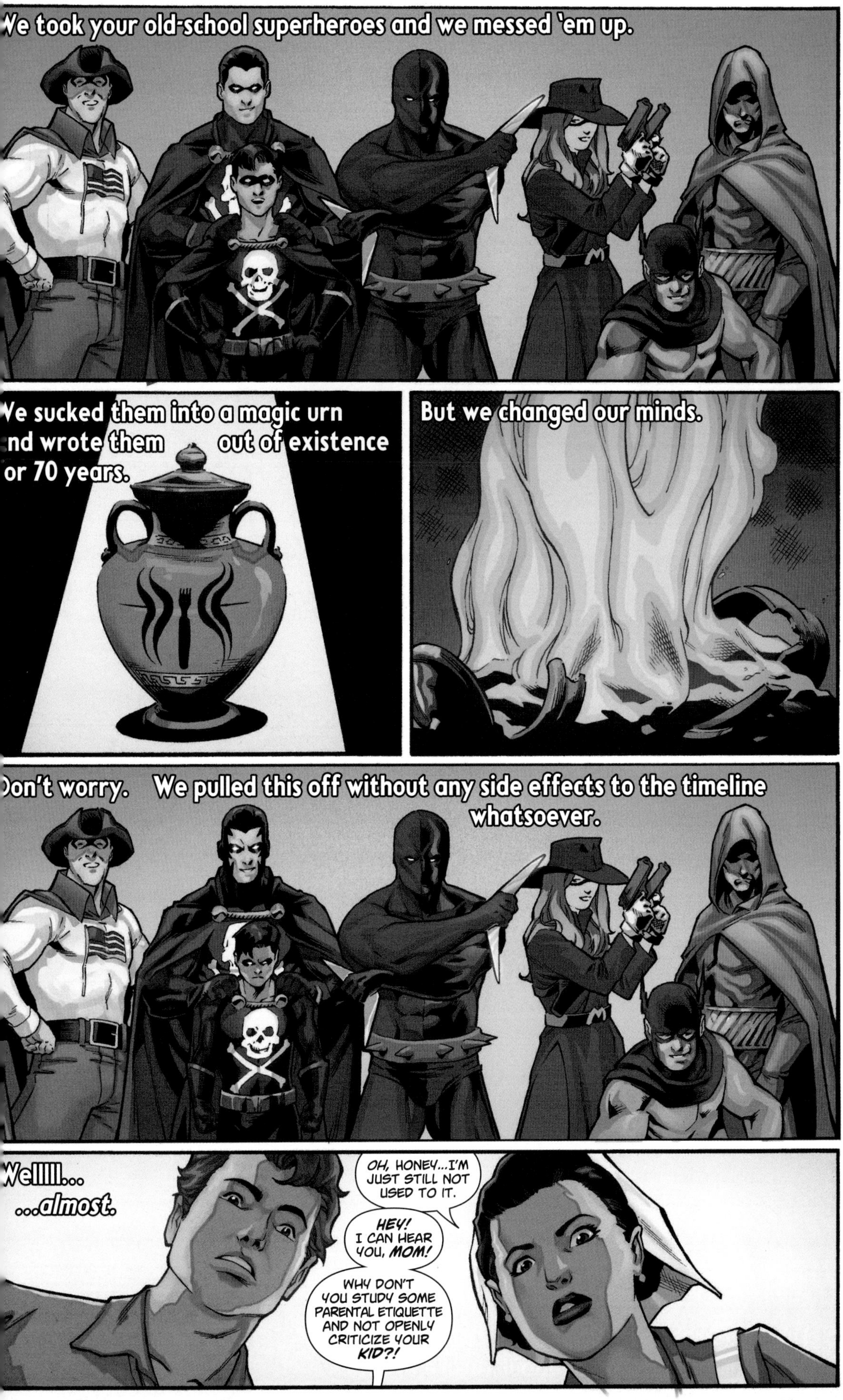

Ve took your old-school superheroes and we messed 'em up.
Ve sucked them into a magic urn
nd wrote them out of existence
or 70 years.
But we changed our minds.
)on't worry. We pulled this off without any side effects to the timeline whatsoever.
Velllll...
...almost.
OH, HONEY...I'M JUST STILL NOT USED TO IT.
HEY! I CAN HEAR YOU, MOM!
WHY DON'T YOU STUDY SOME PARENTAL ETIQUETTE AND NOT OPENLY CRITICIZE YOUR KID?!

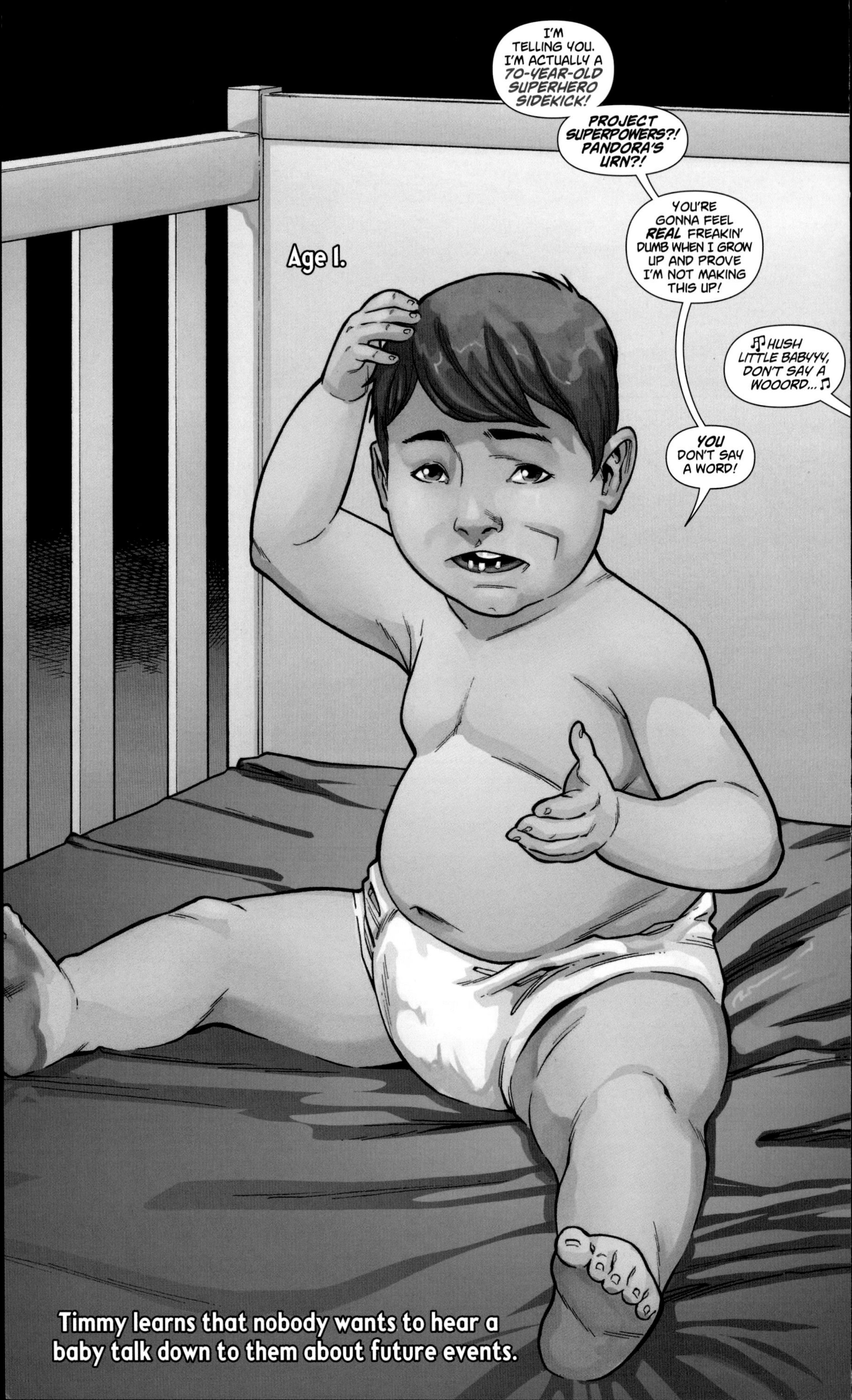

Age 1.
I'M TELLING YOU. I'M ACTUALLY A 70-YEAR-OLD SUPERHERO SIDEKICK!
PROJECT SUPERPOWERS?! PANDORA'S URN?!
YOU'RE GONNA FEEL REAL FREAKIN' DUMB WHEN I GROW UP AND PROVE I'M NOT MAKING THIS UP!
♫ HUSH LITTLE BABYYY, DON'T SAY A WOOORD... ♫
YOU DON'T SAY A WORD!
Timmy learns that nobody wants to hear a baby talk down to them about future events.

HAHAHA! TIMMY IS A DWEEEEEB!

TIMMY TALKS LIKE A WEIRD OL' GEEZER!

AT ME, PHILLIP. YOU HAVE A PHILANDERING, ALCOHOLIC DAD. I DOUBT YOU'LL EVER LEARN HOW TO PLEASURE A WOMAN WITH THAT KIND OF JACKED-UP OEDIPAL HINDERANCE.

APPROVED BY THE COMICS CODE A AUTHORITY

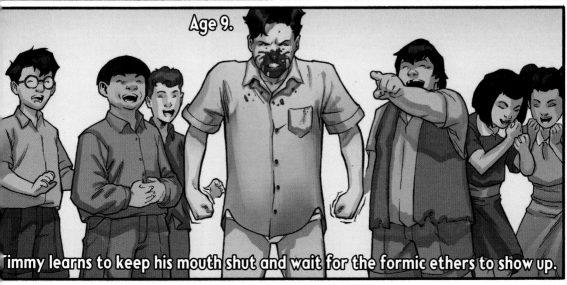

Age 9.

Timmy learns to keep his mouth shut and wait for the formic ethers to show up.

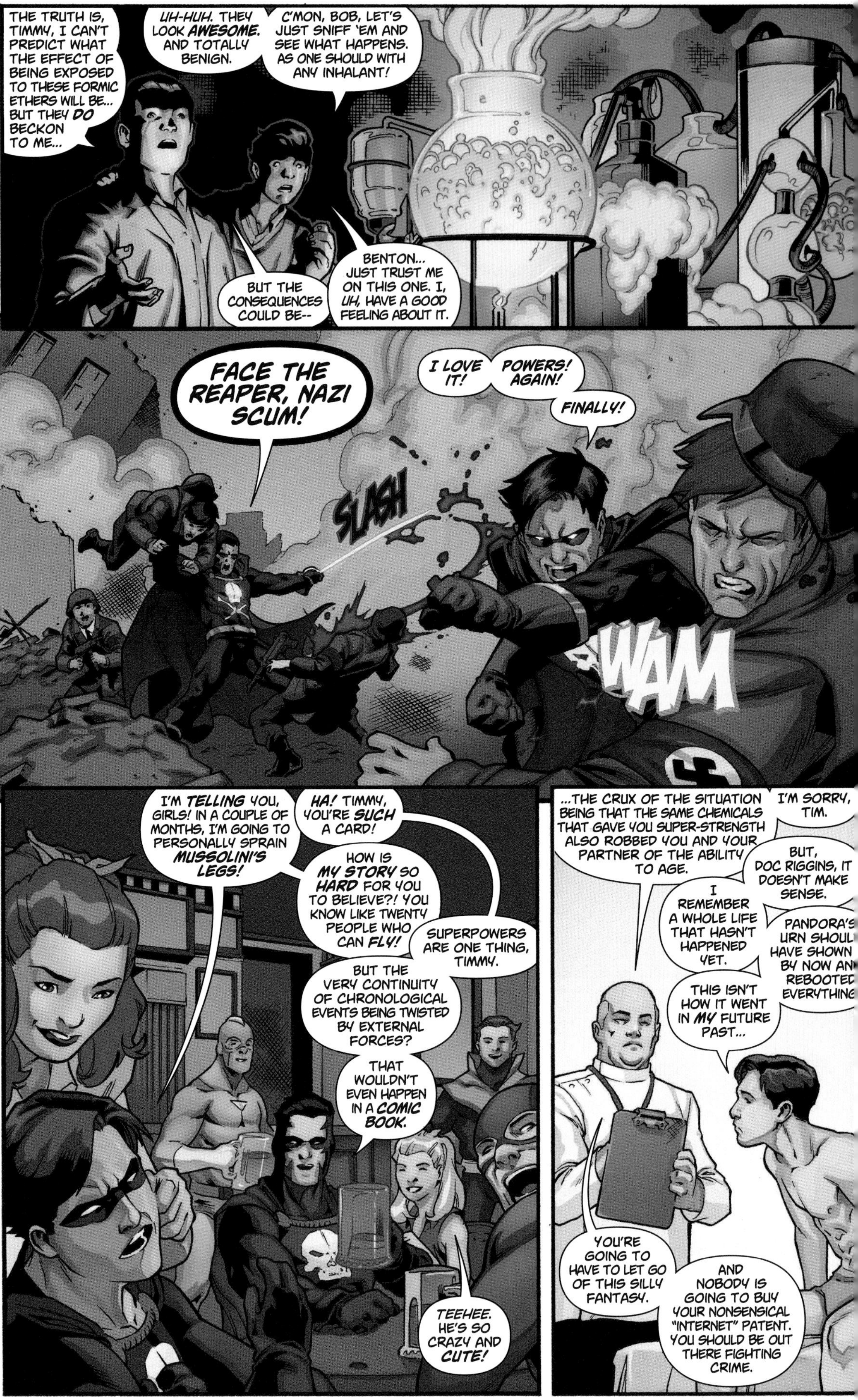
THE TRUTH IS, TIMMY, I CAN'T PREDICT WHAT THE EFFECT OF BEING EXPOSED TO THESE FORMIC ETHERS WILL BE... BUT THEY DO BECKON TO ME...
UH-HUH. THEY LOOK AWESOME. AND TOTALLY BENIGN.
C'MON, BOB, LET'S JUST SNIFF 'EM AND SEE WHAT HAPPENS. AS ONE SHOULD WITH ANY INHALANT!
BUT THE CONSEQUENCES COULD BE--
BENTON... JUST TRUST ME ON THIS ONE. I, UH, HAVE A GOOD FEELING ABOUT IT.
FACE THE REAPER, NAZI SCUM!
I LOVE IT!
POWERS! AGAIN!
FINALLY!
SLASH
WAM
I'M TELLING YOU, GIRLS! IN A COUPLE OF MONTHS, I'M GOING TO PERSONALLY SPRAIN MUSSOLINI'S LEGS!
HA! TIMMY, YOU'RE SUCH A CARD!
HOW IS MY STORY SO HARD FOR YOU TO BELIEVE?! YOU KNOW LIKE TWENTY PEOPLE WHO CAN FLY!
SUPERPOWERS ARE ONE THING, TIMMY.
BUT THE VERY CONTINUITY OF CHRONOLOGICAL EVENTS BEING TWISTED BY EXTERNAL FORCES?
THAT WOULDN'T EVEN HAPPEN IN A COMIC BOOK.
TEEHEE. HE'S SO CRAZY AND CUTE!
...THE CRUX OF THE SITUATION BEING THAT THE SAME CHEMICALS THAT GAVE YOU SUPER-STRENGTH ALSO ROBBED YOU AND YOUR PARTNER OF THE ABILITY TO AGE.
I'M SORRY, TIM.
BUT, DOC RIGGINS, IT DOESN'T MAKE SENSE.
I REMEMBER A WHOLE LIFE THAT HASN'T HAPPENED YET.
PANDORA'S URN SHOUL HAVE SHOWN BY NOW AN REBOOTED EVERYTHING
THIS ISN'T HOW IT WENT IN MY FUTURE PAST...
YOU'RE GOING TO HAVE TO LET GO OF THIS SILLY FANTASY.
AND NOBODY IS GOING TO BUY YOUR NONSENSICAL "INTERNET" PATENT. YOU SHOULD BE OUT THERE FIGHTING CRIME.

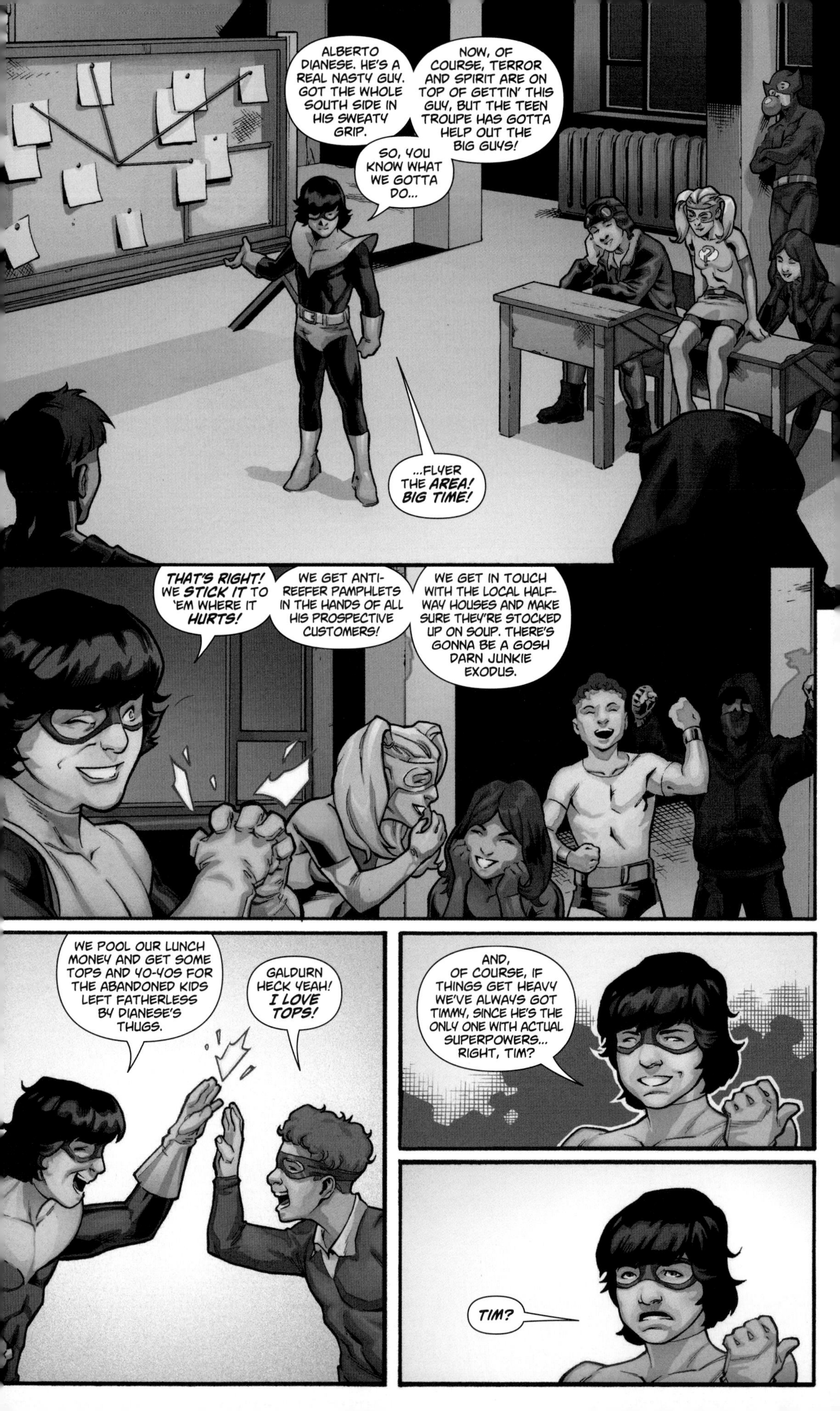
ALBERTO DIANESE. HE'S A REAL NASTY GUY. GOT THE WHOLE SOUTH SIDE IN HIS SWEATY GRIP.
NOW, OF COURSE, TERROR AND SPIRIT ARE ON TOP OF GETTIN' THIS GUY, BUT THE TEEN TROUPE HAS GOTTA HELP OUT THE BIG GUYS!
SO, YOU KNOW WHAT WE GOTTA DO...
...FLYER THE AREA! BIG TIME!
THAT'S RIGHT! WE STICK IT TO 'EM WHERE IT HURTS!
WE GET ANTI-REEFER PAMPHLETS IN THE HANDS OF ALL HIS PROSPECTIVE CUSTOMERS!
WE GET IN TOUCH WITH THE LOCAL HALF-WAY HOUSES AND MAKE SURE THEY'RE STOCKED UP ON SOUP. THERE'S GONNA BE A GOSH DARN JUNKIE EXODUS.
WE POOL OUR LUNCH MONEY AND GET SOME TOPS AND YO-YOS FOR THE ABANDONED KIDS LEFT FATHERLESS BY DIANESE'S THUGS.
GALDURN HECK YEAH! I LOVE TOPS!
AND, OF COURSE, IF THINGS GET HEAVY WE'VE ALWAYS GOT TIMMY, SINCE HE'S THE ONLY ONE WITH ACTUAL SUPERPOWERS... RIGHT, TIM?
TIM?

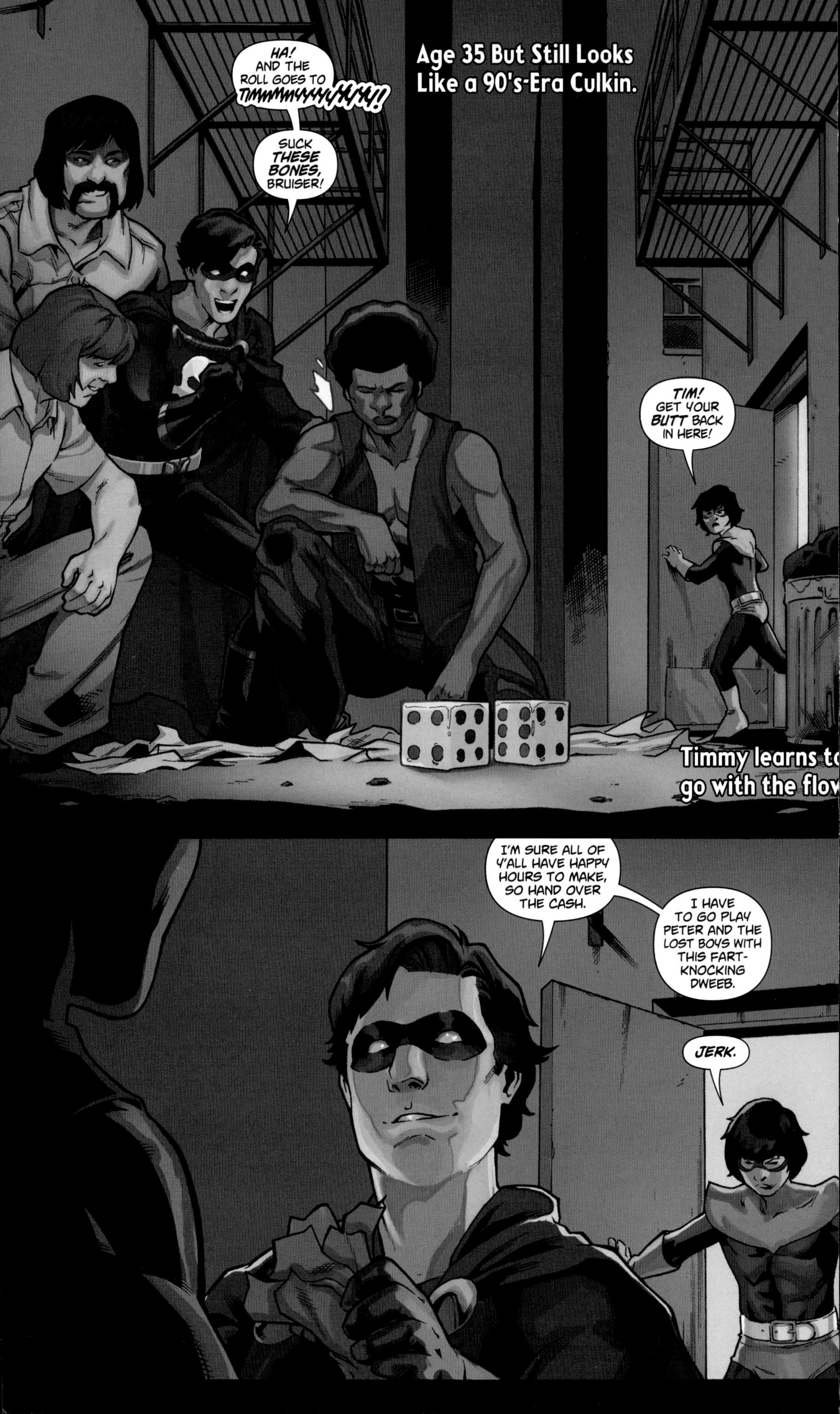
Age 35 But Still Looks Like a 90's-Era Culkin.
HA! AND THE ROLL GOES TO TIMMMMYYYYYYYY!
SUCK THESE BONES, BRUISER!
TIM! GET YOUR BUTT BACK IN HERE!
Timmy learns to go with the flow
I'M SURE ALL OF Y'ALL HAVE HAPPY HOURS TO MAKE, SO HAND OVER THE CASH.
I HAVE TO GO PLAY PETER AND THE LOST BOYS WITH THIS FART-KNOCKING DWEEB.
JERK.

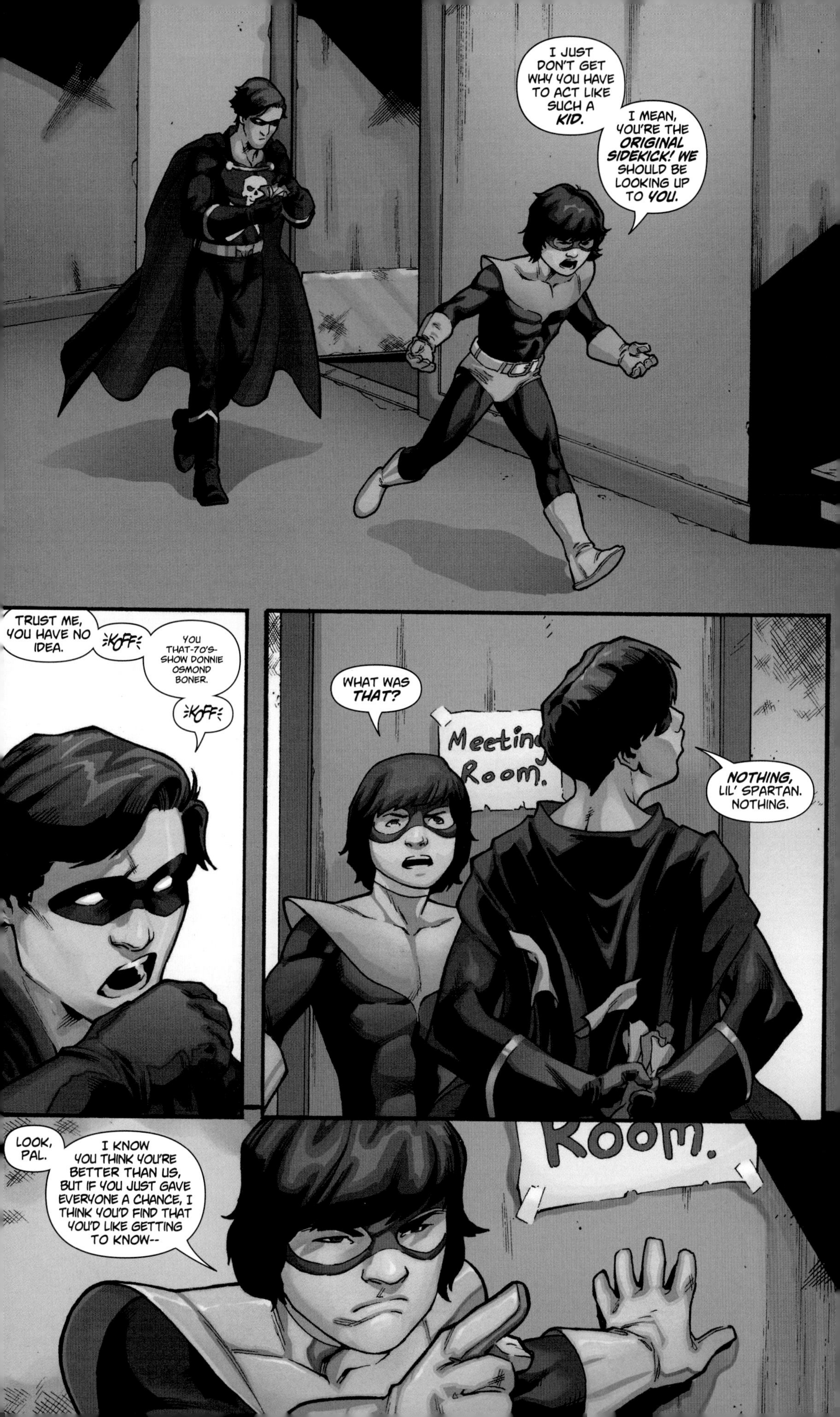
I JUST DON'T GET WHY YOU HAVE TO ACT LIKE SUCH A KID.
I MEAN, YOU'RE THE ORIGINAL SIDEKICK! WE SHOULD BE LOOKING UP TO YOU.
TRUST ME, YOU HAVE NO IDEA.
KOFF
YOU THAT-70'S-SHOW DONNIE OSMOND BONER.
KOFF
WHAT WAS THAT?
Meeting Room.
NOTHING, LIL' SPARTAN. NOTHING.
LOOK, PAL.
I KNOW YOU THINK YOU'RE BETTER THAN US, BUT IF YOU JUST GAVE EVERYONE A CHANCE, I THINK YOU'D FIND THAT YOU'D LIKE GETTING TO KNOW--
ROOM.

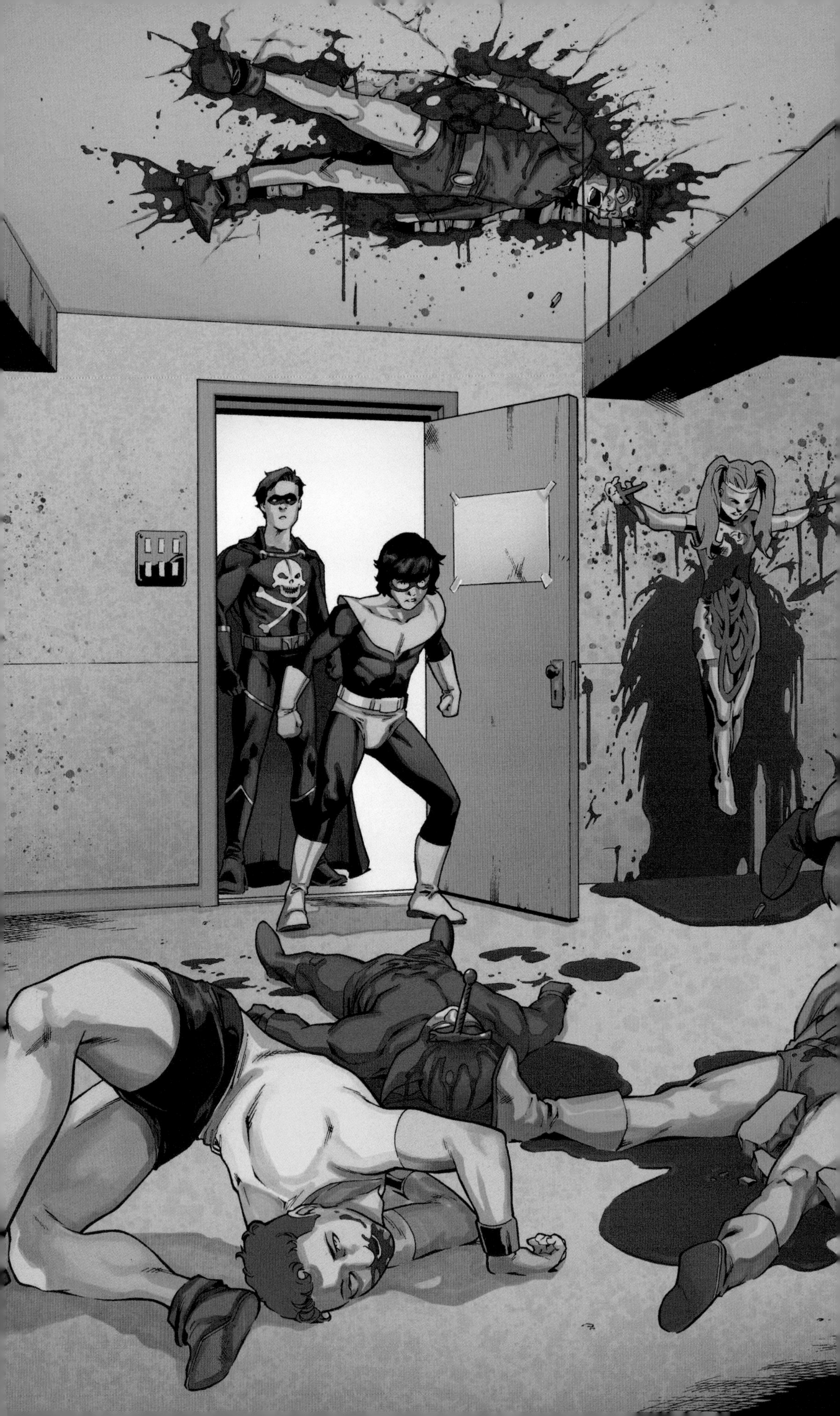

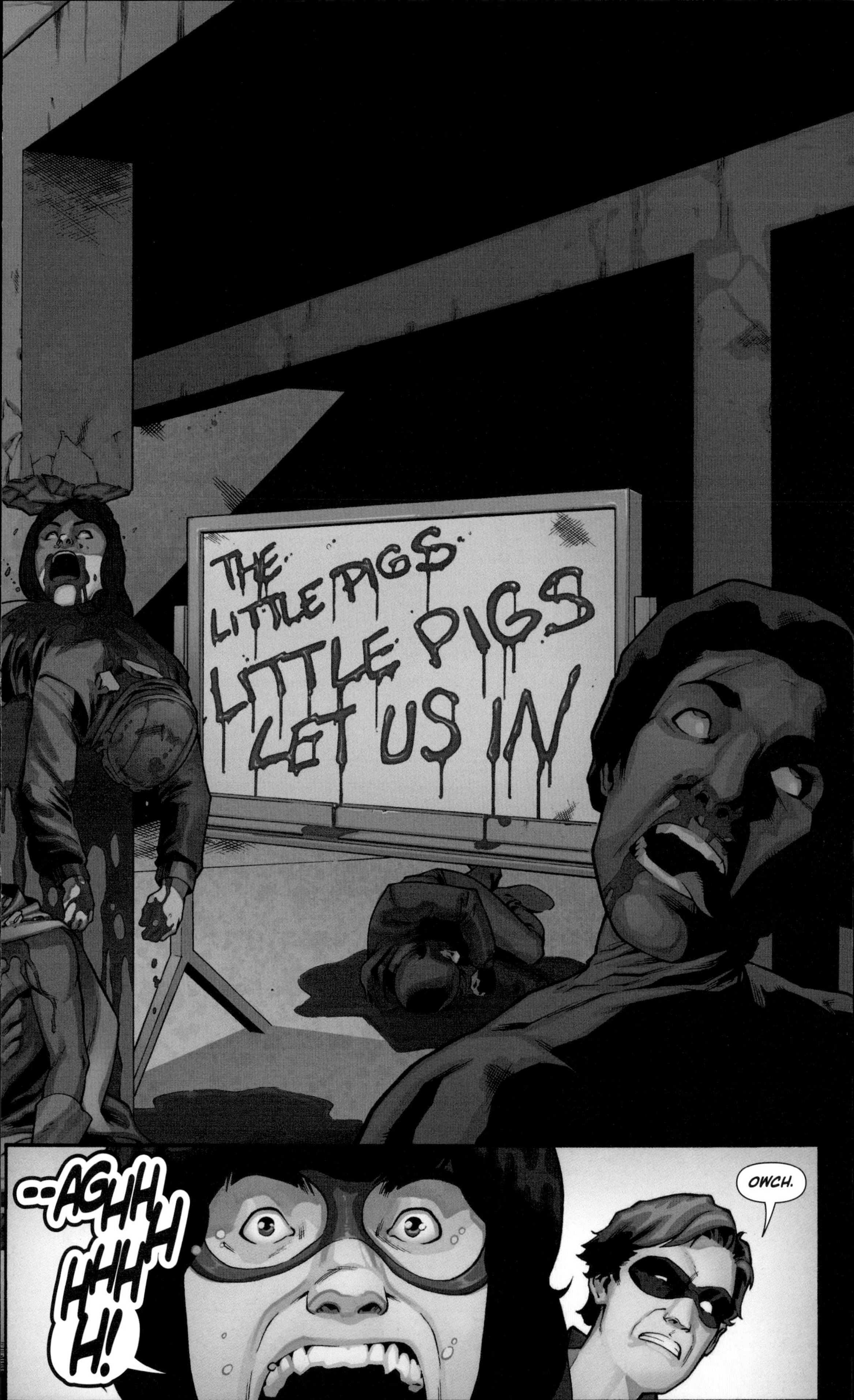
THE LITTLE PIGS LITTLE PIGS LET US IN
--AGHHHHHHH!
OWCH.

MOONBOY?

THROAT SLIT.

MS. MYSTERY?

DISEMBOWELED, SADLY.

WHAT ABOUT THAT LIL' SPARTAN KID?

HE'S ACTUALLY THE ONLY ONE WHO WASN'T BRUTALLY MURDERED.

HMMMPH.

I KNOW. HE'S A PIECE.

MMMF!

ANY LEADS?

WELL, THERE WAS GOING TO BE AN ATTEMPT TO DO SOME DAMAGE TO THE DIANESE FAMILY'S OPERATIONS.

THAT'S AMBITIOUS. THOSE GUYS ARE MONSTERS.

WELL, I SUPPOSE WE SHOULD GO TERRIFY THEM.

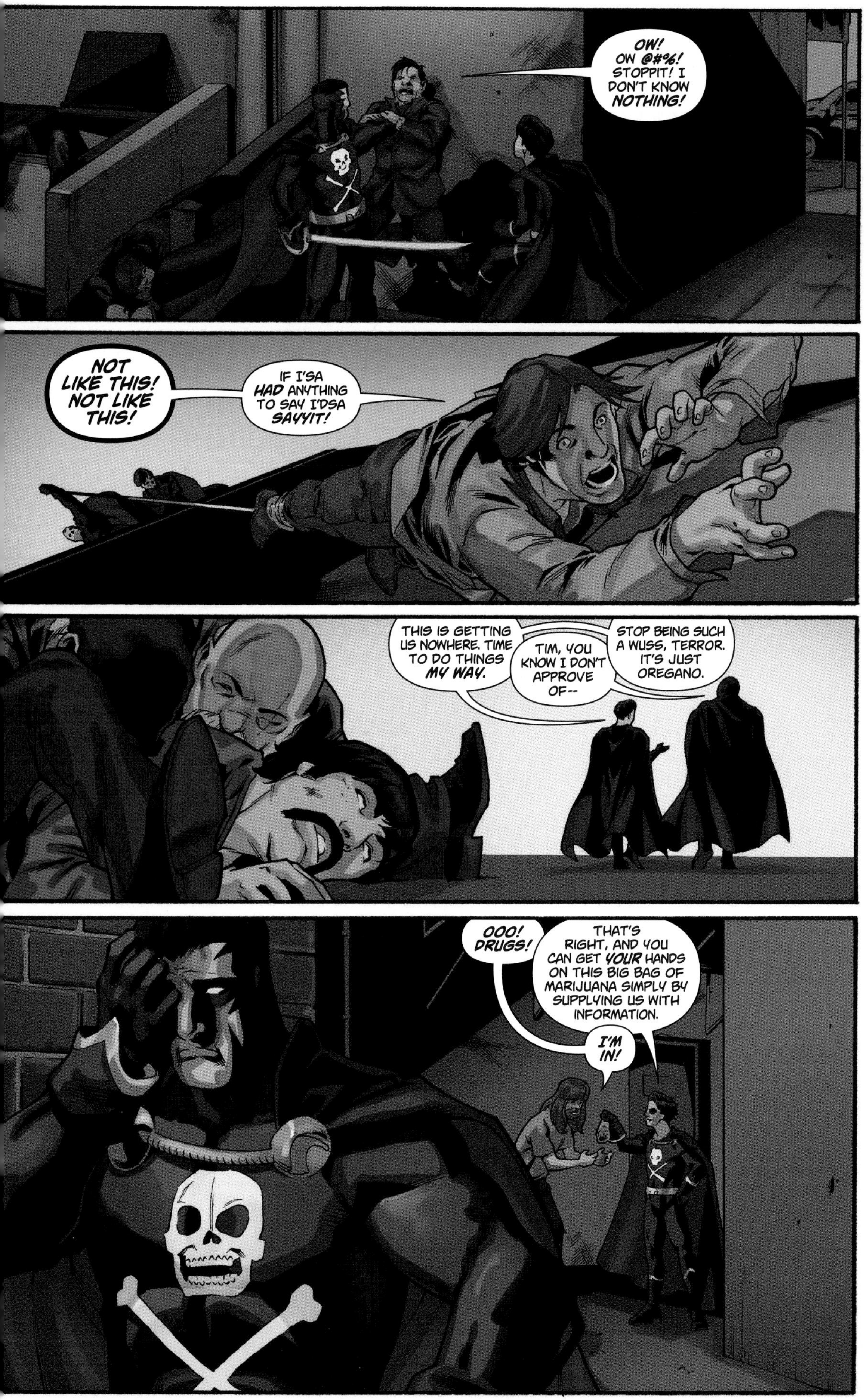
OW! OW @#%! STOPPIT! I DON'T KNOW NOTHING!
NOT LIKE THIS! NOT LIKE THIS!
IF I'SA HAD ANYTHING TO SAY I'DSA SAYYIT!
THIS IS GETTING US NOWHERE. TIME TO DO THINGS MY WAY.
TIM, YOU KNOW I DON'T APPROVE OF--
STOP BEING SUCH A WUSS, TERROR. IT'S JUST OREGANO.
OOO! DRUGS!
THAT'S RIGHT, AND YOU CAN GET YOUR HANDS ON THIS BIG BAG OF MARIJUANA SIMPLY BY SUPPLYING US WITH INFORMATION.
I'M IN!

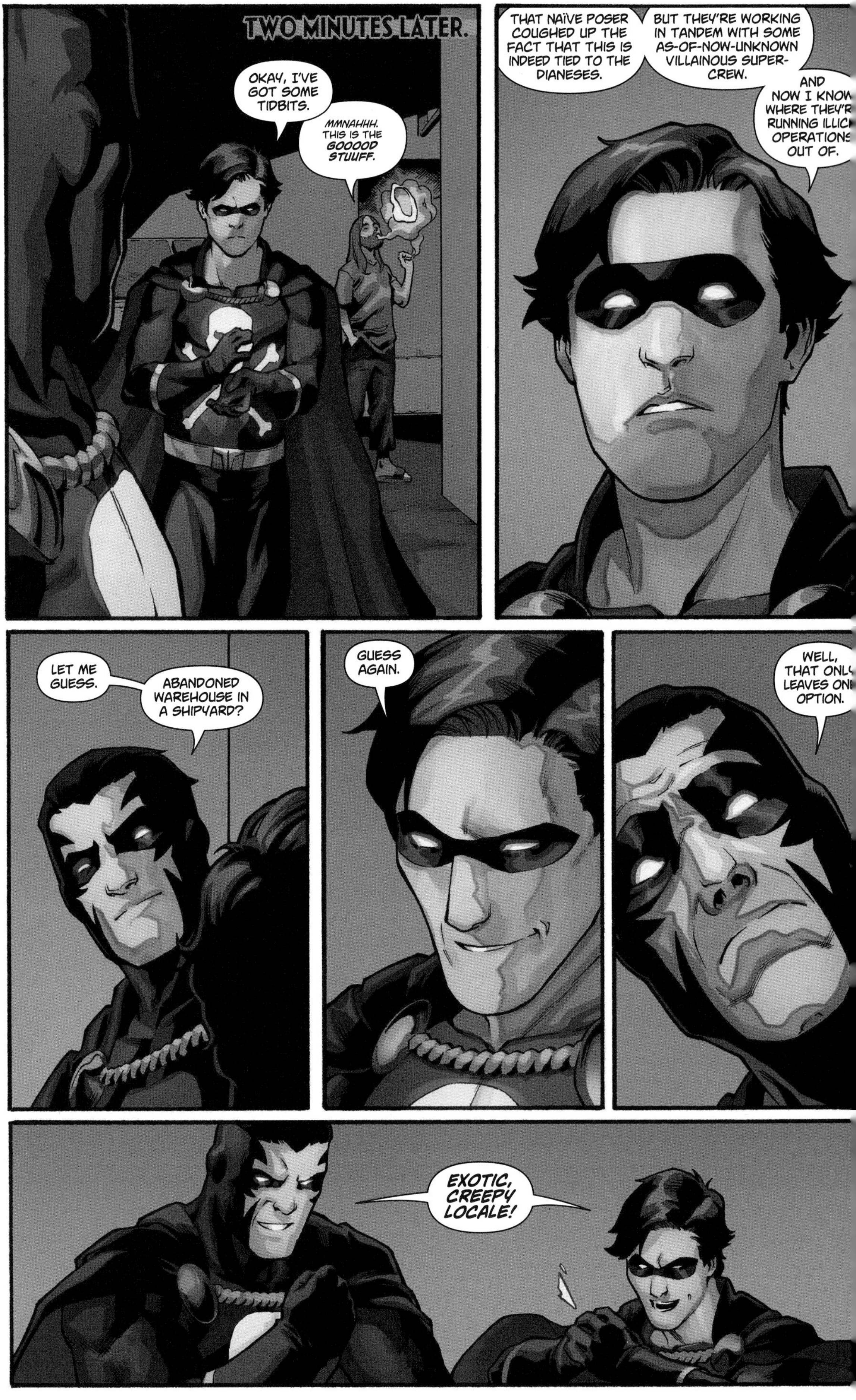
TWO MINUTES LATER.
OKAY, I'VE GOT SOME TIDBITS.
MMNAHHH. THIS IS THE GOOOOD STUUFF.
THAT NAÏVE POSER COUGHED UP THE FACT THAT THIS IS INDEED TIED TO THE DIANESES.
BUT THEY'RE WORKING IN TANDEM WITH SOME AS-OF-NOW-UNKNOWN VILLAINOUS SUPER-CREW.
AND NOW I KNOW WHERE THEY'R RUNNING ILLIC OPERATIONS OUT OF.
LET ME GUESS.
ABANDONED WAREHOUSE IN A SHIPYARD?
GUESS AGAIN.
WELL, THAT ONL LEAVES ON OPTION.
EXOTIC, CREEPY LOCALE!

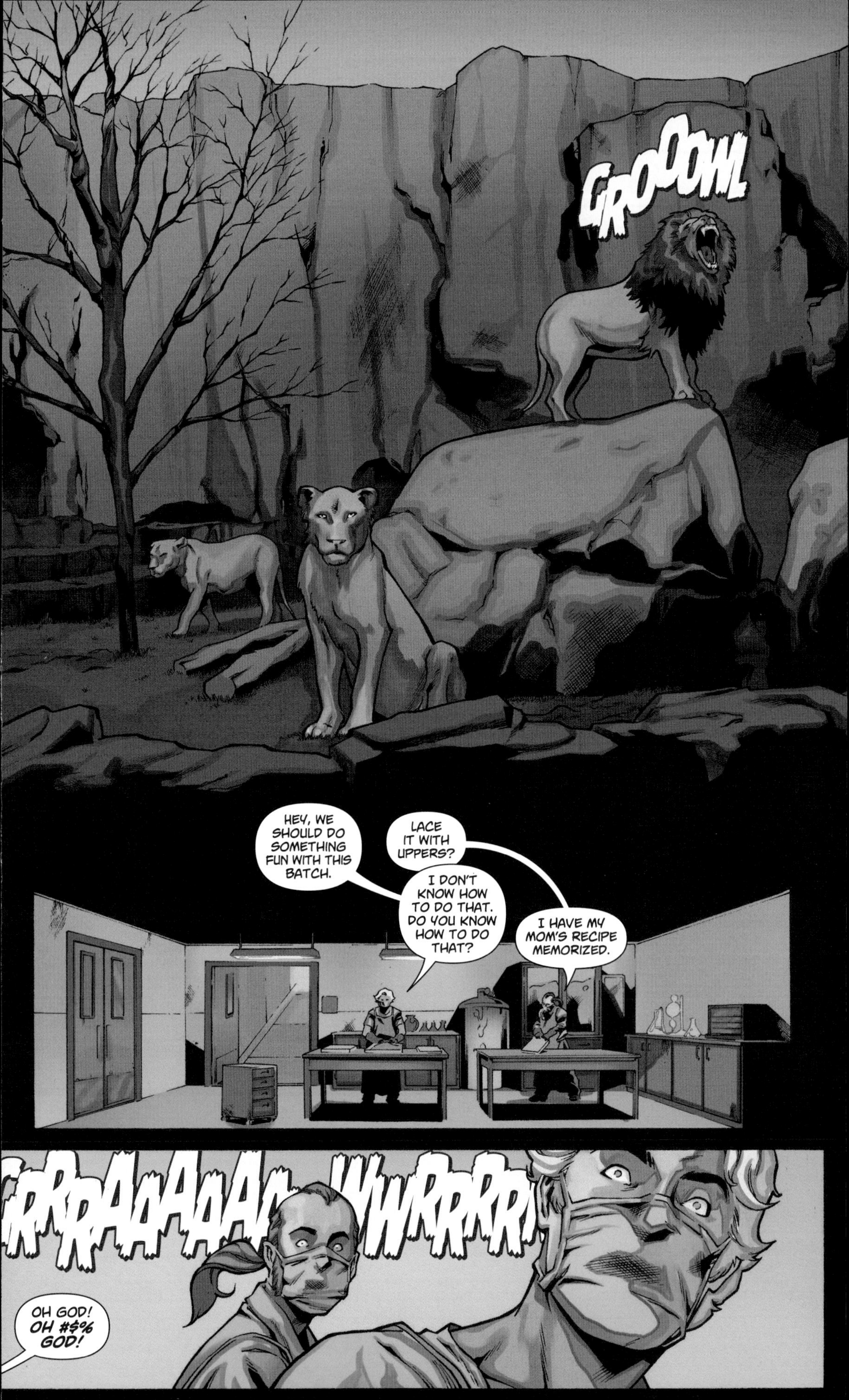
GROOOWL
HEY, WE SHOULD DO SOMETHING FUN WITH THIS BATCH.
LACE IT WITH UPPERS?
I DON'T KNOW HOW TO DO THAT. DO YOU KNOW HOW TO DO THAT?
I HAVE MY MOM'S RECIPE MEMORIZED.
GRRRAAAAAAWRRRR
OH GOD! OH #$% GOD!

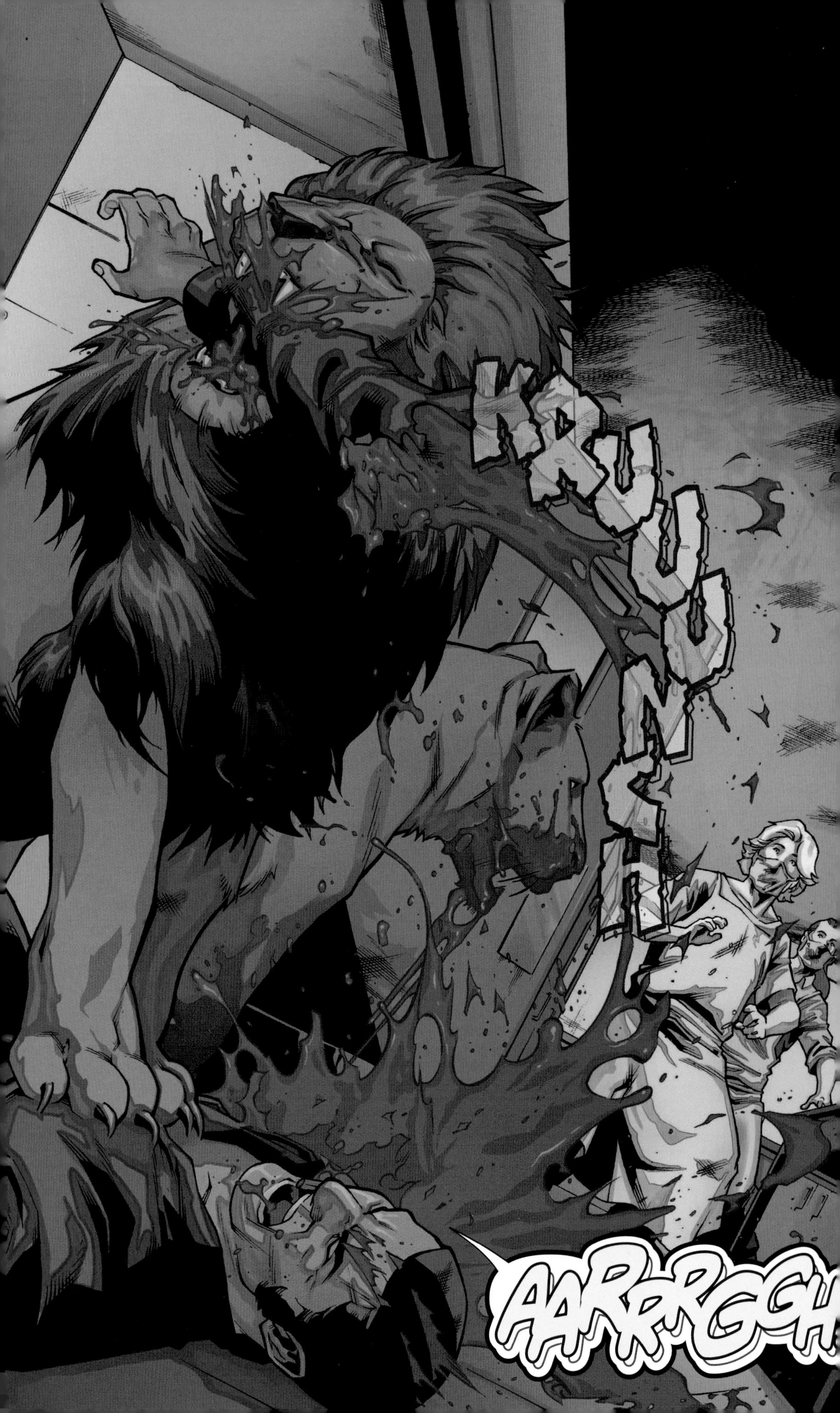
KRUUNCH
AARRRGGH

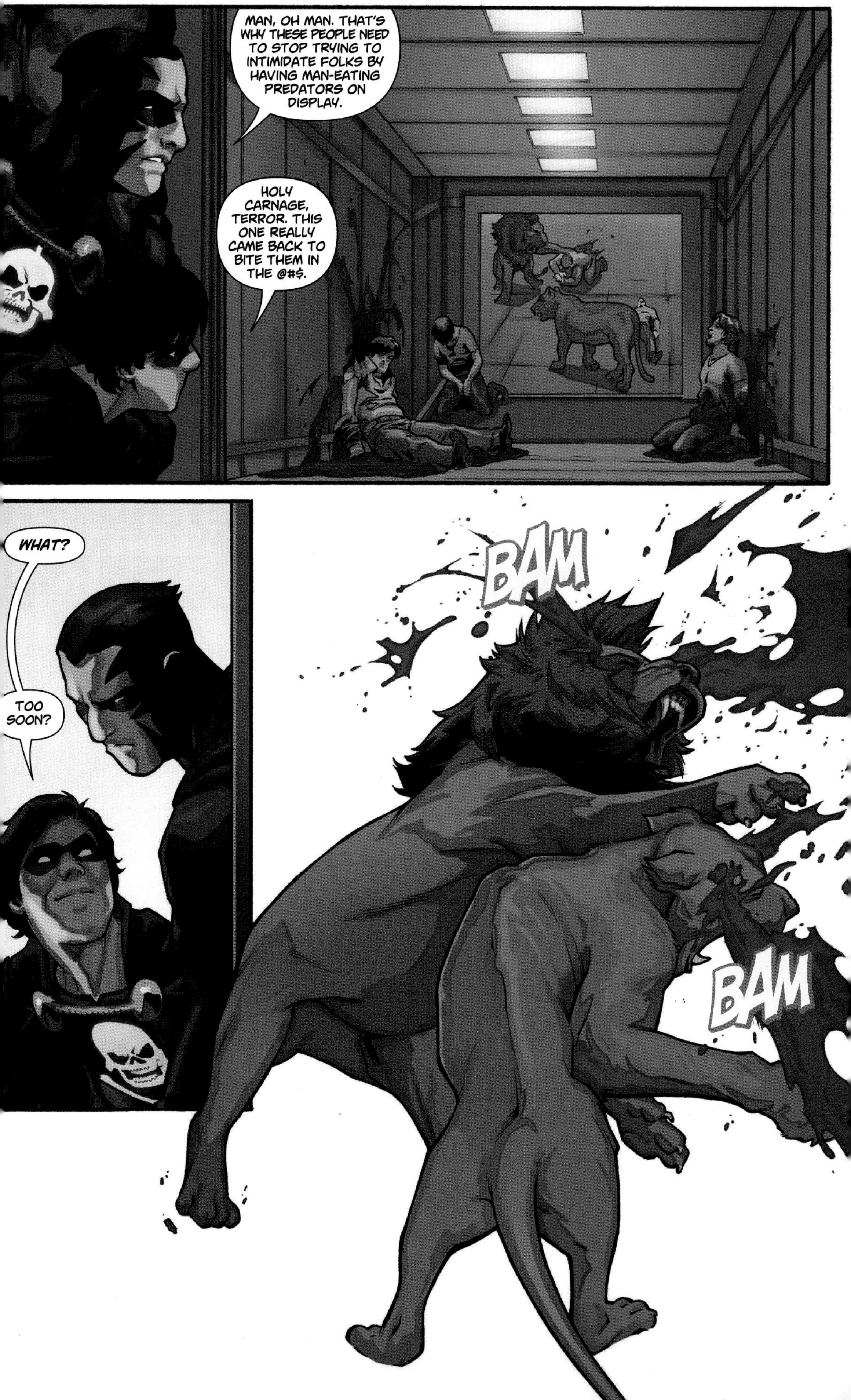
MAN, OH MAN. THAT'S WHY THESE PEOPLE NEED TO STOP TRYING TO INTIMIDATE FOLKS BY HAVING MAN-EATING PREDATORS ON DISPLAY.
HOLY CARNAGE, TERROR. THIS ONE REALLY CAME BACK TO BITE THEM IN THE @#$.
WHAT?
TOO SOON?
BAM
BAM

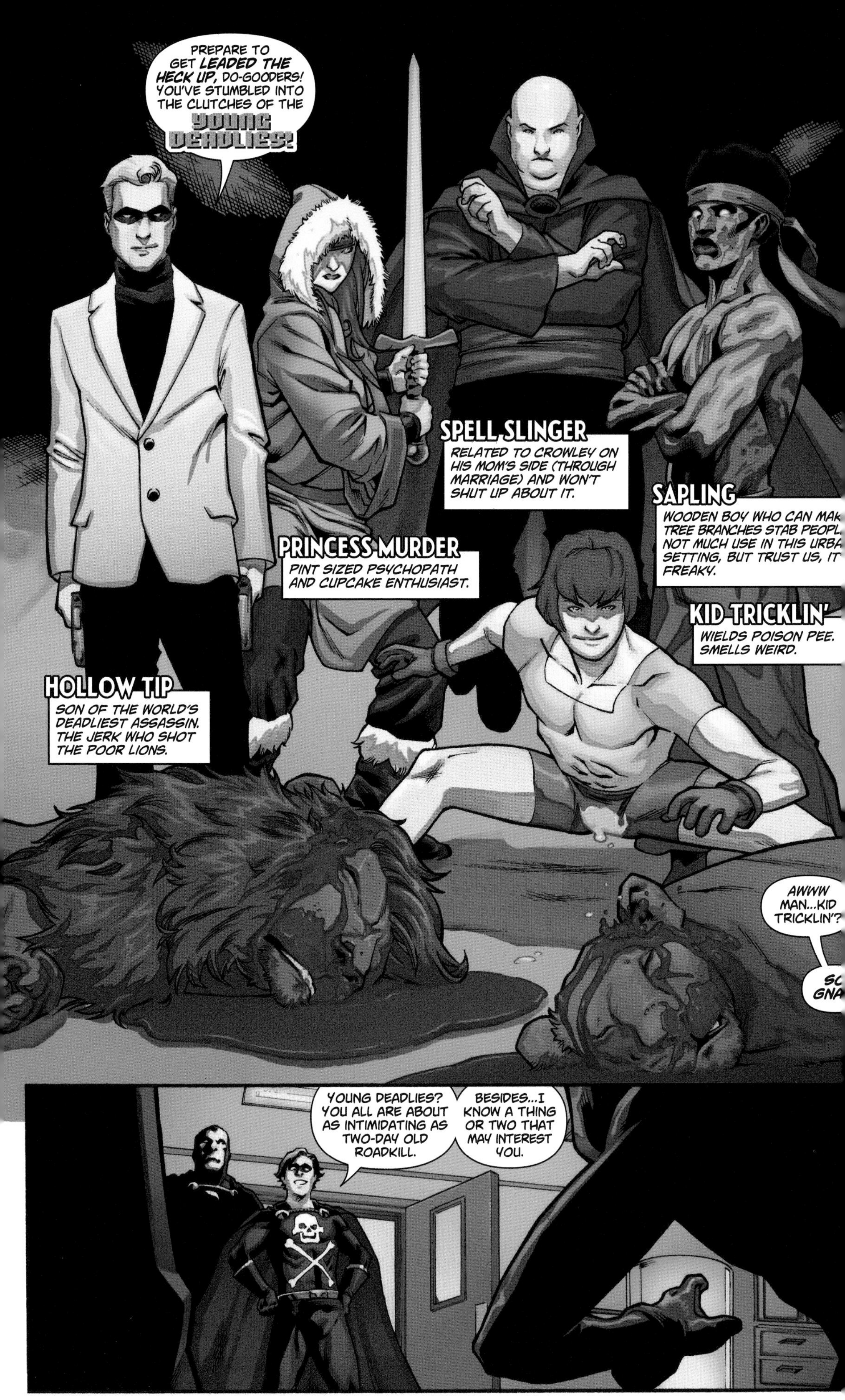
PREPARE TO GET **LEADED THE HECK UP,** DO-GOODERS! YOU'VE STUMBLED INTO THE CLUTCHES OF THE YOUNG DEADLIES!
SPELL SLINGER
RELATED TO CROWLEY ON HIS MOM'S SIDE (THROUGH MARRIAGE) AND WON'T SHUT UP ABOUT IT.
SAPLING
WOODEN BOY WHO CAN MAK TREE BRANCHES STAB PEOPL NOT MUCH USE IN THIS URBA SETTING, BUT TRUST US, IT FREAKY.
PRINCESS MURDER
PINT SIZED PSYCHOPATH AND CUPCAKE ENTHUSIAST.
KID TRICKLIN'
WIELDS POISON PEE. SMELLS WEIRD.
HOLLOW TIP
SON OF THE WORLD'S DEADLIEST ASSASSIN. THE JERK WHO SHOT THE POOR LIONS.
AWWW MAN...KID TRICKLIN'?
YOUNG DEADLIES? YOU ALL ARE ABOUT AS INTIMIDATING AS TWO-DAY OLD ROADKILL.
BESIDES...I KNOW A THING OR TWO THAT MAY INTEREST YOU.

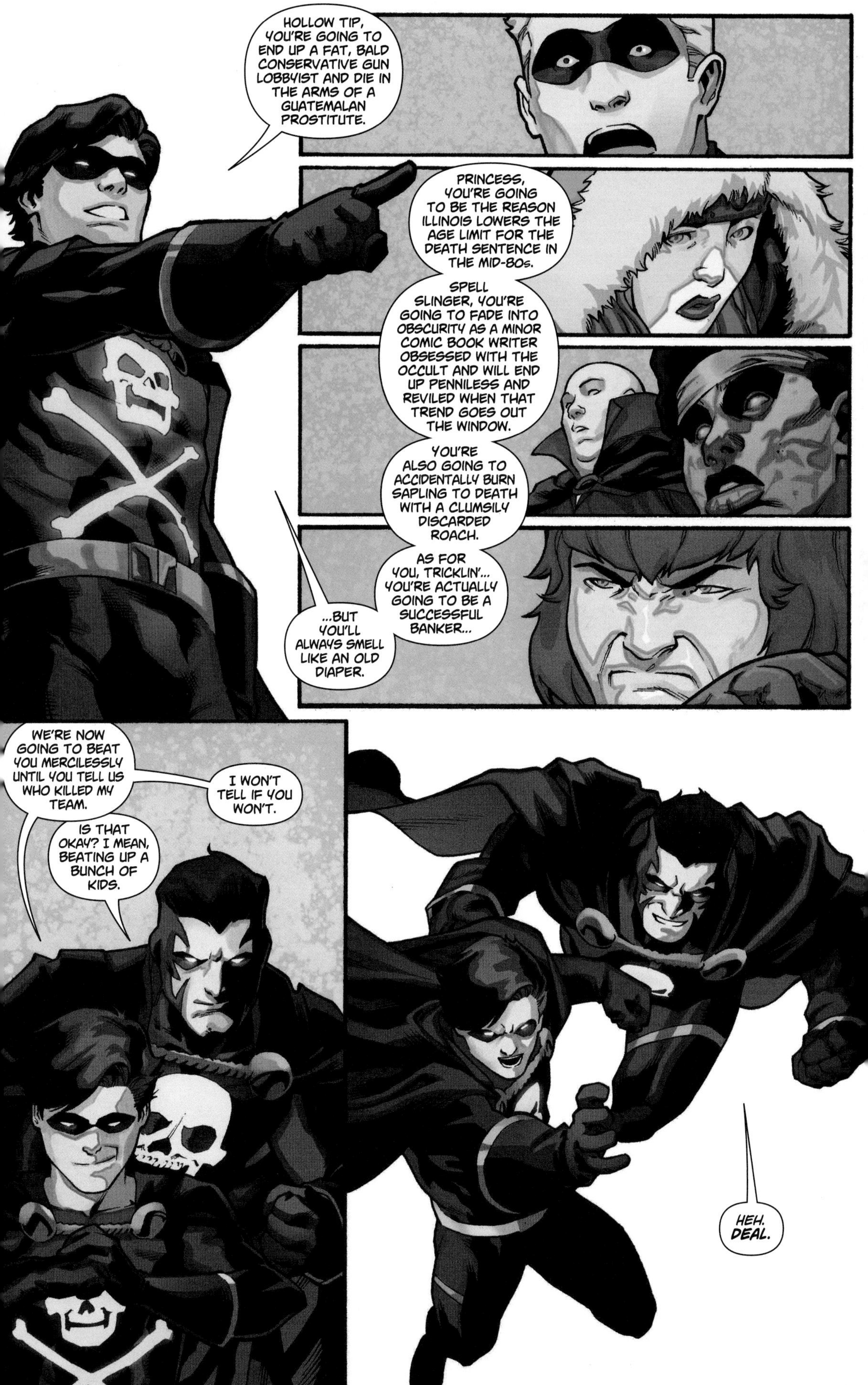
HOLLOW TIP, YOU'RE GOING TO END UP A FAT, BALD CONSERVATIVE GUN LOBBYIST AND DIE IN THE ARMS OF A GUATEMALAN PROSTITUTE.
PRINCESS, YOU'RE GOING TO BE THE REASON ILLINOIS LOWERS THE AGE LIMIT FOR THE DEATH SENTENCE IN THE MID-80s.
SPELL SLINGER, YOU'RE GOING TO FADE INTO OBSCURITY AS A MINOR COMIC BOOK WRITER OBSESSED WITH THE OCCULT AND WILL END UP PENNILESS AND REVILED WHEN THAT TREND GOES OUT THE WINDOW.
YOU'RE ALSO GOING TO ACCIDENTALLY BURN SAPLING TO DEATH WITH A CLUMSILY DISCARDED ROACH.
AS FOR YOU, TRICKLIN'... YOU'RE ACTUALLY GOING TO BE A SUCCESSFUL BANKER...
...BUT YOU'LL ALWAYS SMELL LIKE AN OLD DIAPER.
WE'RE NOW GOING TO BEAT YOU MERCILESSLY UNTIL YOU TELL US WHO KILLED MY TEAM.
IS THAT OKAY? I MEAN, BEATING UP A BUNCH OF KIDS.
I WON'T TELL IF YOU WON'T.
HEH. DEAL.

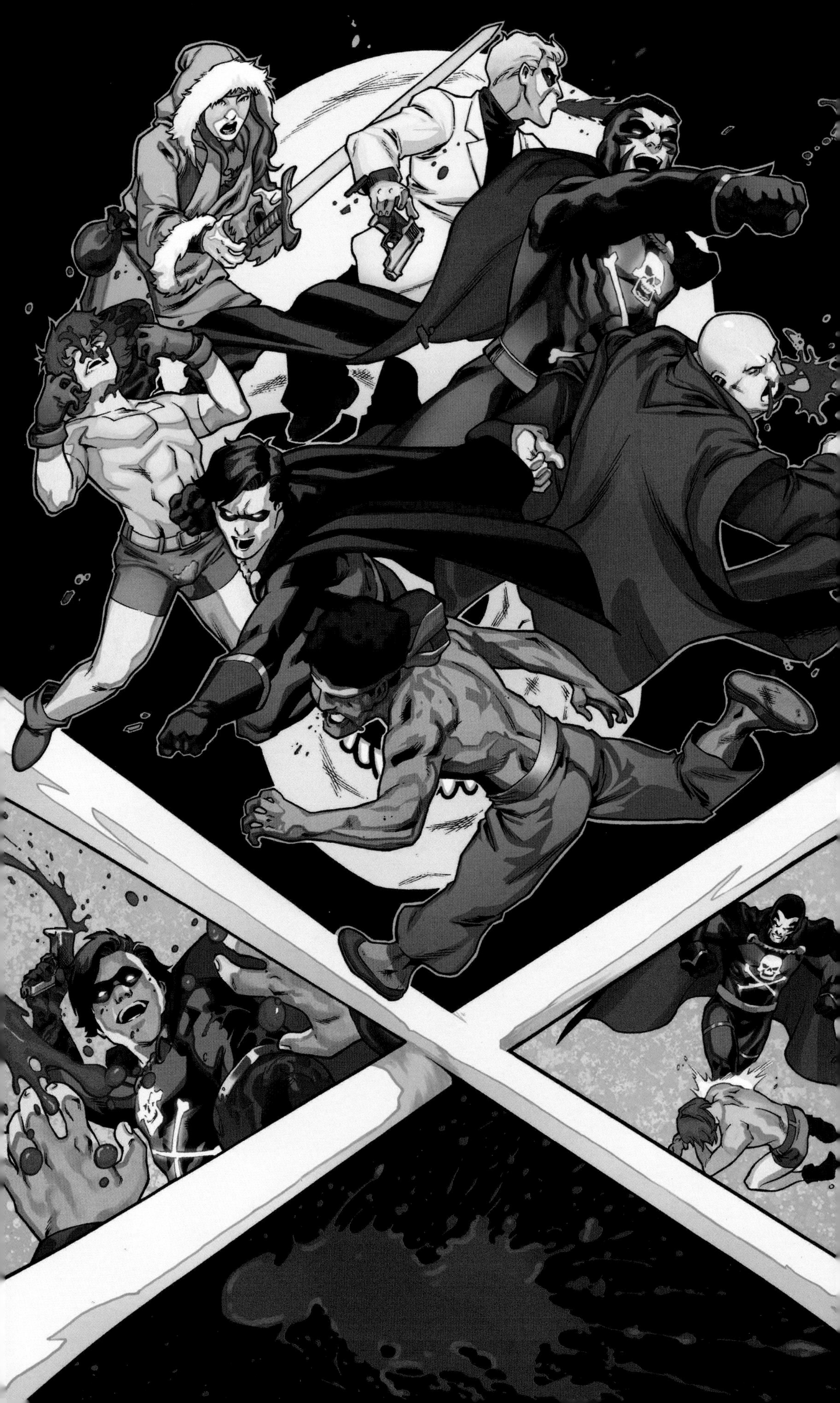

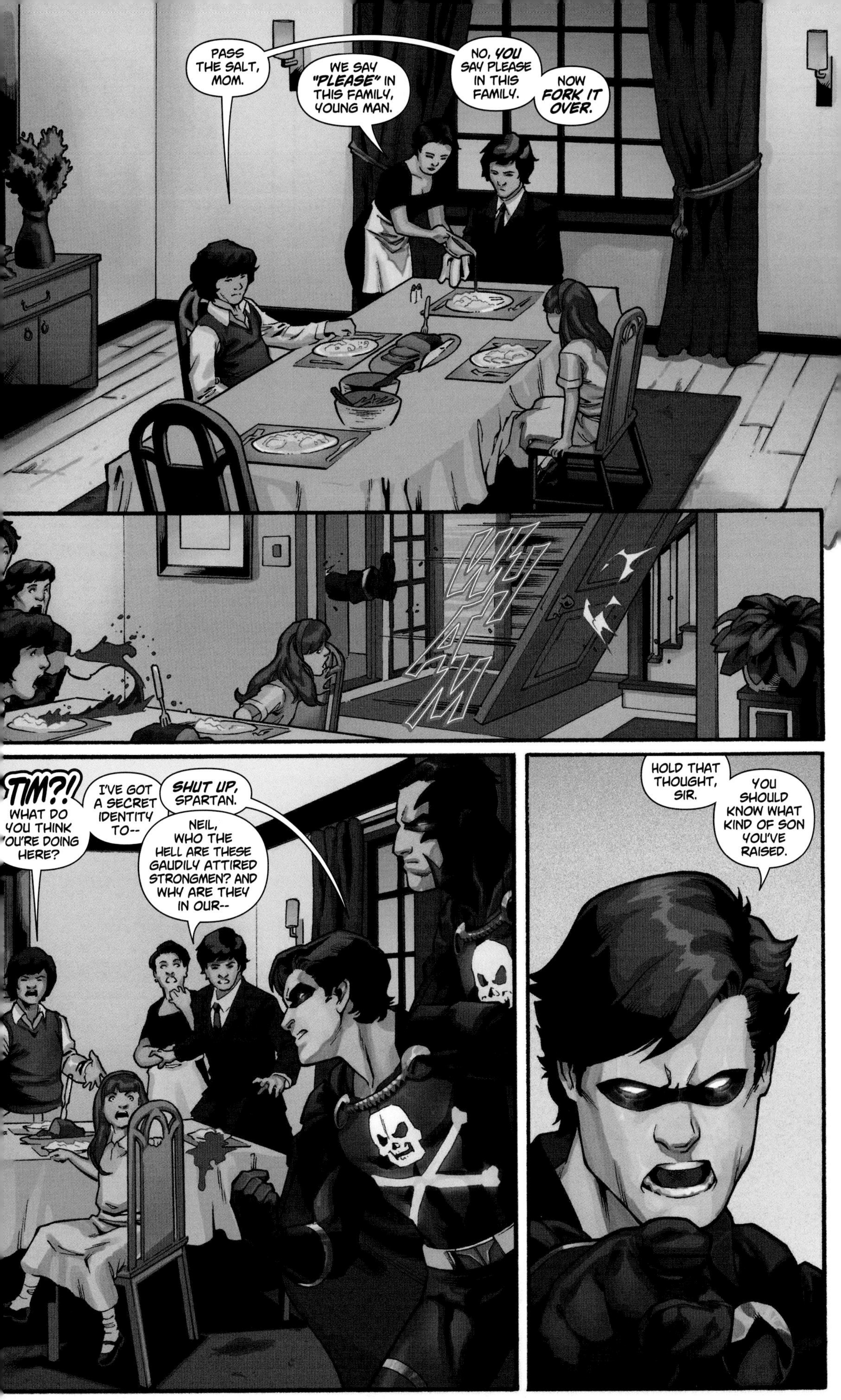
PASS THE SALT, MOM.
WE SAY "PLEASE" IN THIS FAMILY, YOUNG MAN.
NO, YOU SAY PLEASE IN THIS FAMILY.
NOW FORK IT OVER.
TIM?! WHAT DO YOU THINK YOU'RE DOING HERE?
I'VE GOT A SECRET IDENTITY TO--
SHUT UP, SPARTAN.
NEIL, WHO THE HELL ARE THESE GAUDILY ATTIRED STRONGMEN? AND WHY ARE THEY IN OUR--
HOLD THAT THOUGHT, SIR.
YOU SHOULD KNOW WHAT KIND OF SON YOU'VE RAISED.

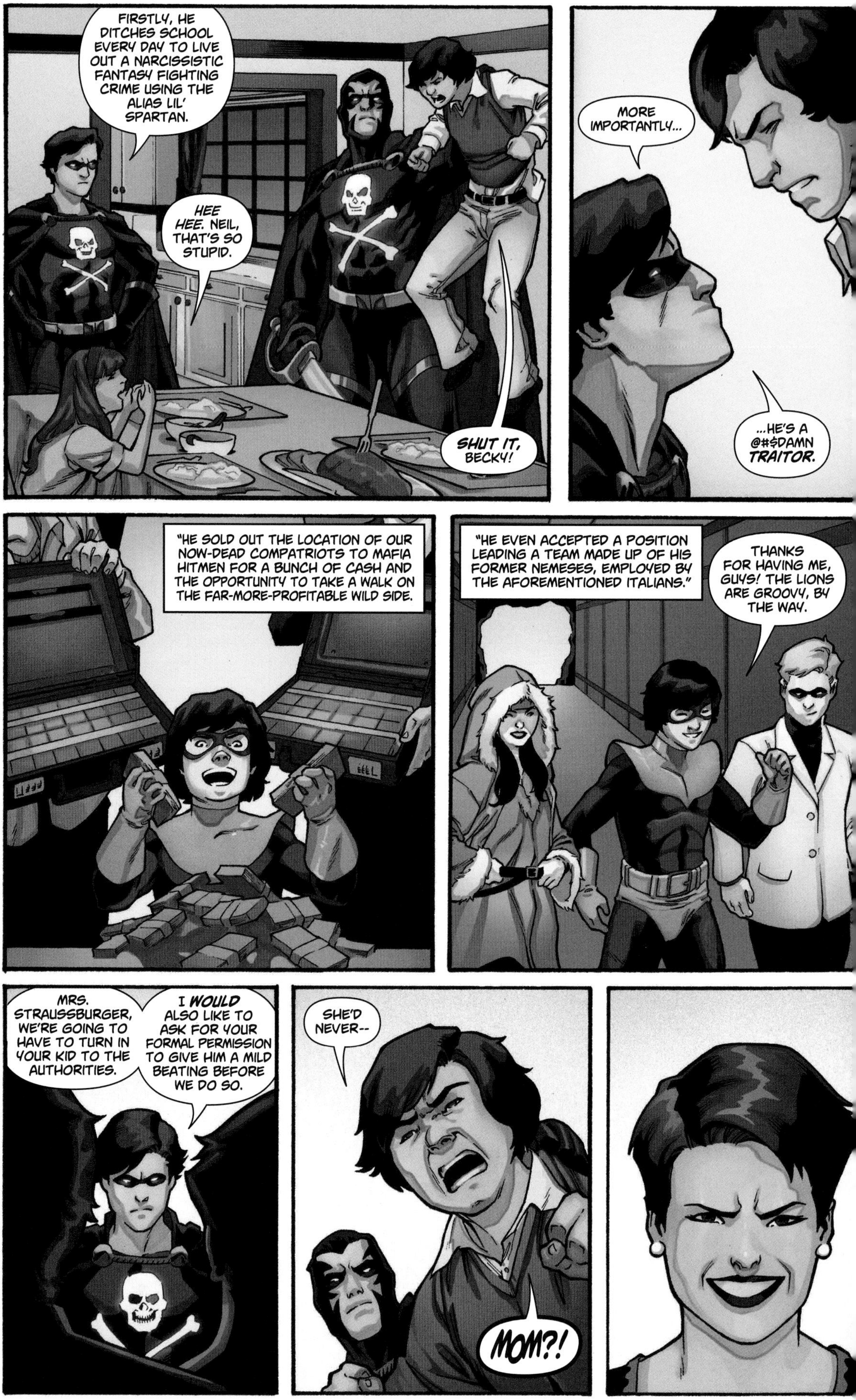
FIRSTLY, HE DITCHES SCHOOL EVERY DAY TO LIVE OUT A NARCISSISTIC FANTASY FIGHTING CRIME USING THE ALIAS LIL' SPARTAN.
HEE HEE. NEIL, THAT'S SO STUPID.
SHUT IT, BECKY!
MORE IMPORTANTLY...
...HE'S A @#$DAMN TRAITOR.
"HE SOLD OUT THE LOCATION OF OUR NOW-DEAD COMPATRIOTS TO MAFIA HITMEN FOR A BUNCH OF CASH AND THE OPPORTUNITY TO TAKE A WALK ON THE FAR-MORE-PROFITABLE WILD SIDE.
"HE EVEN ACCEPTED A POSITION LEADING A TEAM MADE UP OF HIS FORMER NEMESES, EMPLOYED BY THE AFOREMENTIONED ITALIANS."
THANKS FOR HAVING ME, GUYS! THE LIONS ARE GROOVY, BY THE WAY.
MRS. STRAUSSBURGER, WE'RE GOING TO HAVE TO TURN IN YOUR KID TO THE AUTHORITIES.
I WOULD ALSO LIKE TO ASK FOR YOUR FORMAL PERMISSION TO GIVE HIM A MILD BEATING BEFORE WE DO SO.
SHE'D NEVER--
MOM?!

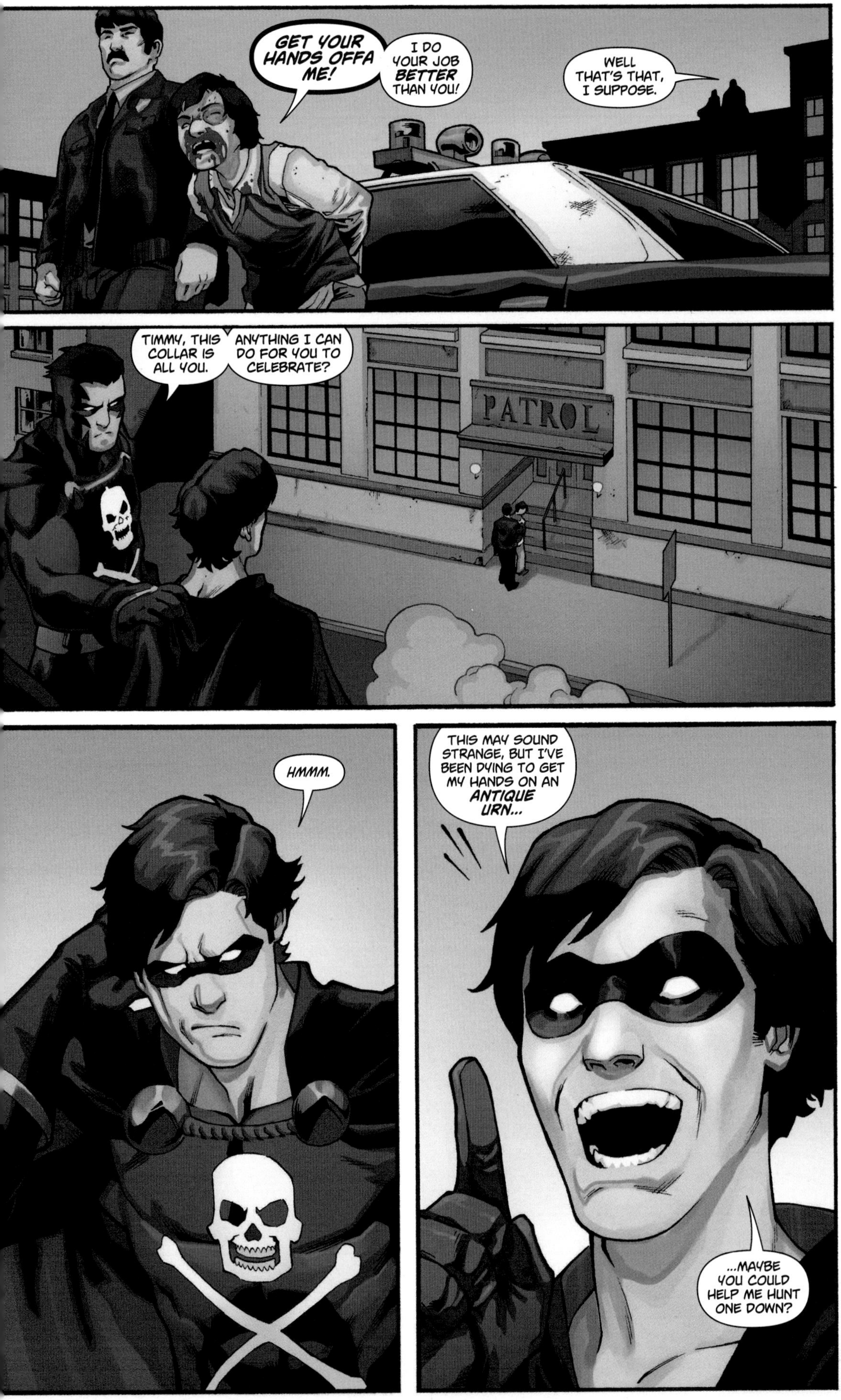
GET YOUR HANDS OFFA ME!
I DO YOUR JOB BETTER THAN YOU!
WELL THAT'S THAT, I SUPPOSE.
PATROL
TIMMY, THIS COLLAR IS ALL YOU.
ANYTHING I CAN DO FOR YOU TO CELEBRATE?
HMMM.
THIS MAY SOUND STRANGE, BUT I'VE BEEN DYING TO GET MY HANDS ON AN ANTIQUE URN...
...MAYBE YOU COULD HELP ME HUNT ONE DOWN?

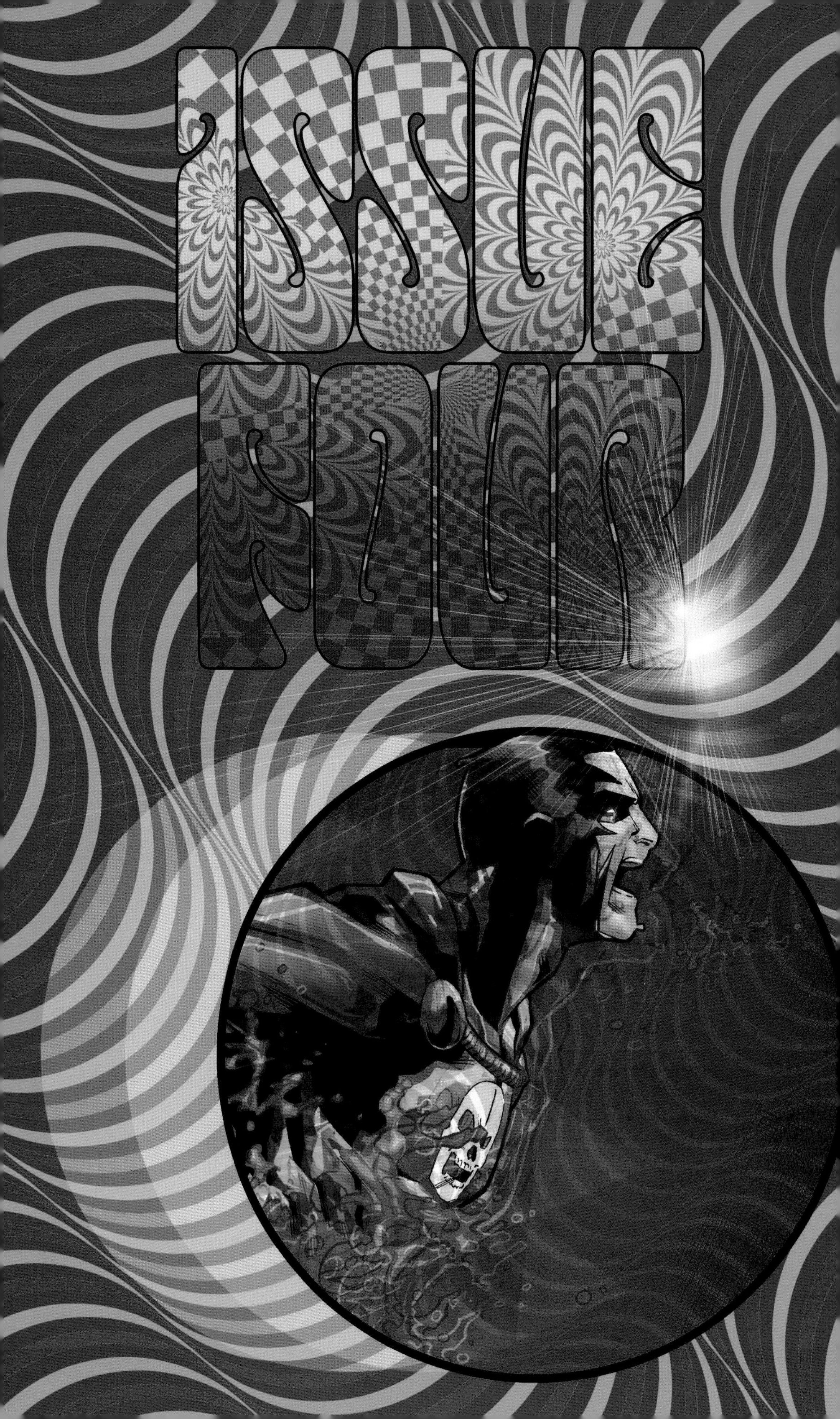
ISSUE
FOUR

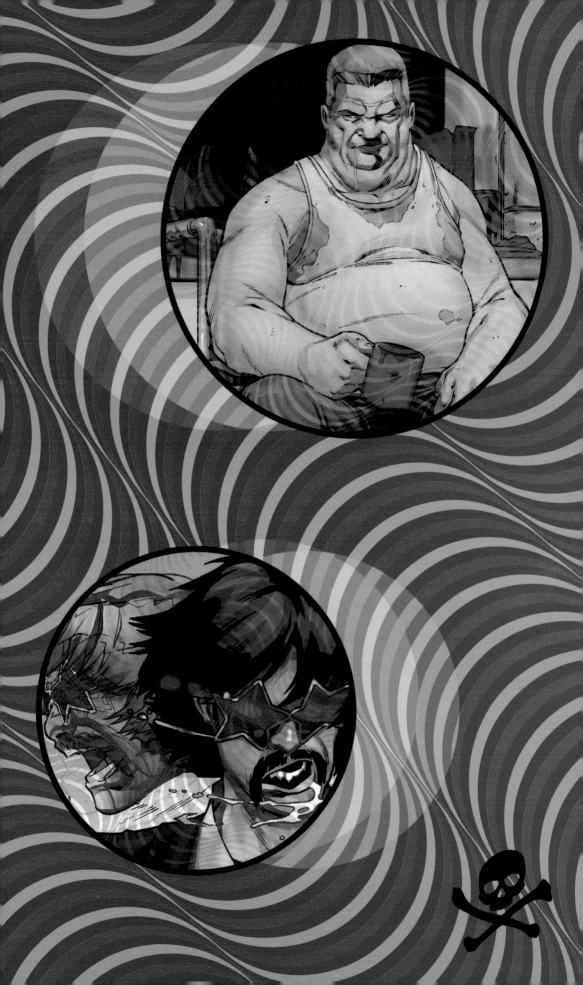

ISSUE 4
COVER ART BY RAHZZAH

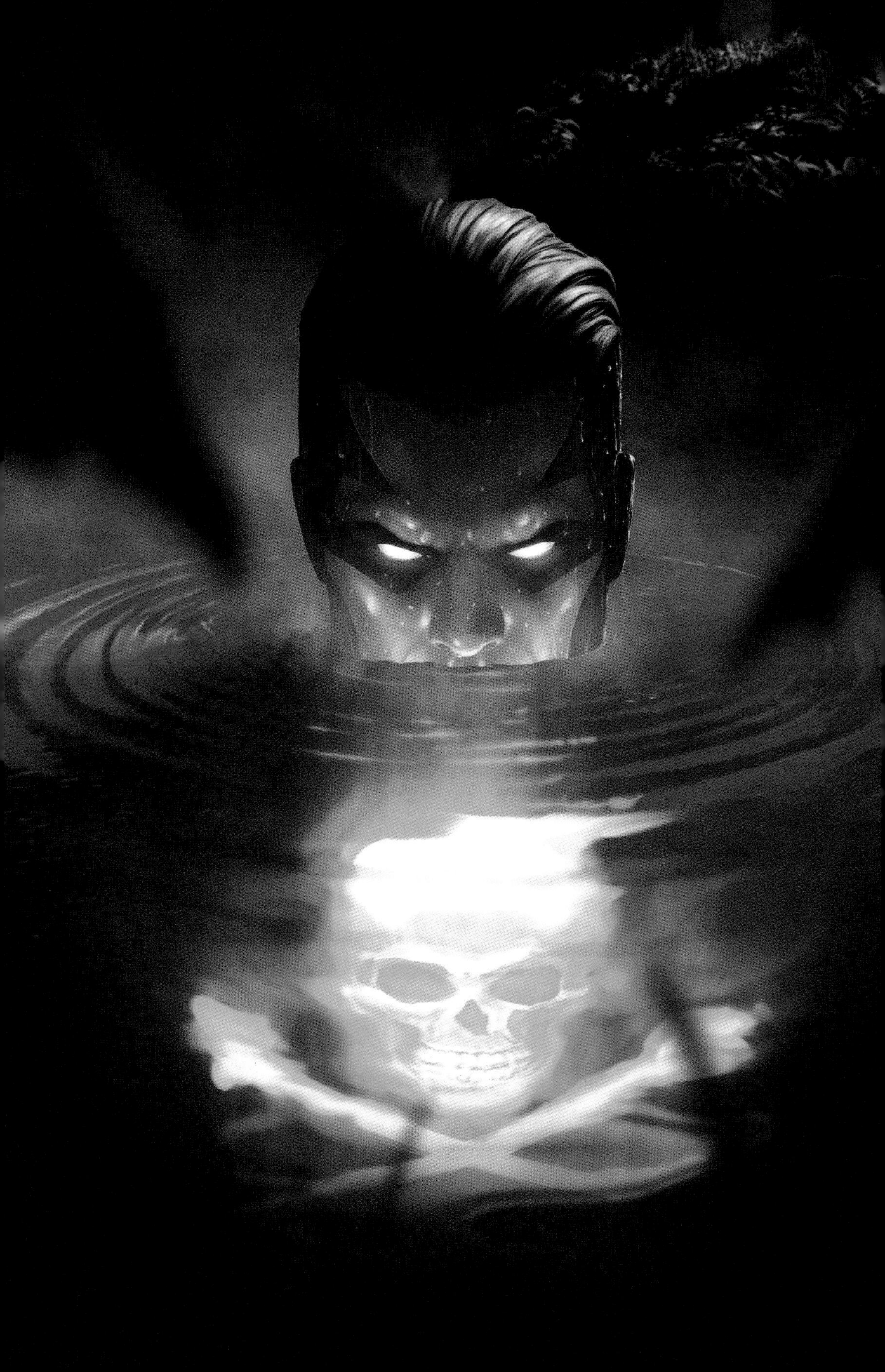

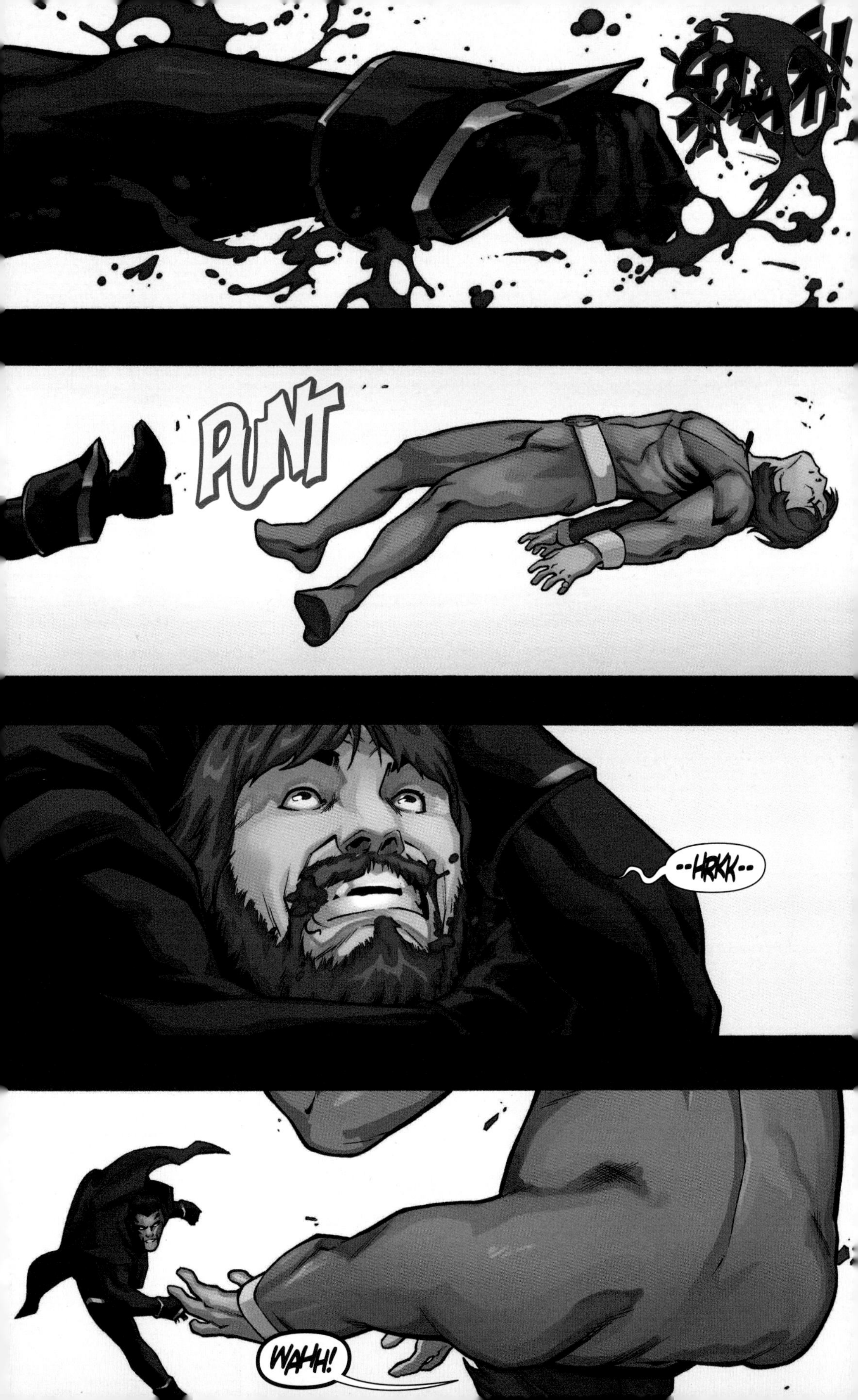
PUNT
--HRKK--
WAHH!

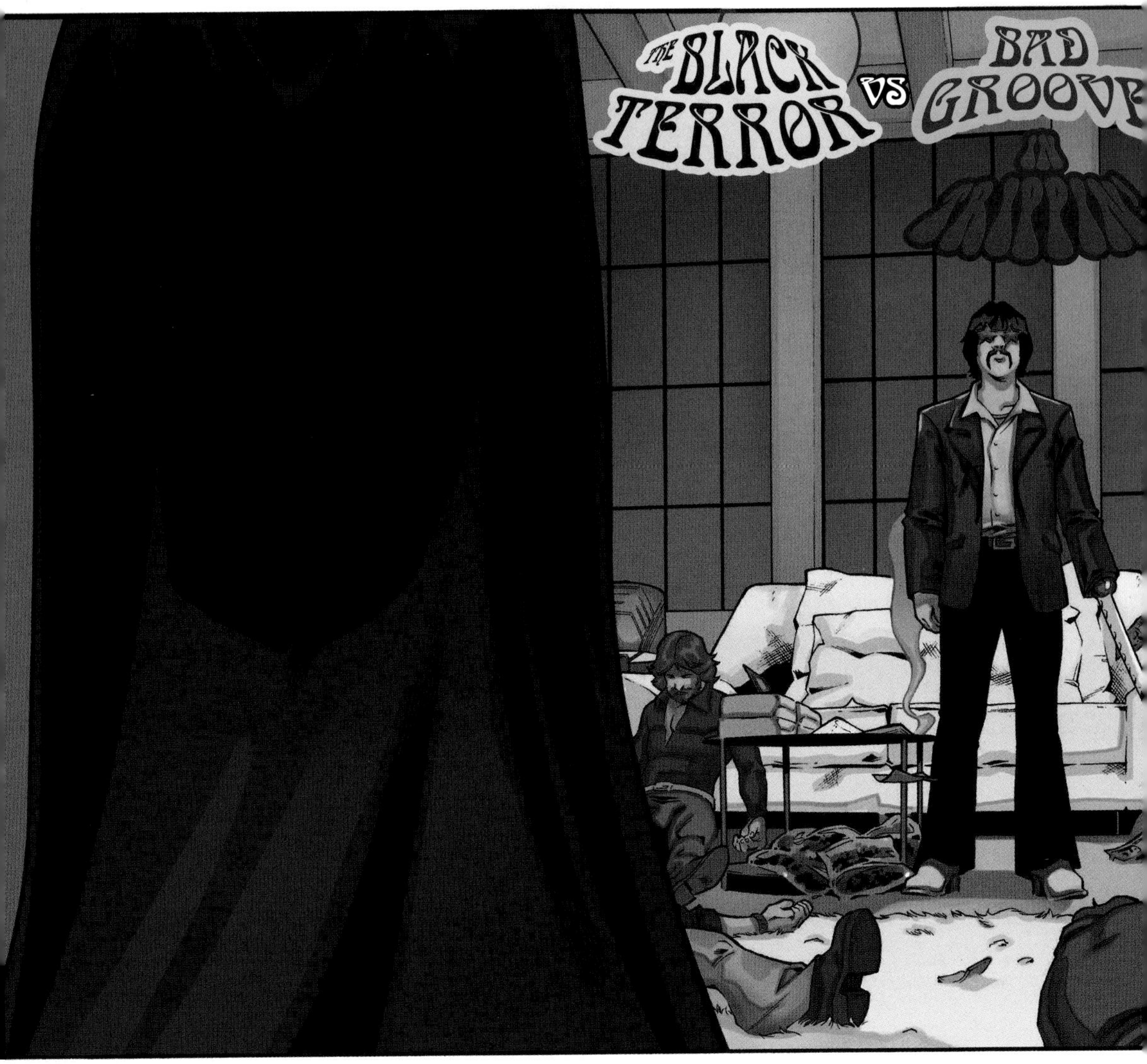
THE BLACK TERROR
VS
BAD GROOV

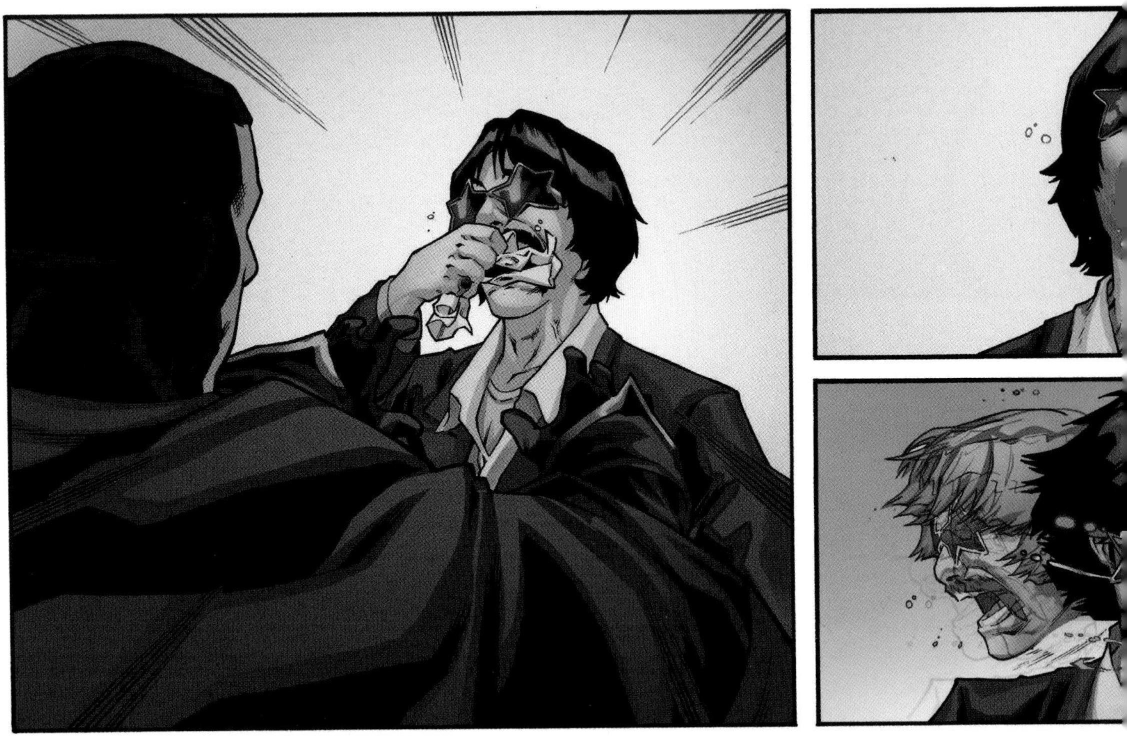

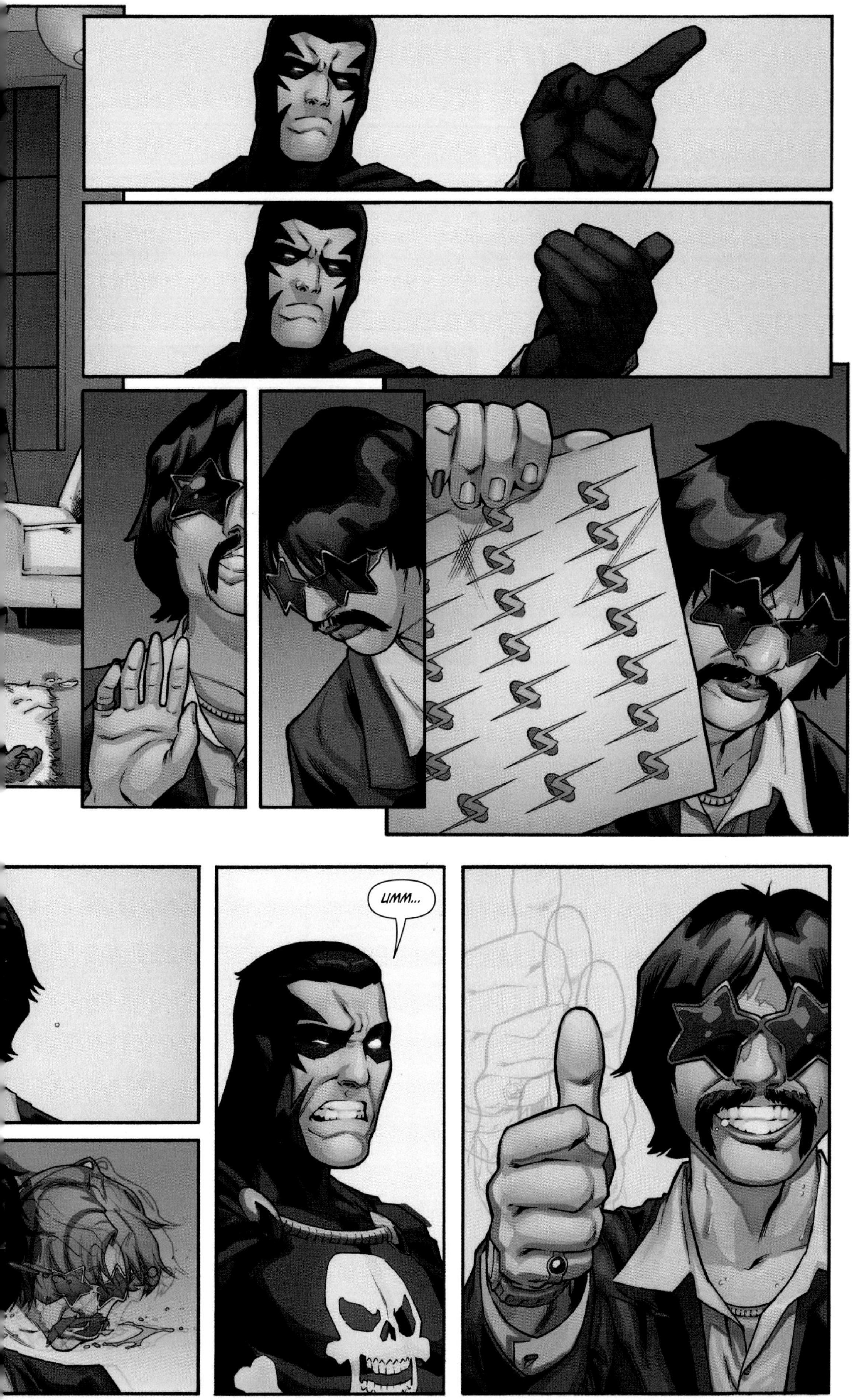
UMM...

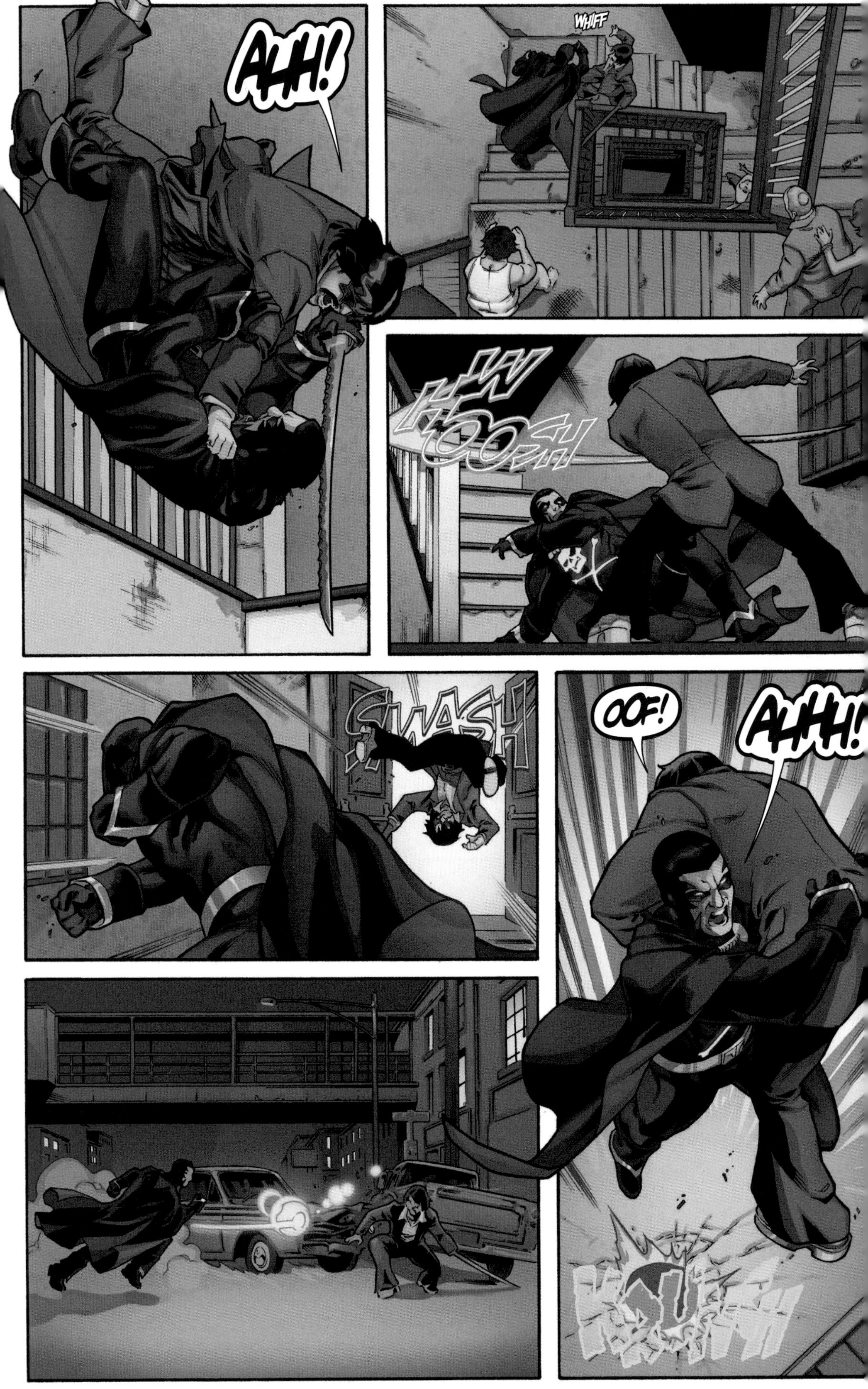
AHH!
WHIFF
HWOOSH
SWASH
OOF!
AHHH!

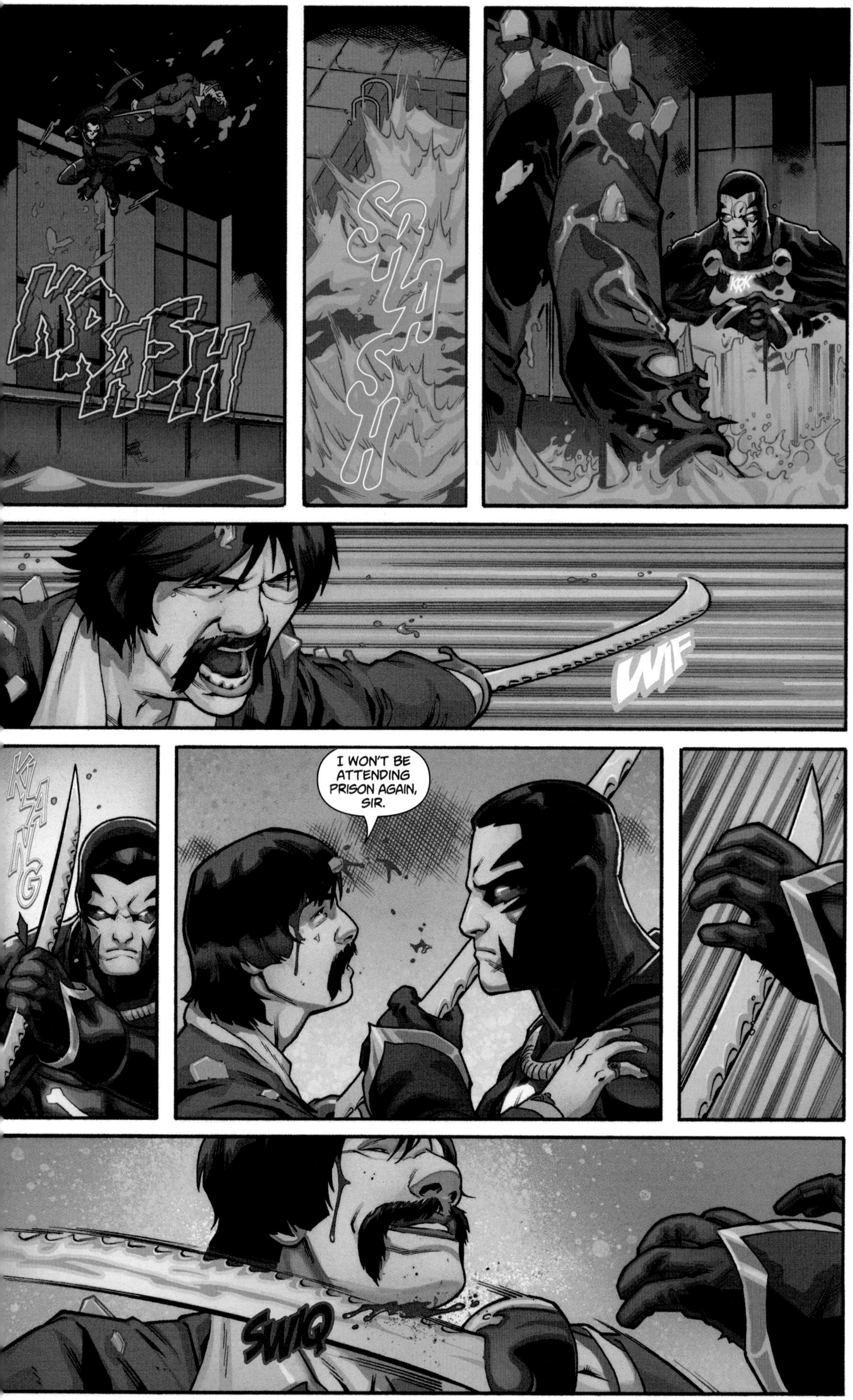
KRASH
SPLASH
KRK
WIF
KLANG
I WON'T BE ATTENDING PRISON AGAIN, SIR.
SWIQ

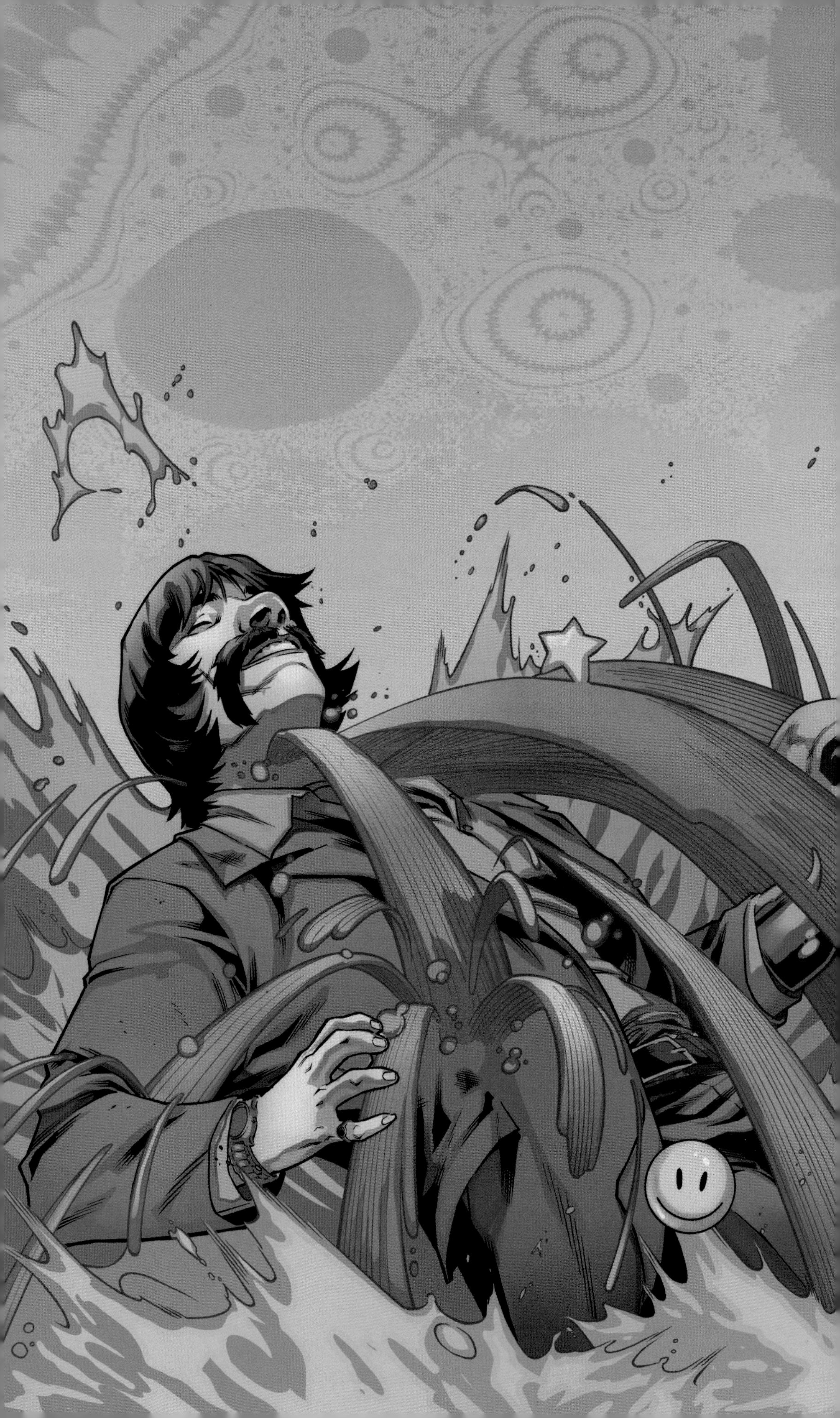

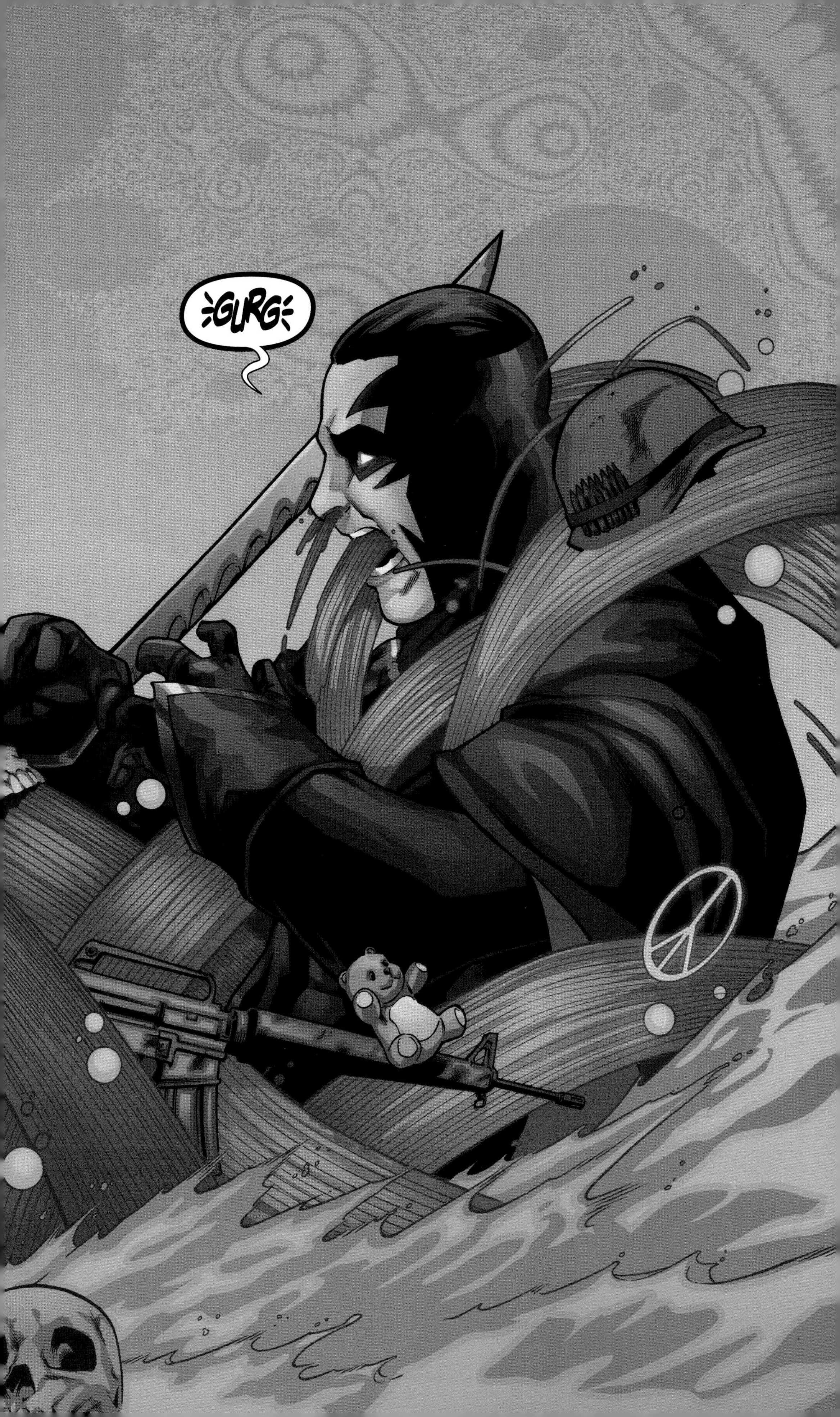
GURG

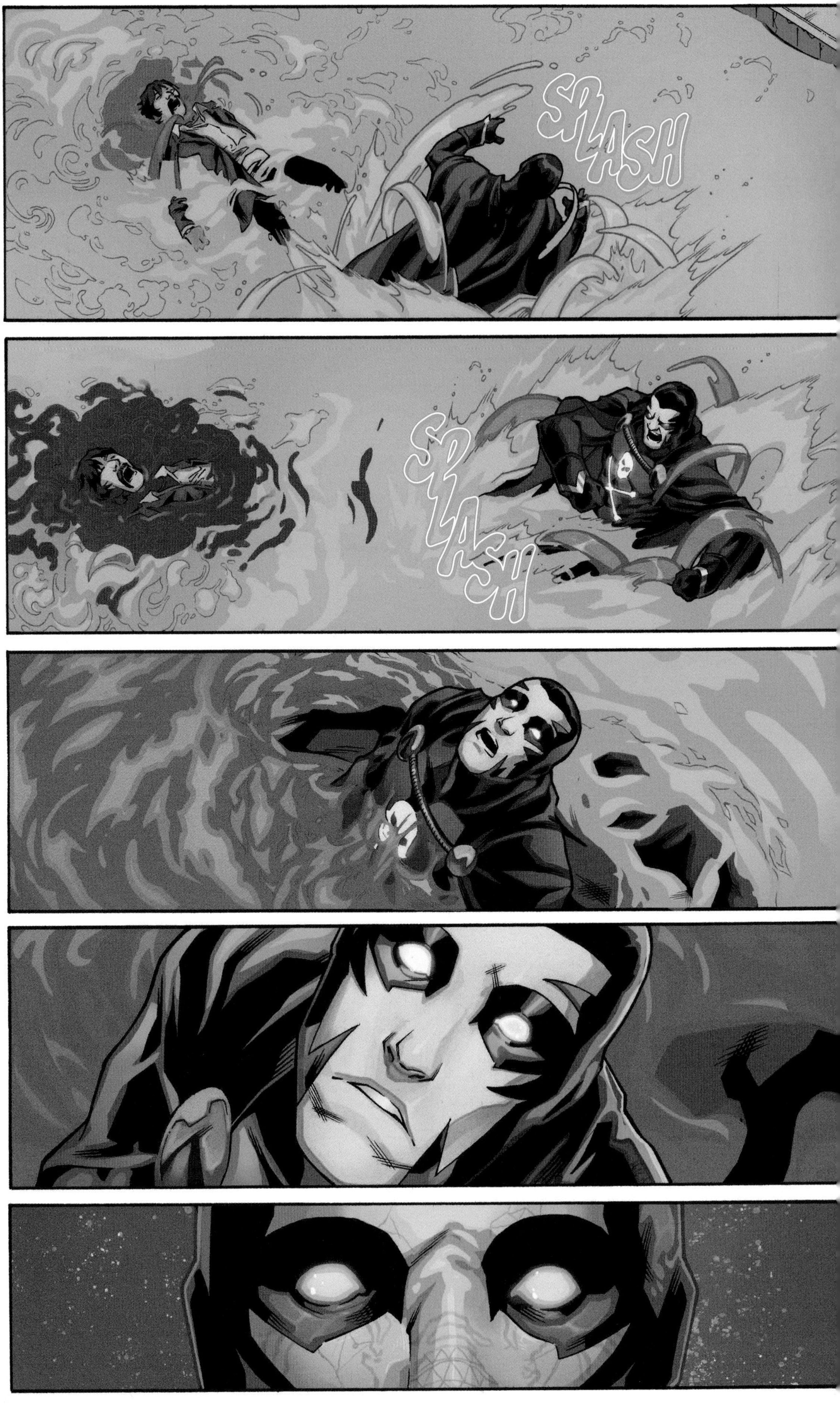
SPLASH
SPLASH

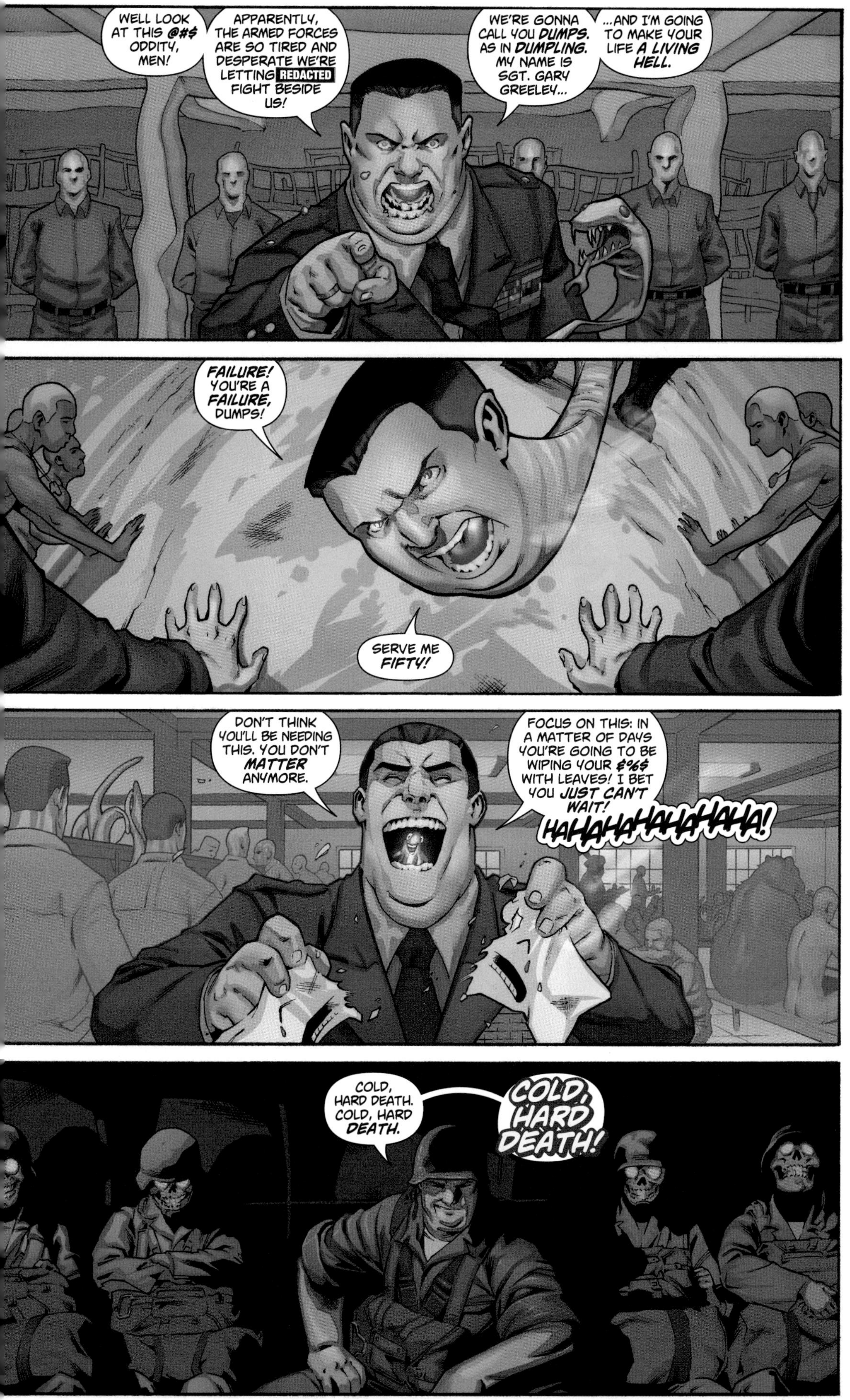
WELL LOOK AT THIS @#$ ODDITY, MEN!
APPARENTLY, THE ARMED FORCES ARE SO TIRED AND DESPERATE WE'RE LETTING REDACTED FIGHT BESIDE US!
WE'RE GONNA CALL YOU DUMPS. AS IN DUMPLING. MY NAME IS SGT. GARY GREELEY...
...AND I'M GOING TO MAKE YOUR LIFE A LIVING HELL.
FAILURE! YOU'RE A FAILURE, DUMPS!
SERVE ME FIFTY!
DON'T THINK YOU'LL BE NEEDING THIS. YOU DON'T MATTER ANYMORE.
FOCUS ON THIS: IN A MATTER OF DAYS YOU'RE GOING TO BE WIPING YOUR $%$ WITH LEAVES! I BET YOU JUST CAN'T WAIT!
HAHAHAHAHAHAHA!
COLD, HARD DEATH. COLD, HARD DEATH.
COLD, HARD DEATH!

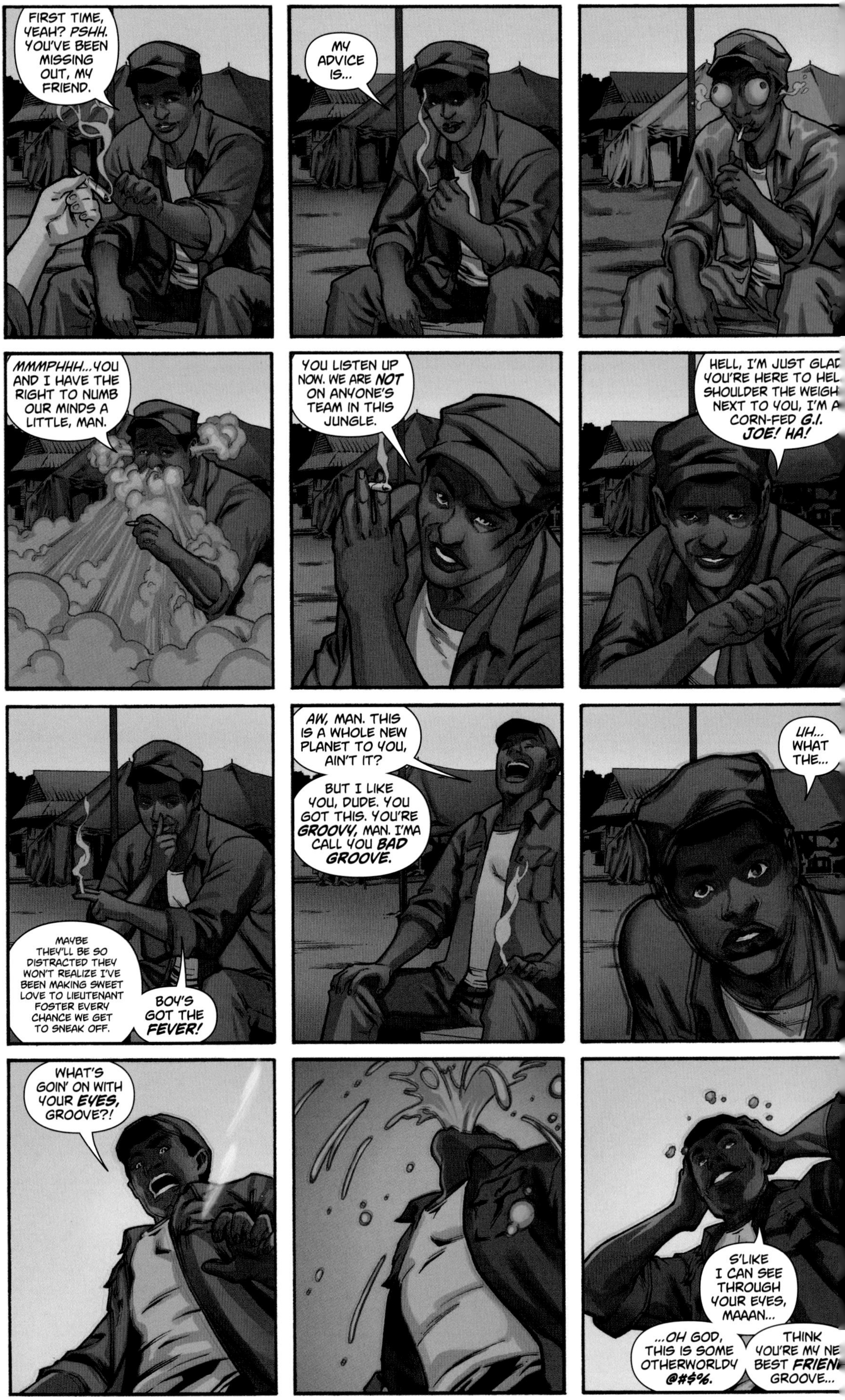
FIRST TIME, YEAH? PSHH. YOU'VE BEEN MISSING OUT, MY FRIEND.
MY ADVICE IS...
MMMPHHH...YOU AND I HAVE THE RIGHT TO NUMB OUR MINDS A LITTLE, MAN.
YOU LISTEN UP NOW. WE ARE NOT ON ANYONE'S TEAM IN THIS JUNGLE.
HELL, I'M JUST GLAD YOU'RE HERE TO HEL SHOULDER THE WEIGH NEXT TO YOU, I'M A CORN-FED G.I. JOE! HA!
MAYBE THEY'LL BE SO DISTRACTED THEY WON'T REALIZE I'VE BEEN MAKING SWEET LOVE TO LIEUTENANT FOSTER EVERY CHANCE WE GET TO SNEAK OFF.
BOY'S GOT THE FEVER!
AW, MAN. THIS IS A WHOLE NEW PLANET TO YOU, AIN'T IT?
BUT I LIKE YOU, DUDE. YOU GOT THIS. YOU'RE GROOVY, MAN. I'MA CALL YOU BAD GROOVE.
UH... WHAT THE...
WHAT'S GOIN' ON WITH YOUR EYES, GROOVE?!
S'LIKE I CAN SEE THROUGH YOUR EYES, MAAAN...
...OH GOD, THIS IS SOME OTHERWORLDY @#$%.
THINK YOU'RE MY NE BEST FRIEN GROOVE...

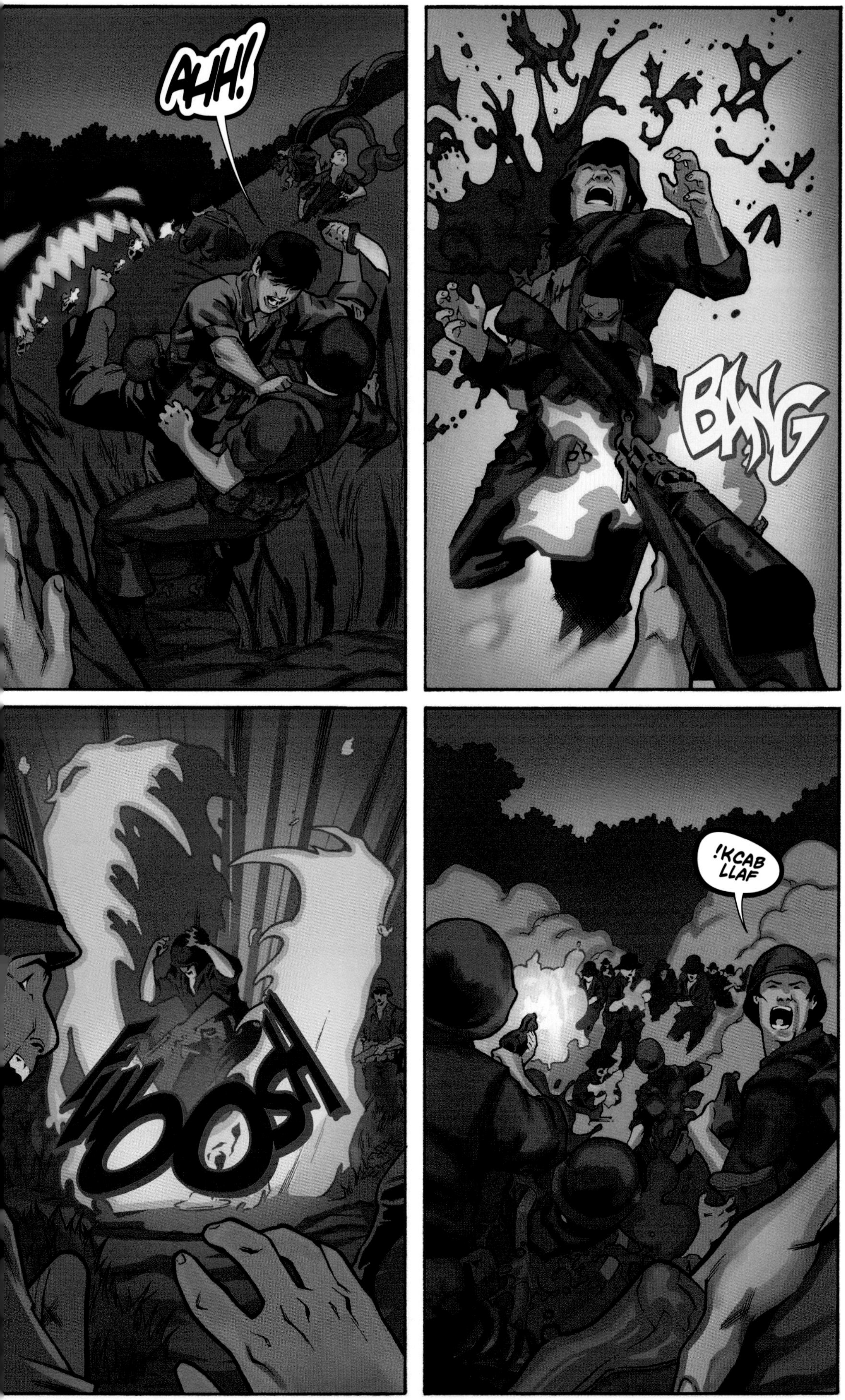
AHH!
BANG
WHOOSH
!KCAB LLAF

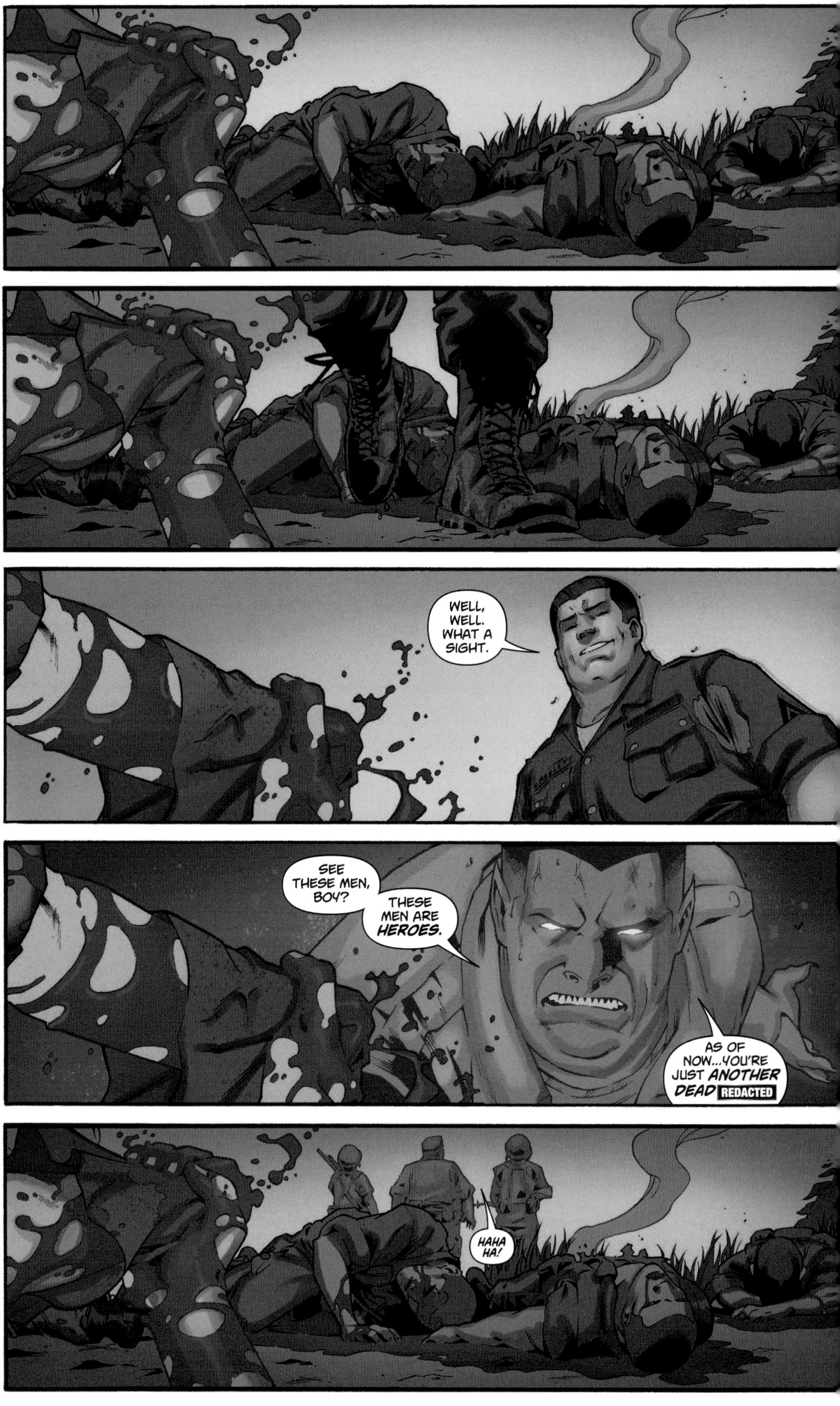
WELL, WELL. WHAT A SIGHT.
SEE THESE MEN, BOY?
THESE MEN ARE **HEROES.**
AS OF NOW...YOU'RE JUST **ANOTHER DEAD** REDACTED
HAHA HA!

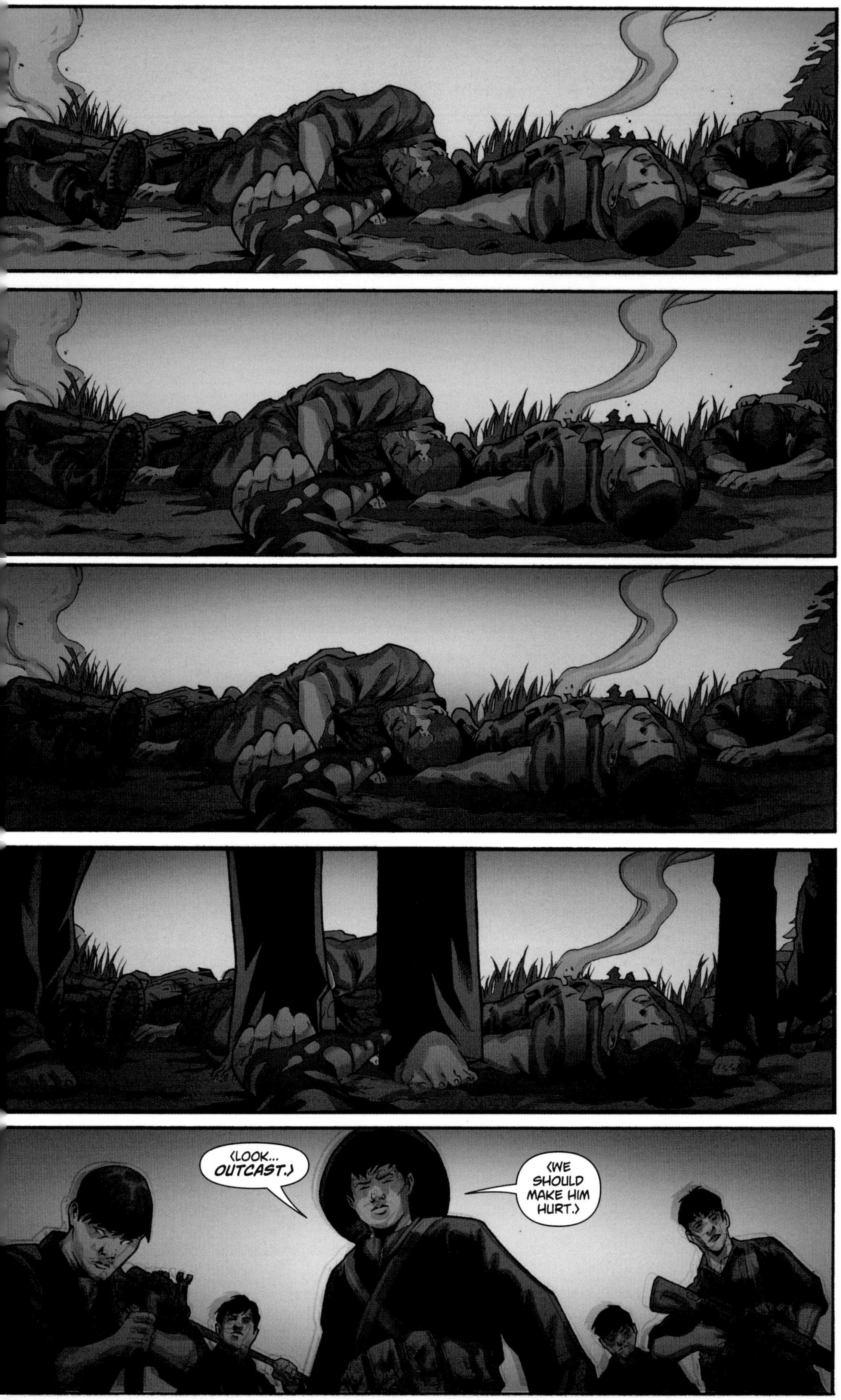
‹LOOK... OUTCAST.›
‹WE SHOULD MAKE HIM HURT.›

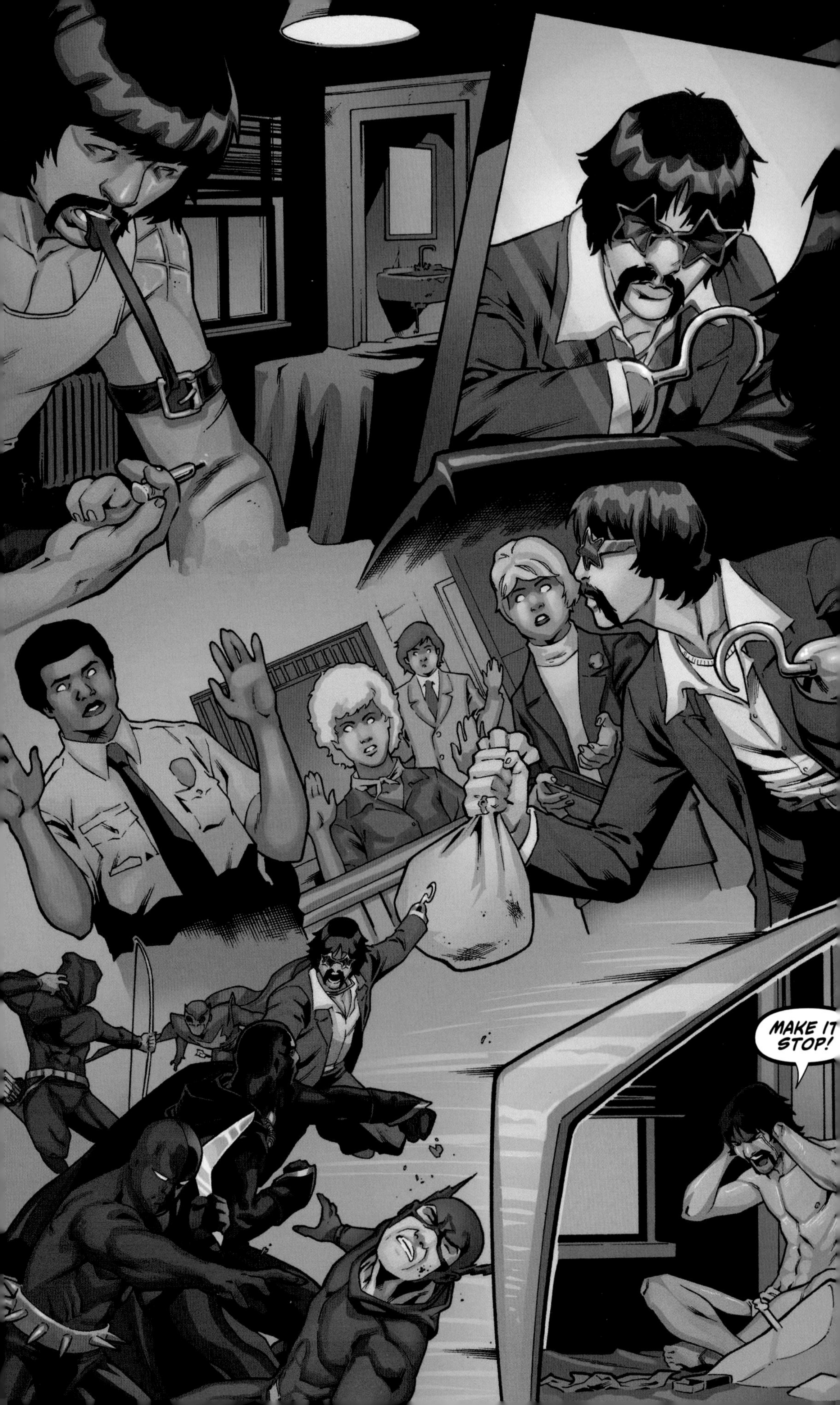
MAKE IT STOP!

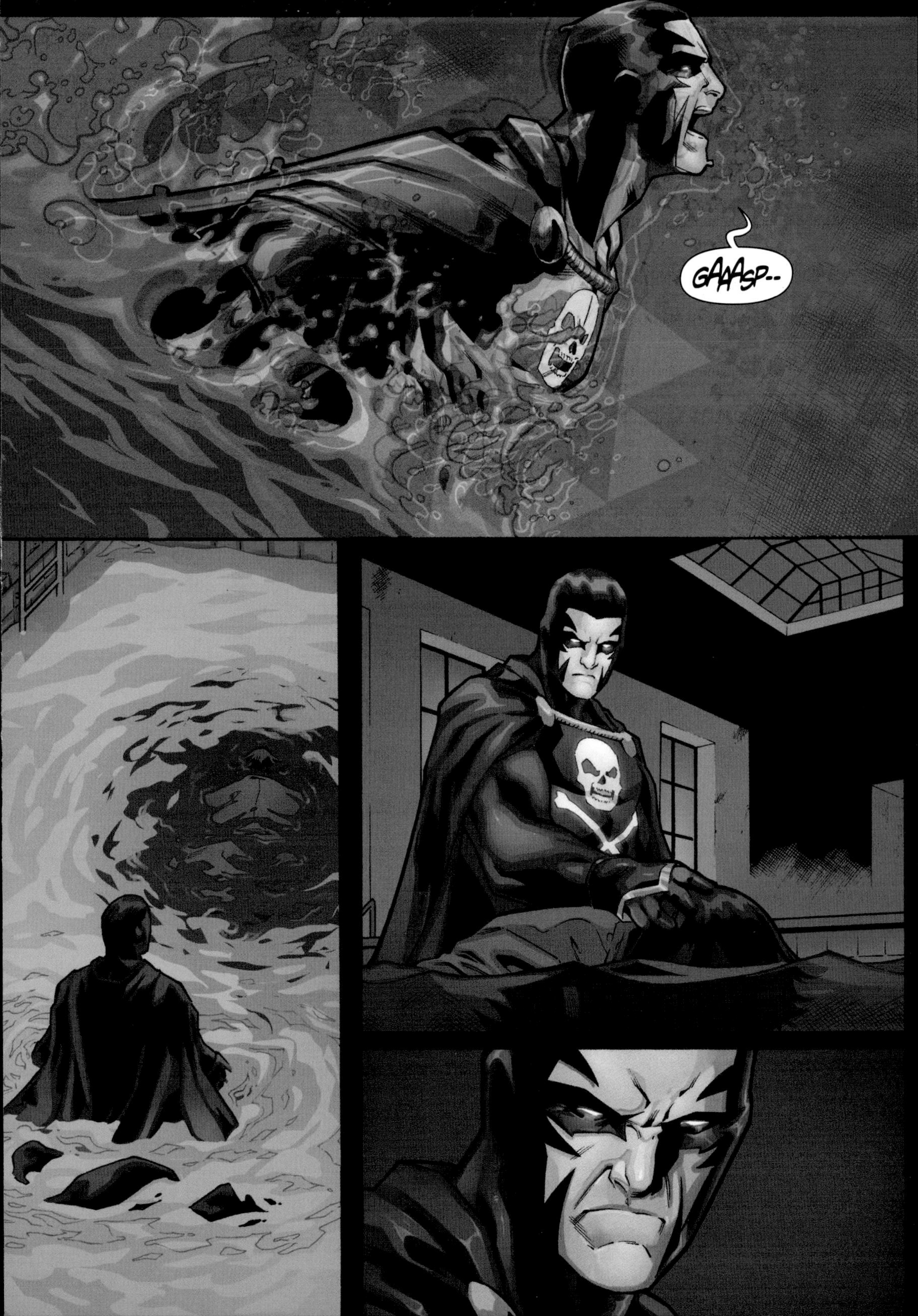
GAAASP--

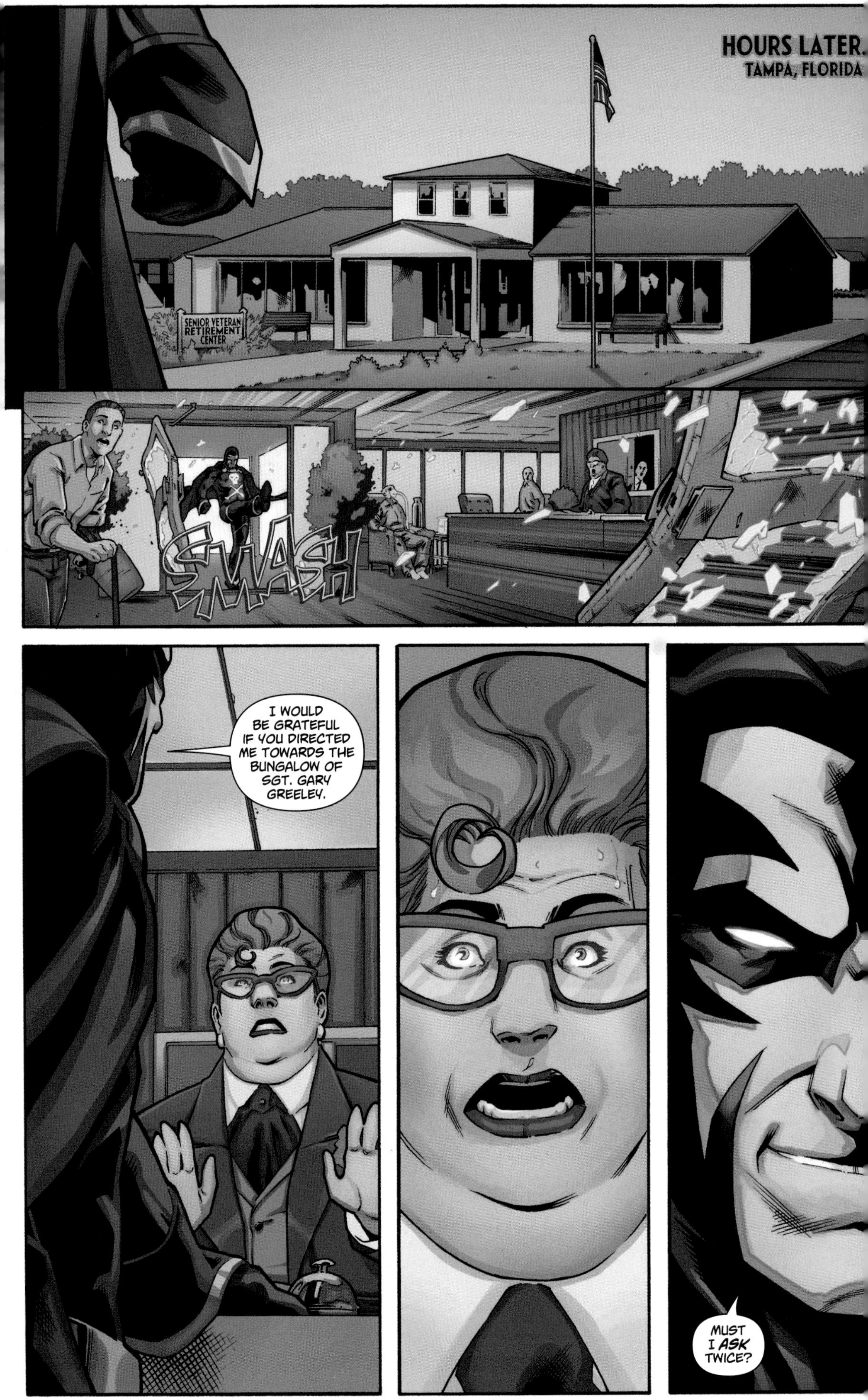
HOURS LATER.
TAMPA, FLORIDA
SENIOR VETERAN RETIREMENT CENTER
SMASH
I WOULD BE GRATEFUL IF YOU DIRECTED ME TOWARDS THE BUNGALOW OF SGT. GARY GREELEY.
MUST I ASK TWICE?

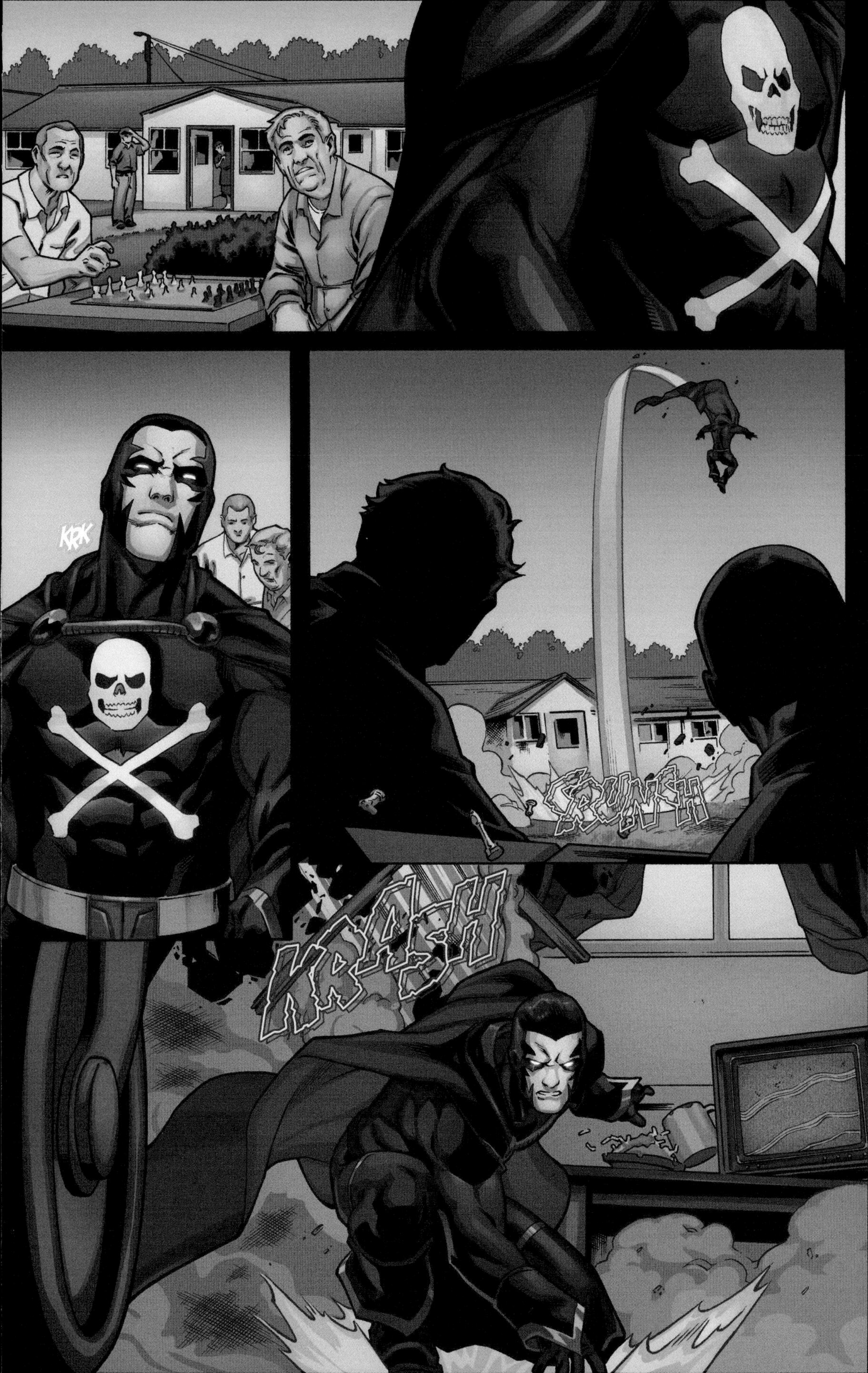
KRK
SKRUNCH
KRASH

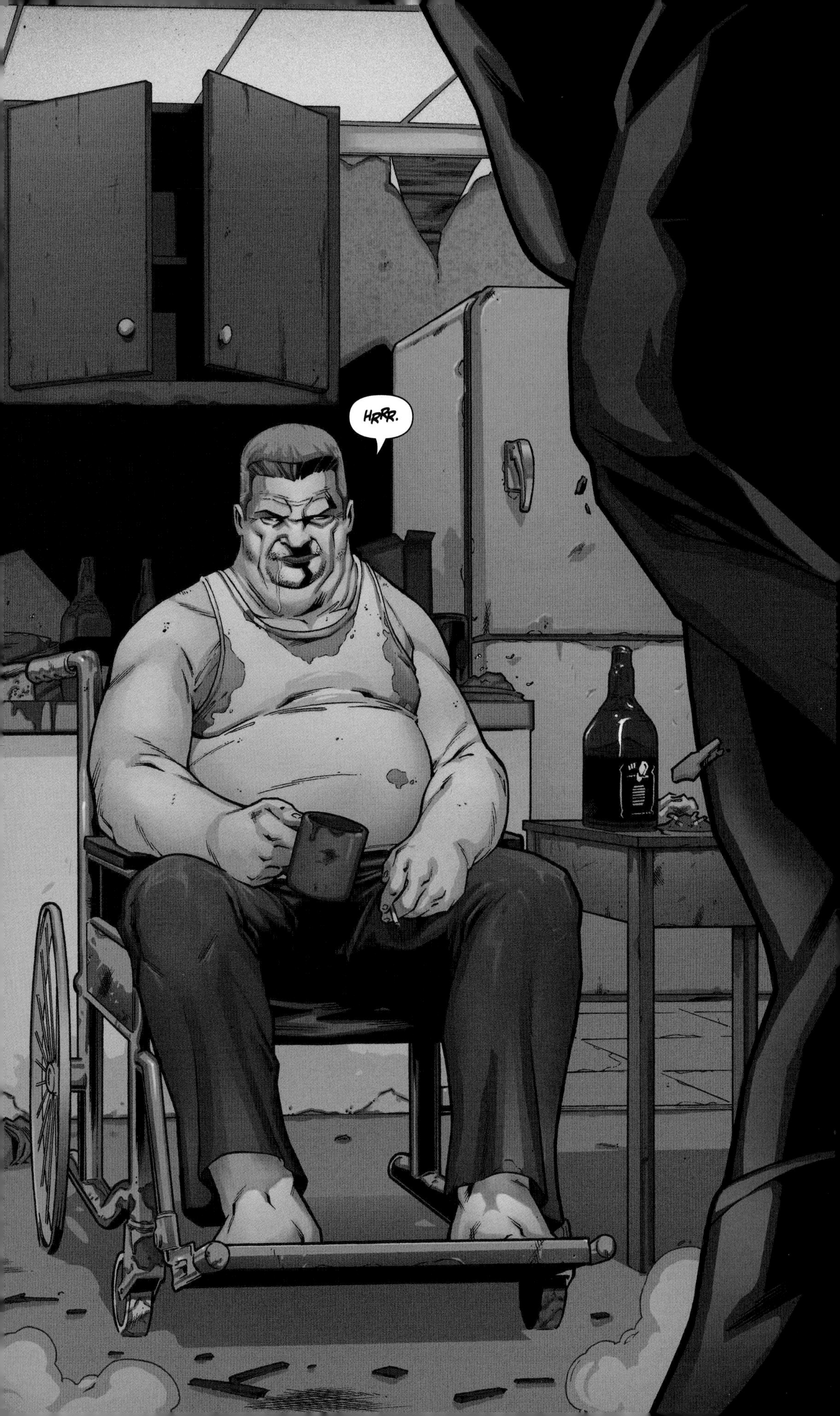
HRRR.

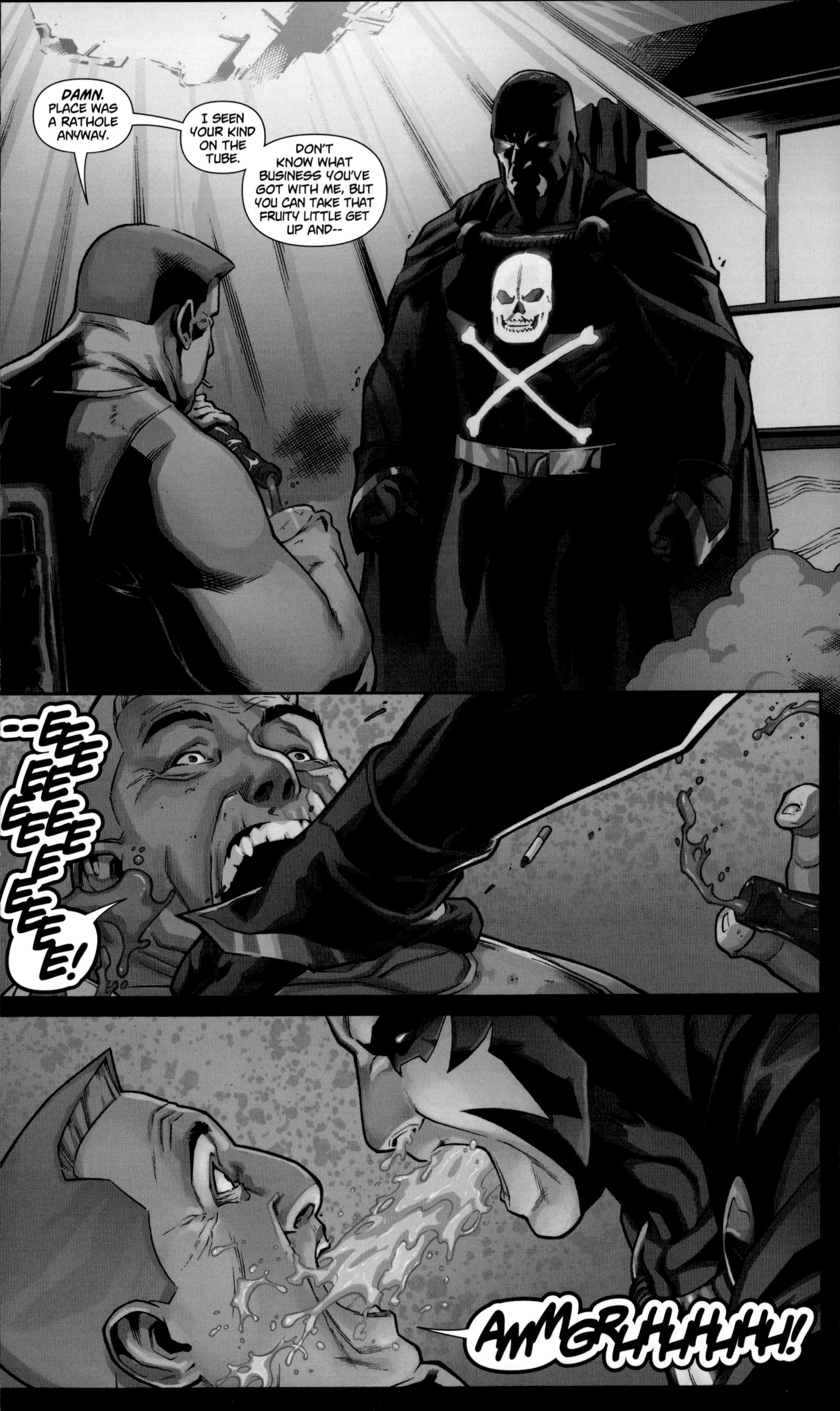
DAMN. PLACE WAS A RATHOLE ANYWAY.
I SEEN YOUR KIND ON THE TUBE.
DON'T KNOW WHAT BUSINESS YOU'VE GOT WITH ME, BUT YOU CAN TAKE THAT FRUITY LITTLE GET UP AND--
--EEEEEEEEEEEEEEEEE!
AMMGRHHHHH!

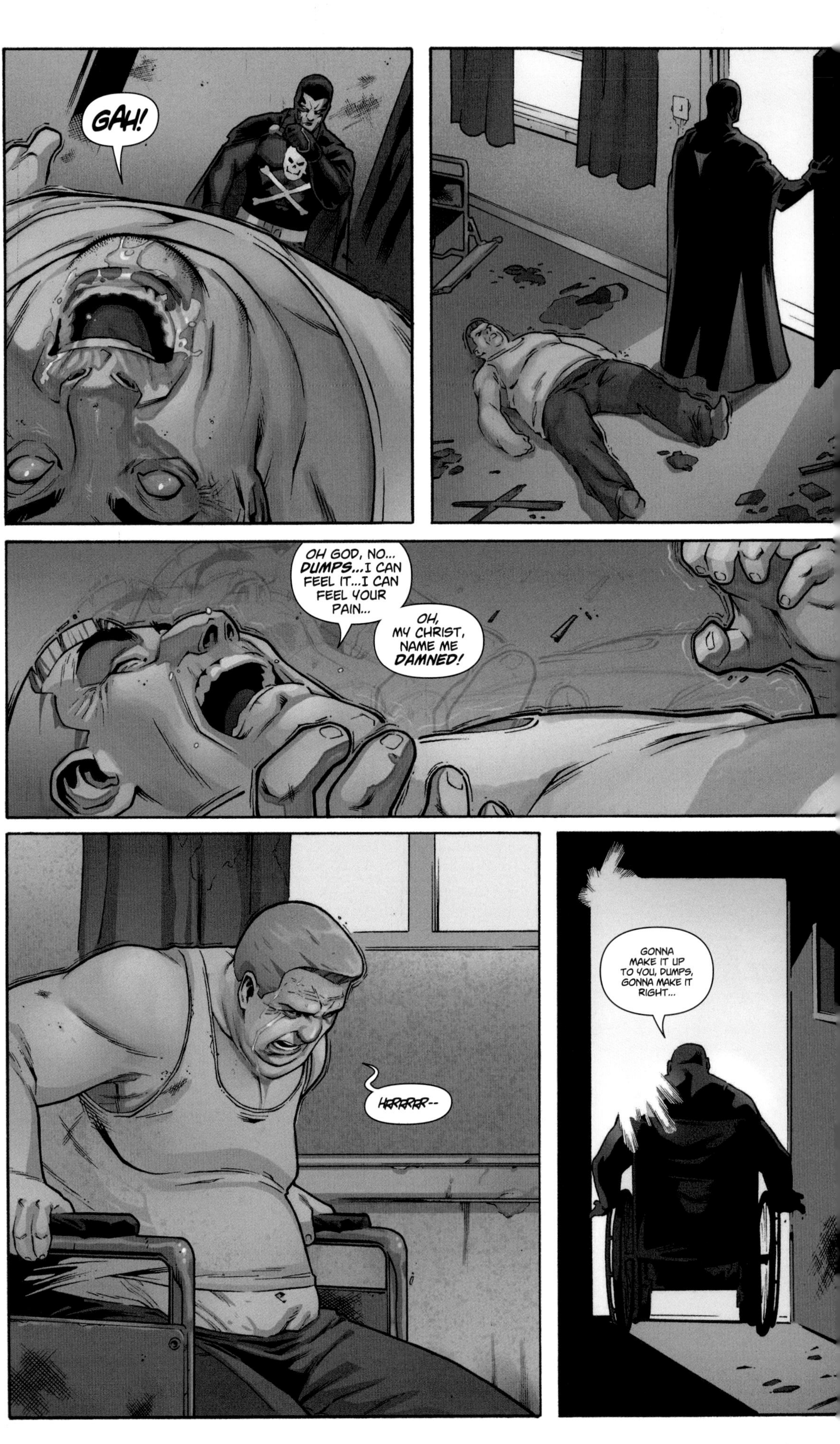
GAH!
OH GOD, NO... DUMPS...I CAN FEEL IT...I CAN FEEL YOUR PAIN...
OH, MY CHRIST, NAME ME DAMNED!
HRRRRR--
GONNA MAKE IT UP TO YOU, DUMPS, GONNA MAKE IT RIGHT...

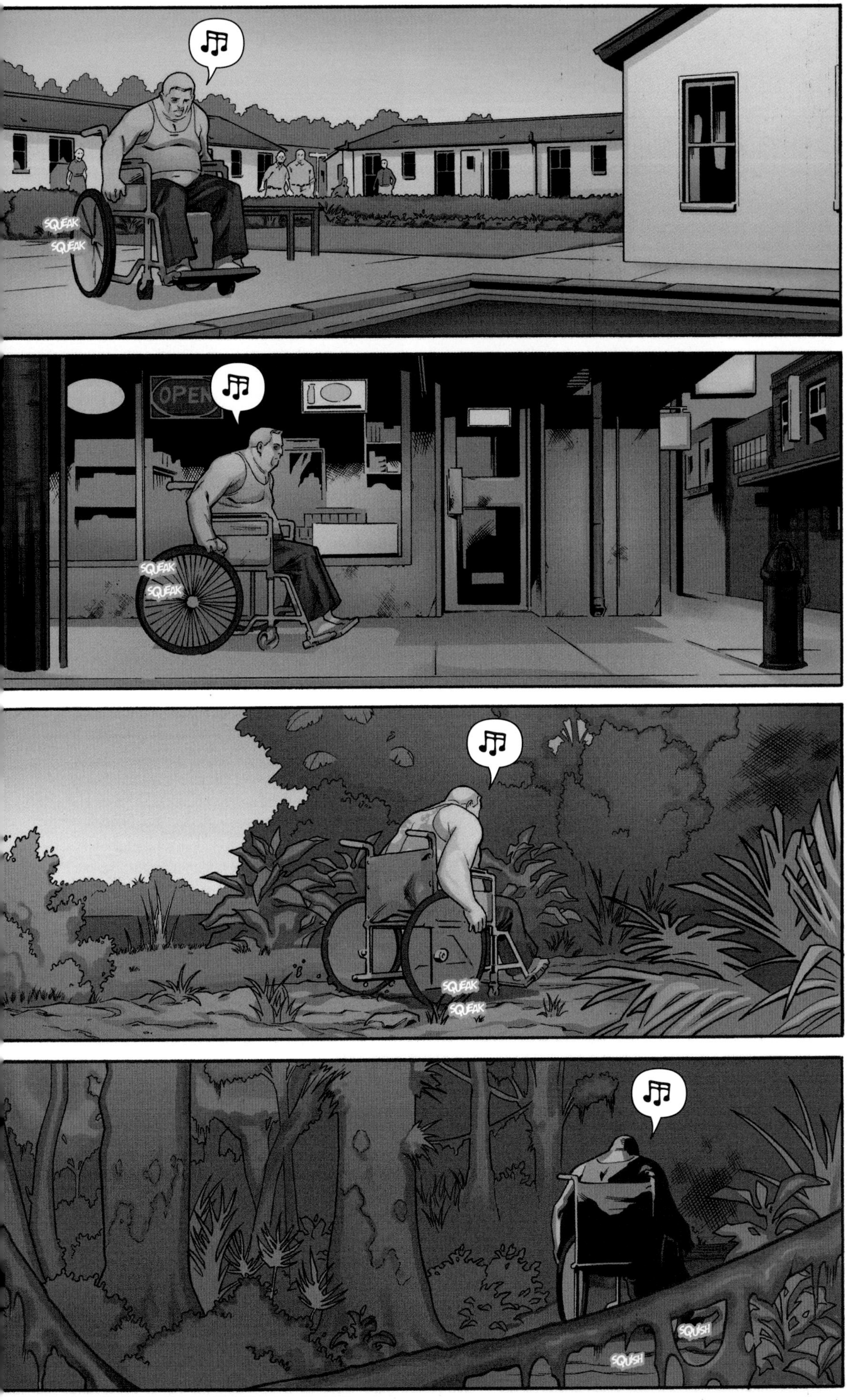

SQUEAK
SQUEAK
SQUEAK
SQUEAK
SQUEAK
SQUEAK
SQUISH
SQUISH

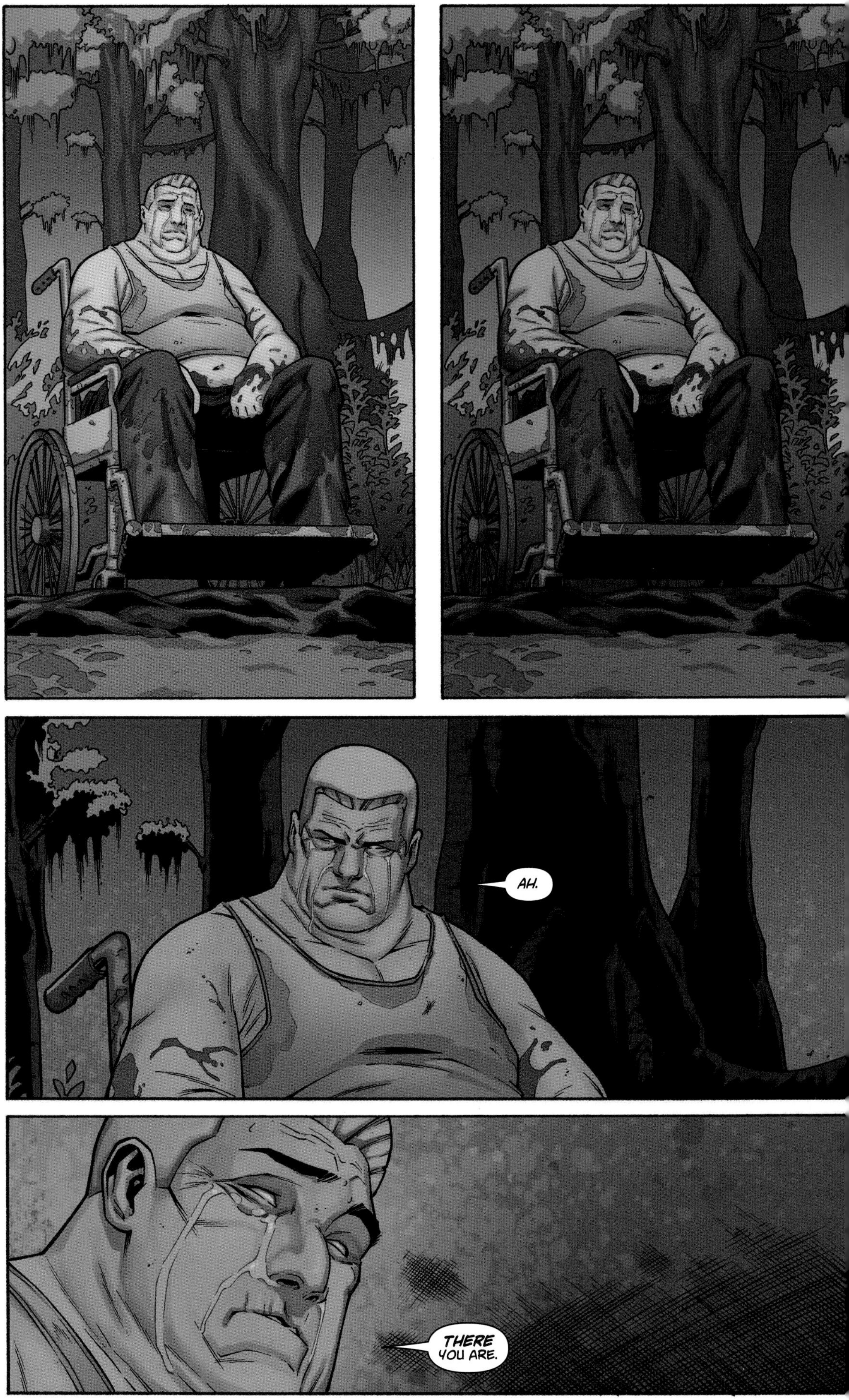
AH.
THERE YOU ARE.

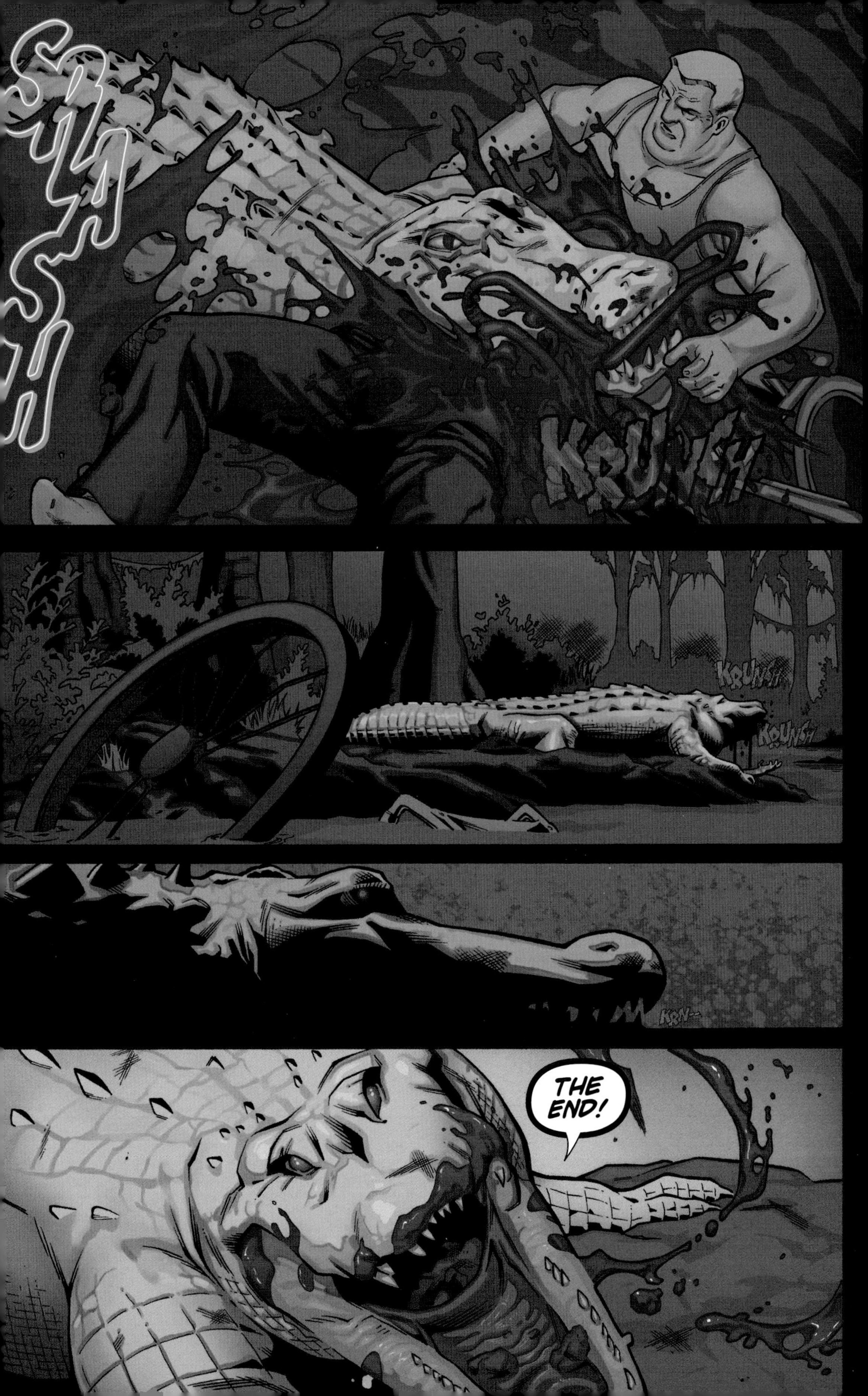
SPLASH
KRUNCH
KRUNCH
KRUNCH
KRN--
THE END!

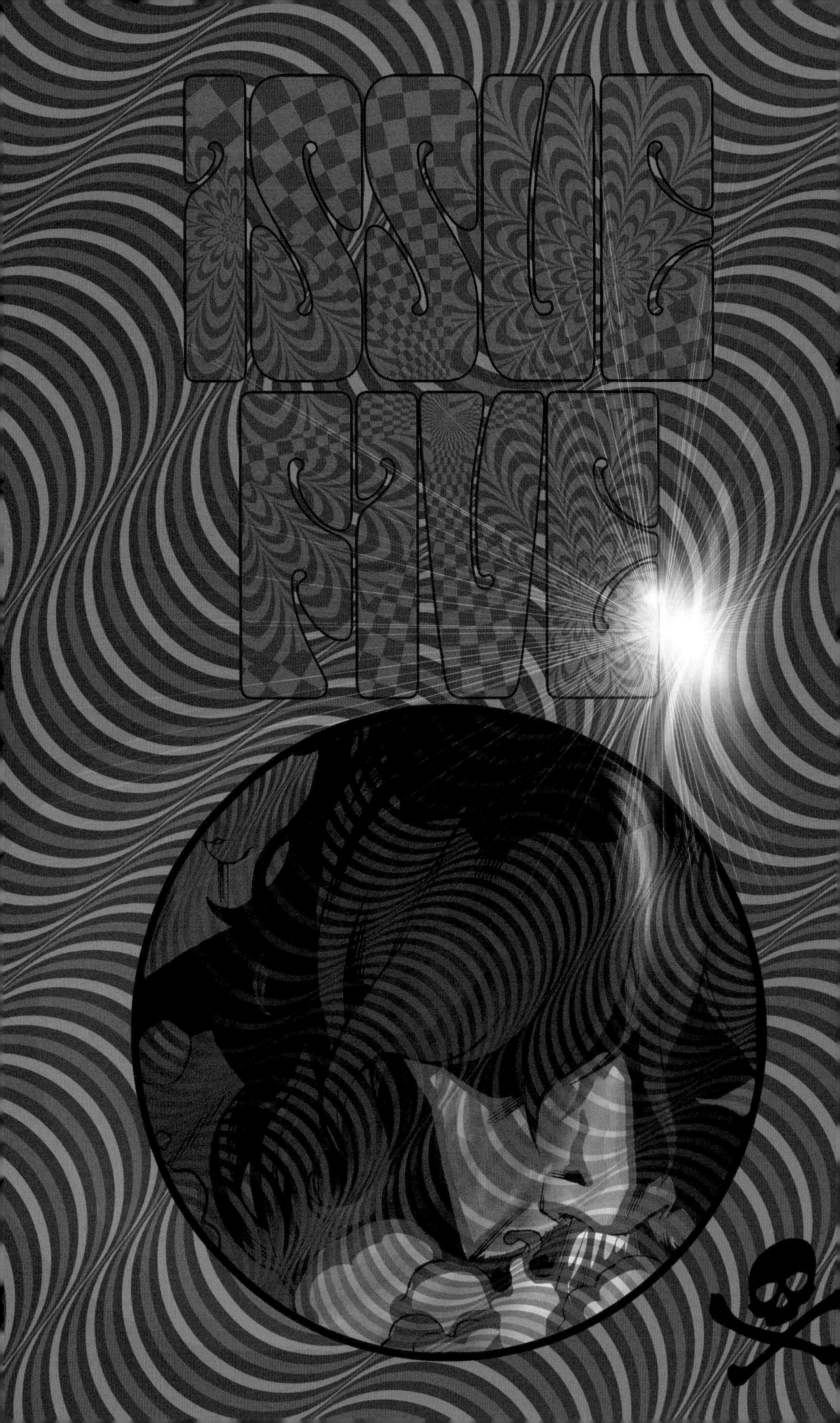
ISSUE
FIVE

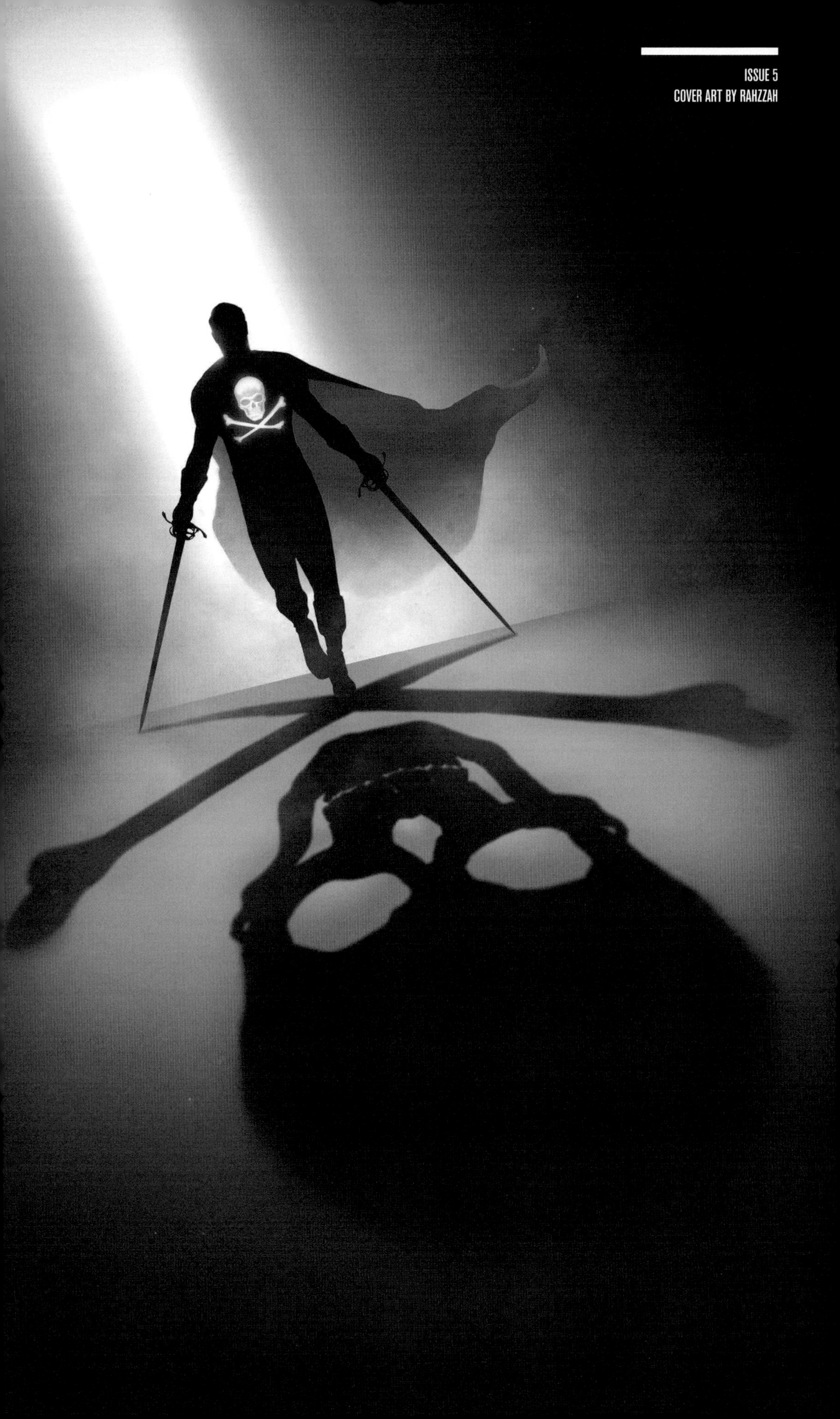

ISSUE 5
COVER ART BY RAHZZAH

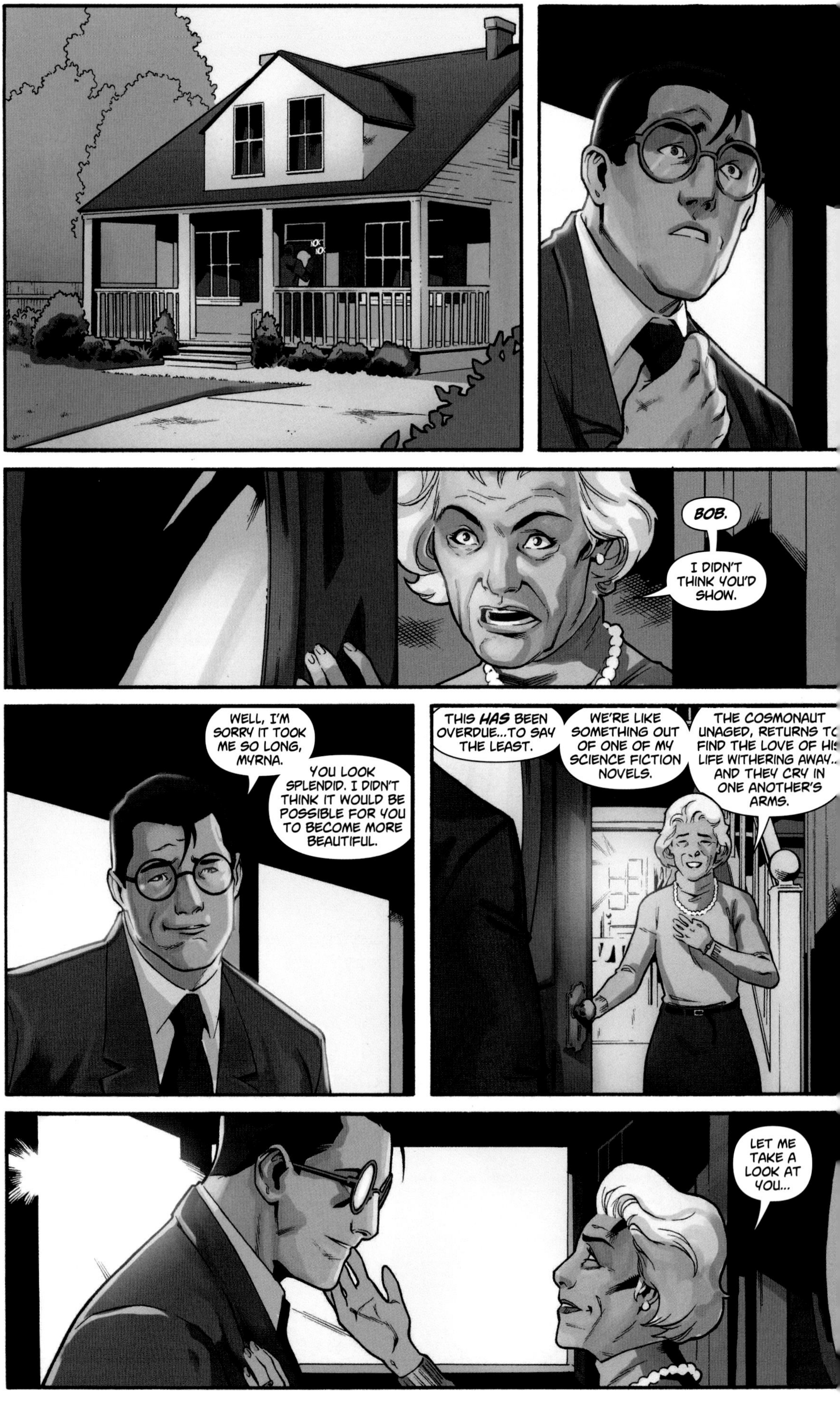
BOB.
I DIDN'T THINK YOU'D SHOW.
WELL, I'M SORRY IT TOOK ME SO LONG, MYRNA.
YOU LOOK SPLENDID. I DIDN'T THINK IT WOULD BE POSSIBLE FOR YOU TO BECOME MORE BEAUTIFUL.
THIS HAS BEEN OVERDUE...TO SAY THE LEAST.
WE'RE LIKE SOMETHING OUT OF ONE OF MY SCIENCE FICTION NOVELS.
THE COSMONAUT UNAGED, RETURNS TO FIND THE LOVE OF HIS LIFE WITHERING AWAY... AND THEY CRY IN ONE ANOTHER'S ARMS.
LET ME TAKE A LOOK AT YOU...

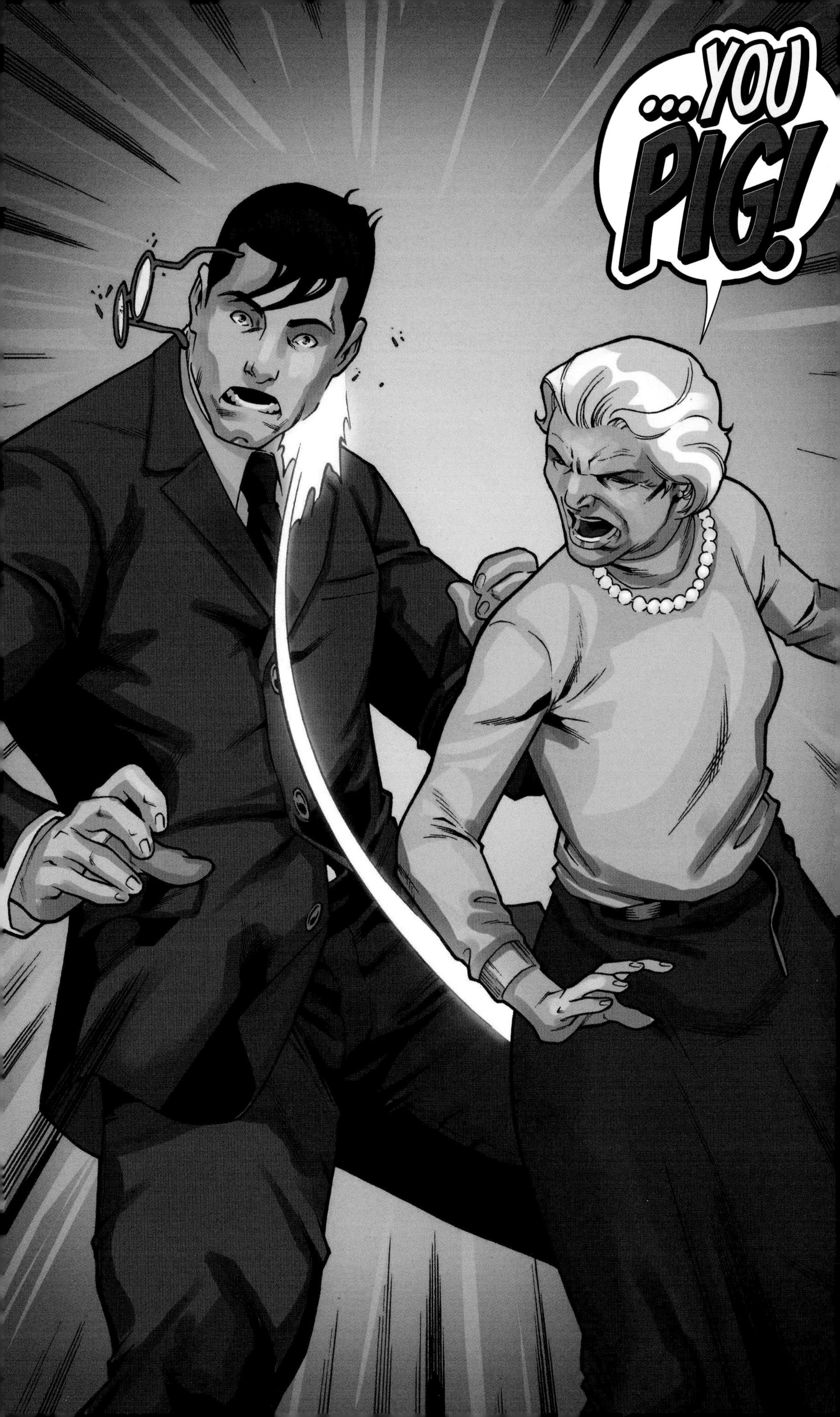
...YOU PIG!

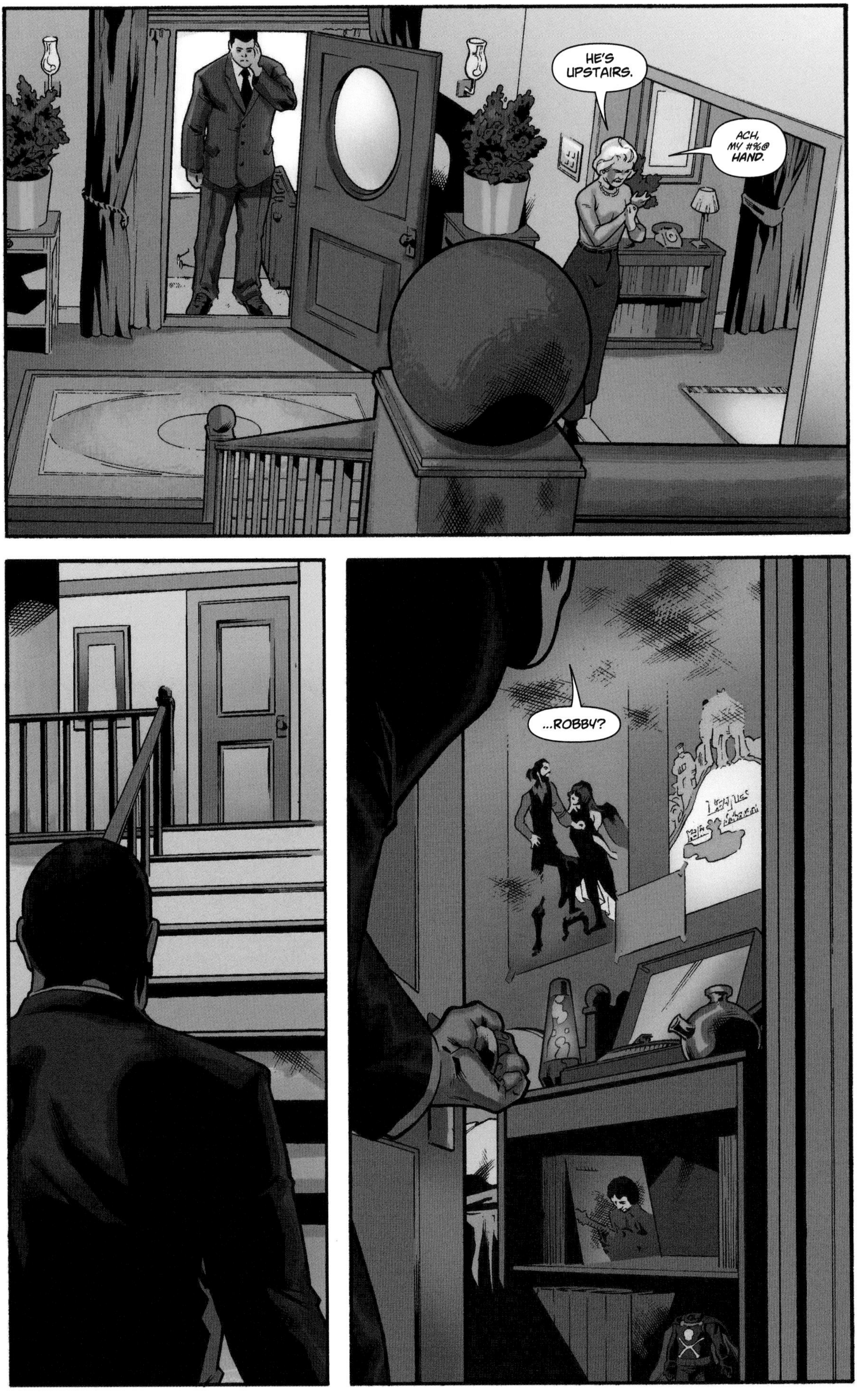
HE'S UPSTAIRS.
ACH, MY #%@ HAND.
...ROBBY?

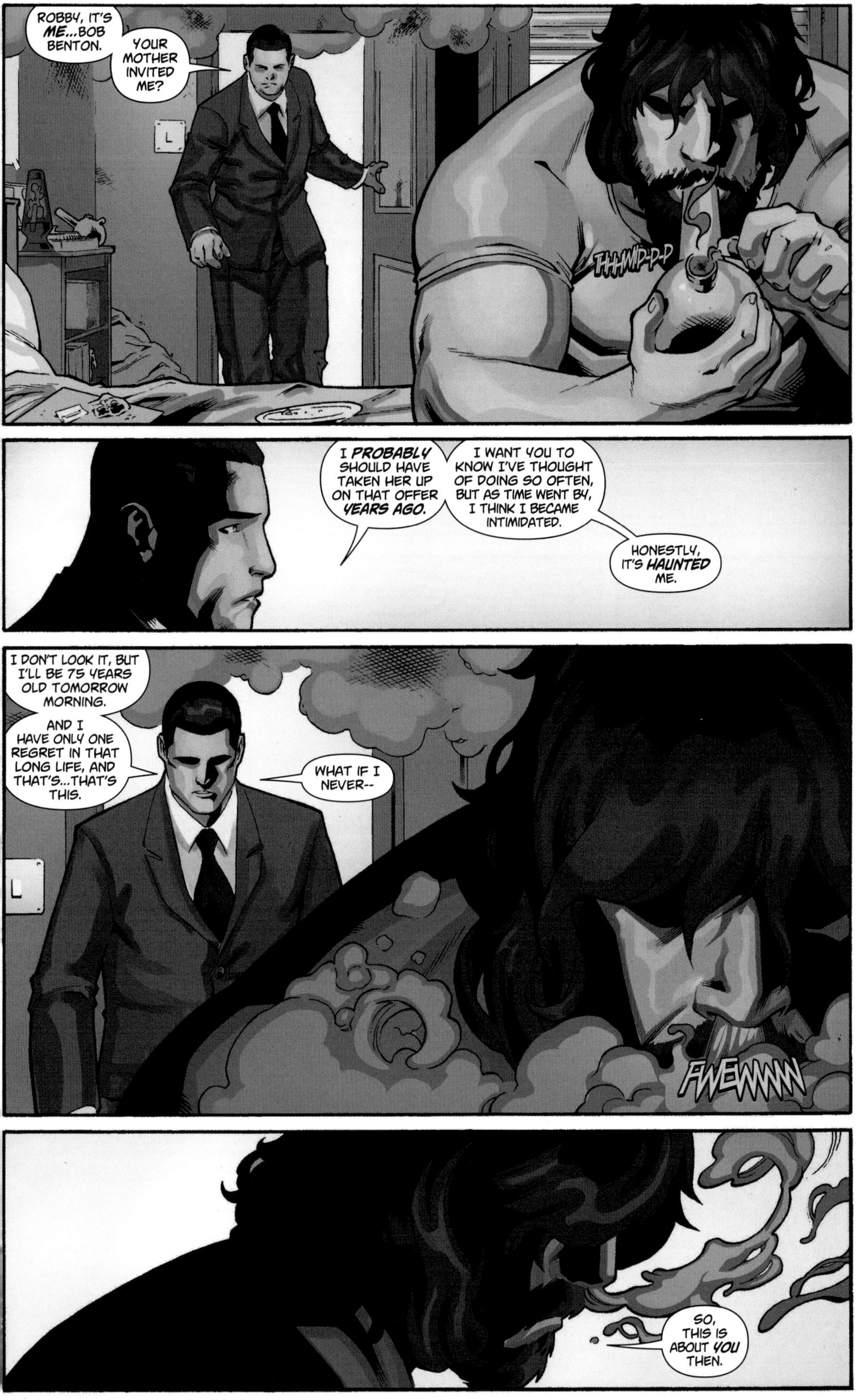
ROBBY, IT'S ME...BOB BENTON.
YOUR MOTHER INVITED ME?
THHHWIP-P-P
I PROBABLY SHOULD HAVE TAKEN HER UP ON THAT OFFER YEARS AGO.
I WANT YOU TO KNOW I'VE THOUGHT OF DOING SO OFTEN, BUT AS TIME WENT BY, I THINK I BECAME INTIMIDATED.
HONESTLY, IT'S HAUNTED ME.
I DON'T LOOK IT, BUT I'LL BE 75 YEARS OLD TOMORROW MORNING.
AND I HAVE ONLY ONE REGRET IN THAT LONG LIFE, AND THAT'S...THAT'S THIS.
WHAT IF I NEVER--
FWEWWW
SO, THIS IS ABOUT YOU THEN.

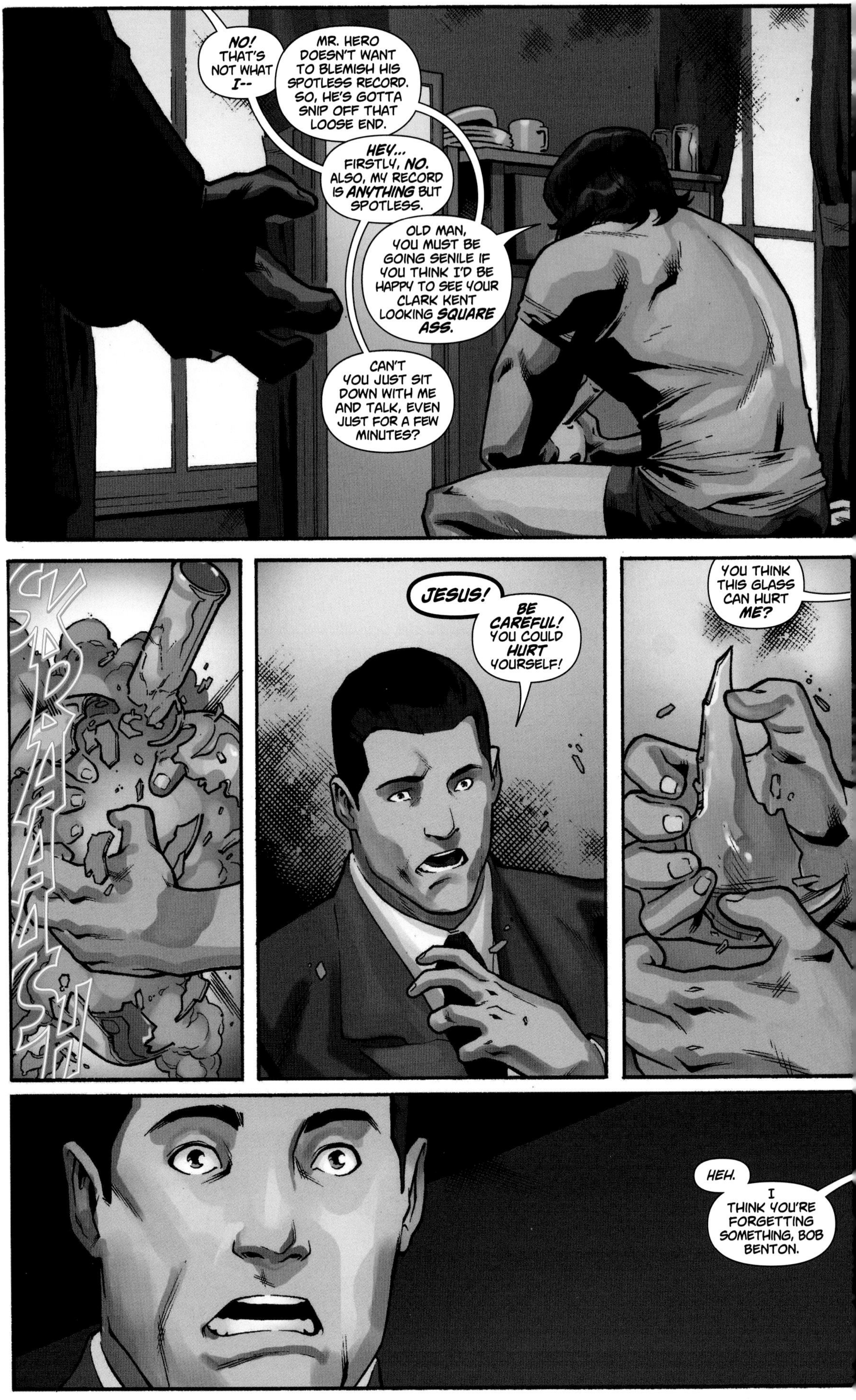
NO! THAT'S NOT WHAT I--
MR. HERO DOESN'T WANT TO BLEMISH HIS SPOTLESS RECORD. SO, HE'S GOTTA SNIP OFF THAT LOOSE END.
HEY... FIRSTLY, NO. ALSO, MY RECORD IS ANYTHING BUT SPOTLESS.
OLD MAN, YOU MUST BE GOING SENILE IF YOU THINK I'D BE HAPPY TO SEE YOUR CLARK KENT LOOKING SQUARE ASS.
CAN'T YOU JUST SIT DOWN WITH ME AND TALK, EVEN JUST FOR A FEW MINUTES?
JESUS!
BE CAREFUL! YOU COULD HURT YOURSELF!
YOU THINK THIS GLASS CAN HURT ME?
HEH.
I THINK YOU'RE FORGETTING SOMETHING, BOB BENTON.

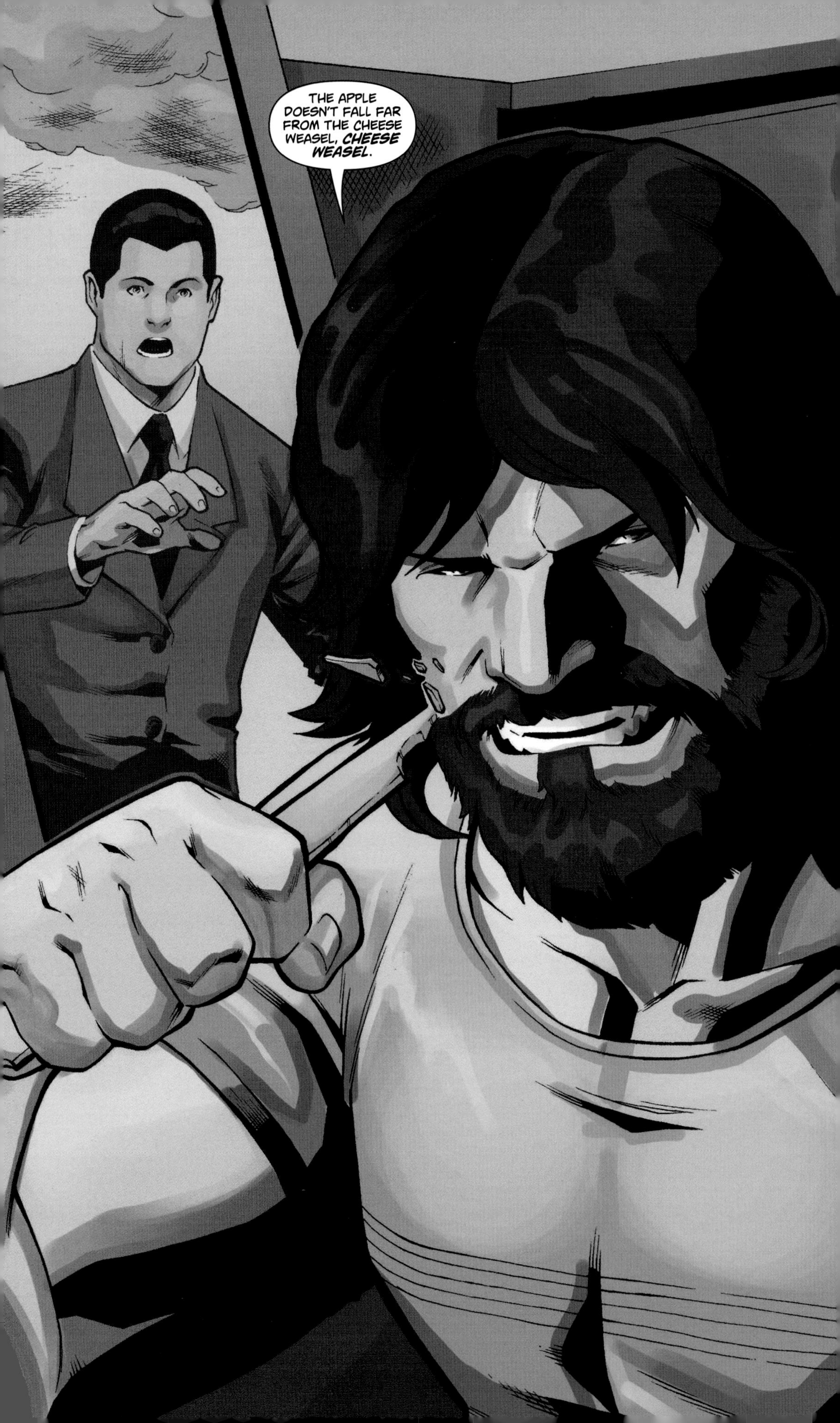
THE APPLE DOESN'T FALL FAR FROM THE CHEESE WEASEL, *CHEESE WEASEL*.

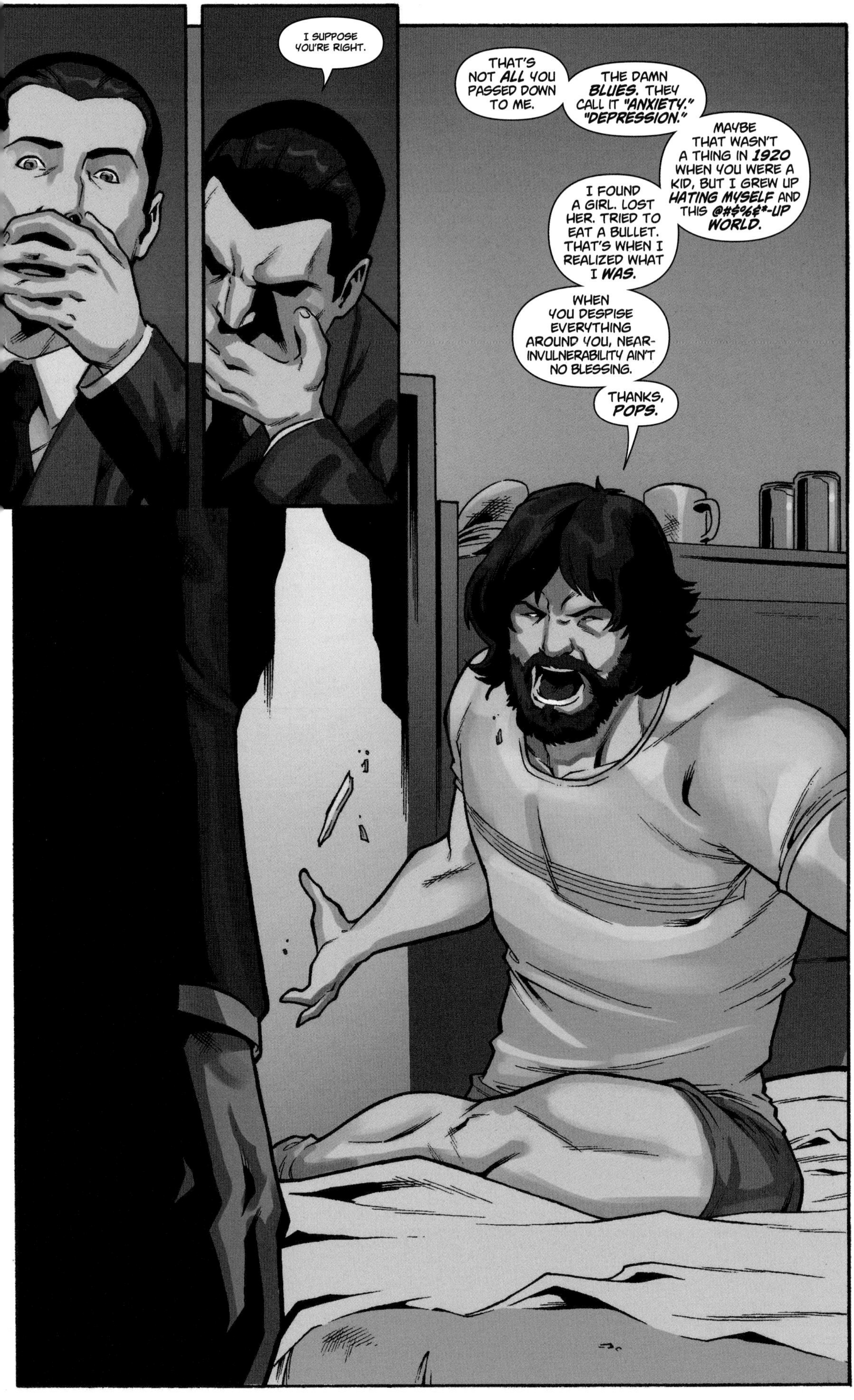
I SUPPOSE YOU'RE RIGHT.
THAT'S NOT ALL YOU PASSED DOWN TO ME.
THE DAMN BLUES. THEY CALL IT "ANXIETY." "DEPRESSION."
MAYBE THAT WASN'T A THING IN 1920 WHEN YOU WERE A KID, BUT I GREW UP HATING MYSELF AND THIS @#$%&*-UP WORLD.
I FOUND A GIRL. LOST HER. TRIED TO EAT A BULLET. THAT'S WHEN I REALIZED WHAT I WAS.
WHEN YOU DESPISE EVERYTHING AROUND YOU, NEAR-INVULNERABILITY AIN'T NO BLESSING.
THANKS, POPS.

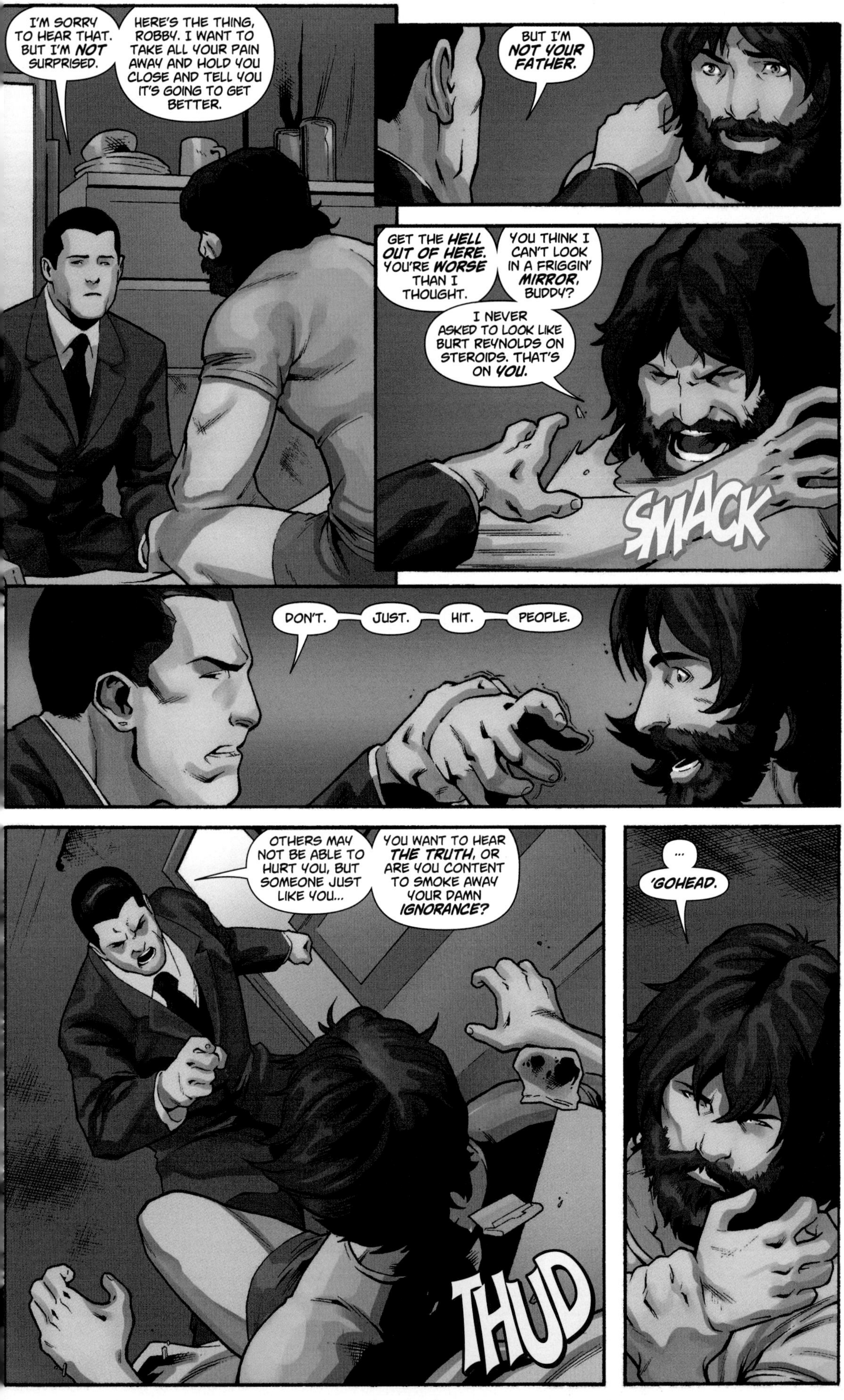
I'M SORRY TO HEAR THAT. BUT I'M NOT SURPRISED.
HERE'S THE THING, ROBBY. I WANT TO TAKE ALL YOUR PAIN AWAY AND HOLD YOU CLOSE AND TELL YOU IT'S GOING TO GET BETTER.
BUT I'M NOT YOUR FATHER.
GET THE HELL OUT OF HERE. YOU'RE WORSE THAN I THOUGHT.
YOU THINK I CAN'T LOOK IN A FRIGGIN' MIRROR, BUDDY?
I NEVER ASKED TO LOOK LIKE BURT REYNOLDS ON STEROIDS. THAT'S ON YOU.
SMACK
DON'T.
JUST.
HIT.
PEOPLE.
OTHERS MAY NOT BE ABLE TO HURT YOU, BUT SOMEONE JUST LIKE YOU...
YOU WANT TO HEAR THE TRUTH, OR ARE YOU CONTENT TO SMOKE AWAY YOUR DAMN IGNORANCE?
THUD
...
'GOHEAD.

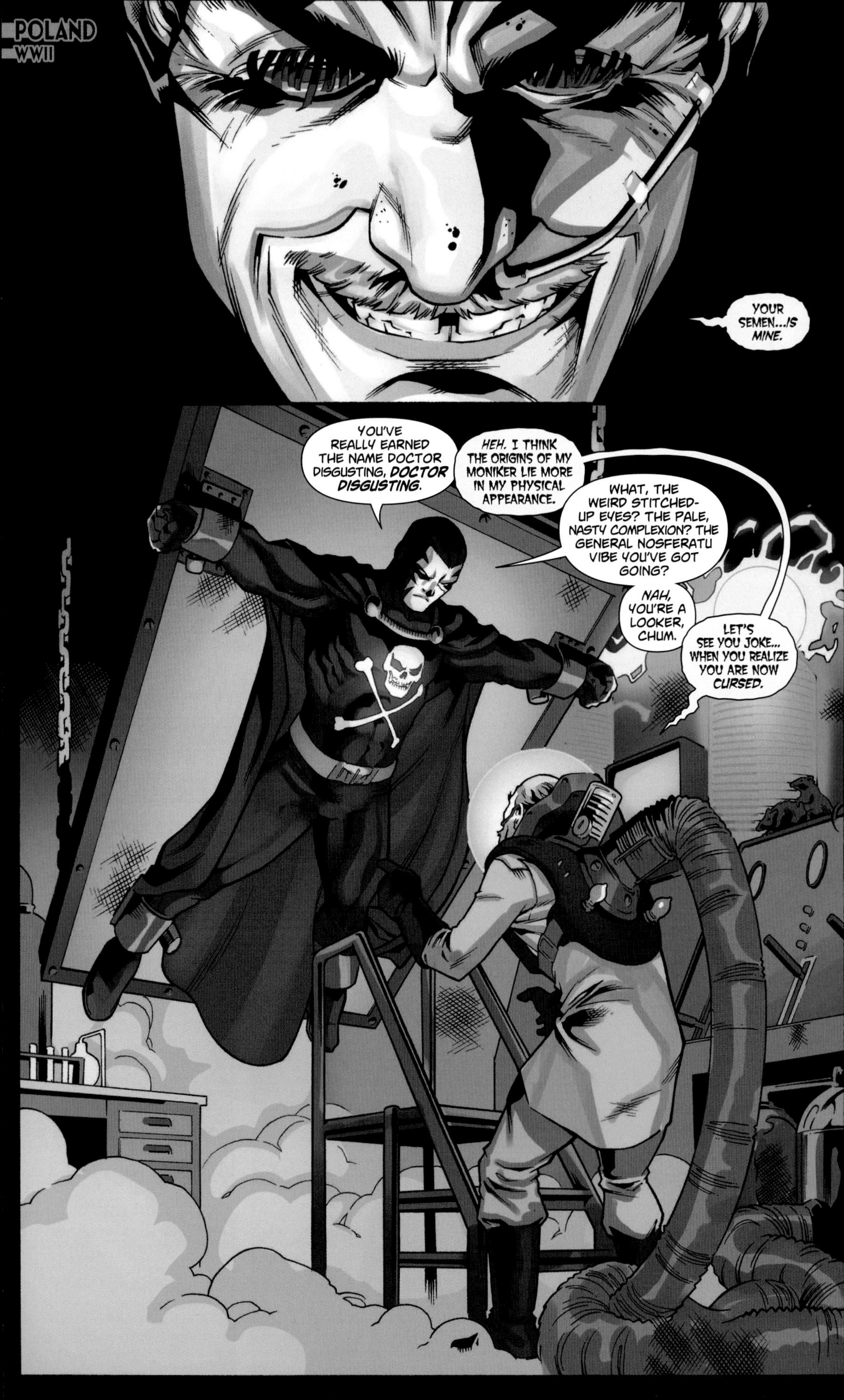
POLAND
WWII
YOUR SEMEN...IS MINE.
YOU'VE REALLY EARNED THE NAME DOCTOR DISGUSTING, DOCTOR DISGUSTING.
HEH. I THINK THE ORIGINS OF MY MONIKER LIE MORE IN MY PHYSICAL APPEARANCE.
WHAT, THE WEIRD STITCHED-UP EYES? THE PALE, NASTY COMPLEXION? THE GENERAL NOSFERATU VIBE YOU'VE GOT GOING?
NAH, YOU'RE A LOOKER, CHUM.
LET'S SEE YOU JOKE... WHEN YOU REALIZE YOU ARE NOW CURSED.

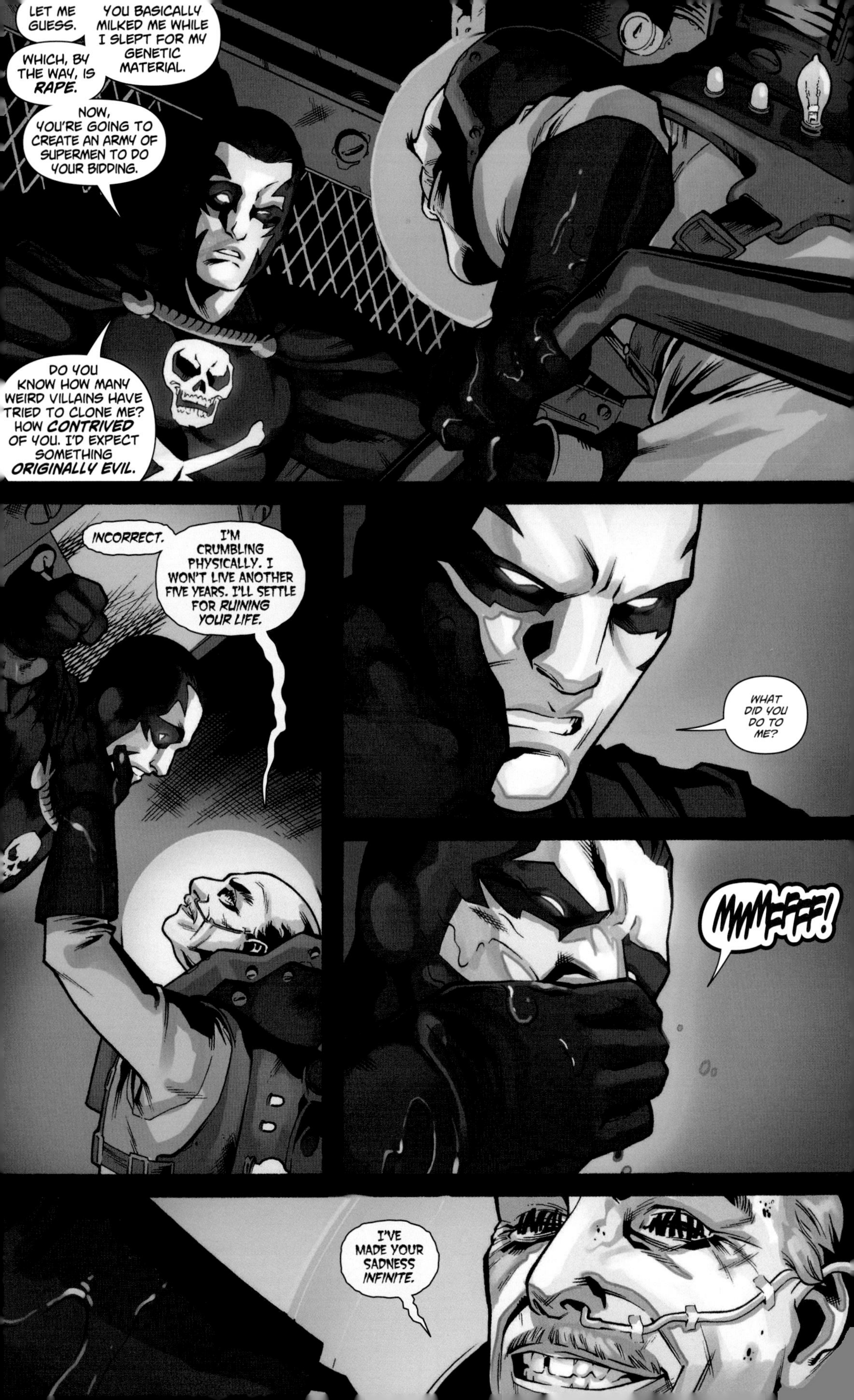
LET ME GUESS.
YOU BASICALLY MILKED ME WHILE I SLEPT FOR MY GENETIC MATERIAL.
WHICH, BY THE WAY, IS RAPE.
NOW, YOU'RE GOING TO CREATE AN ARMY OF SUPERMEN TO DO YOUR BIDDING.
DO YOU KNOW HOW MANY WEIRD VILLAINS HAVE TRIED TO CLONE ME? HOW CONTRIVED OF YOU. I'D EXPECT SOMETHING ORIGINALLY EVIL.
INCORRECT.
I'M CRUMBLING PHYSICALLY. I WON'T LIVE ANOTHER FIVE YEARS. I'LL SETTLE FOR RUINING YOUR LIFE.
WHAT DID YOU DO TO ME?
MMMFFF!
I'VE MADE YOUR SADNESS INFINITE.

"I DON'T *NEED* TO CLONE YOU."

"BECAUSE YOU'LL DO IT FOR ME *YOURSELF.*"

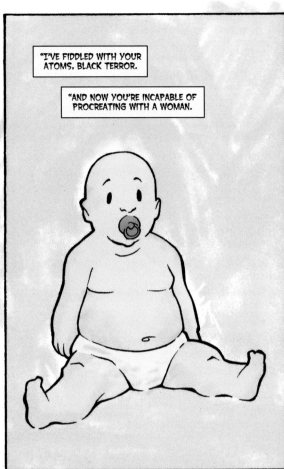

"I'VE FIDDLED WITH YOUR ATOMS, BLACK TERROR."

"AND NOW YOU'RE INCAPABLE OF PROCREATING WITH A WOMAN."

"I KNOW OF YOUR PROMISCUOUS NATURE...YOU MAY SEE THIS AS A BOON."

"BUT YOU'RE STILL FERTILE."

"ANY CHILD YOU FATHER...WILL SIMPLY BE AN *EXACT COPY OF YOU.*"

"A MALE REPRODUCTION OF YOU PHYSICALLY, MENTALLY, AND GENETICALLY. EVEN MORE SO THAN A CLONE."

"UNLESS YOU PLAN ON REMAINING CHASTE OR CHANGING YOUR WOMANIZING WAYS..."

"CHANCES ARE YOU'RE GOING TO KNOCK SOME POOR COW UP. AND WHEN THAT CHILD IS BORN, IT WILL GROW UP WITH YOUR POWERS."

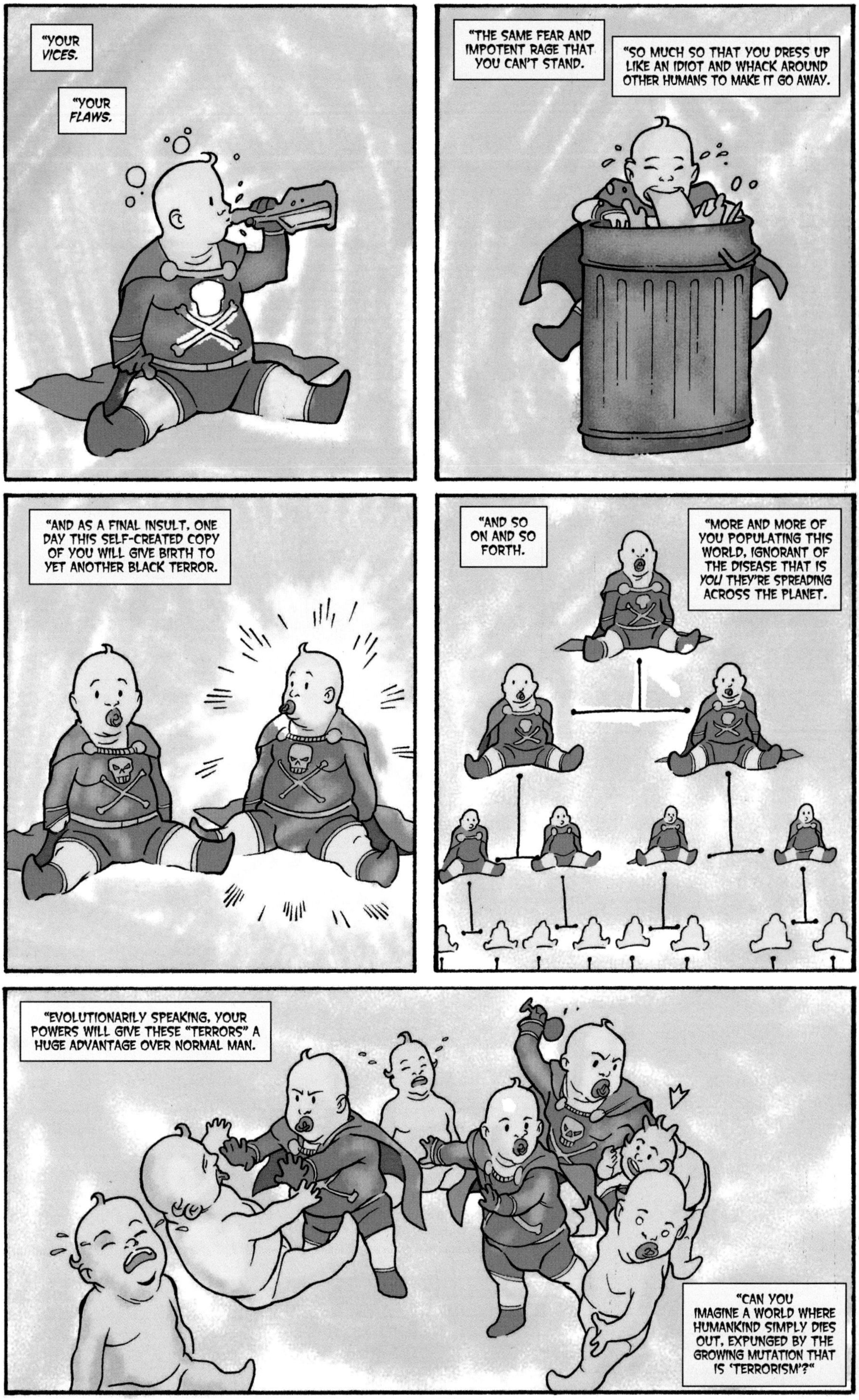
"YOUR VICES.
"YOUR FLAWS.
"THE SAME FEAR AND IMPOTENT RAGE THAT YOU CAN'T STAND.
"SO MUCH SO THAT YOU DRESS UP LIKE AN IDIOT AND WHACK AROUND OTHER HUMANS TO MAKE IT GO AWAY.
"AND AS A FINAL INSULT, ONE DAY THIS SELF-CREATED COPY OF YOU WILL GIVE BIRTH TO YET ANOTHER BLACK TERROR.
"AND SO ON AND SO FORTH.
"MORE AND MORE OF YOU POPULATING THIS WORLD, IGNORANT OF THE DISEASE THAT IS YOU THEY'RE SPREADING ACROSS THE PLANET.
"EVOLUTIONARILY SPEAKING, YOUR POWERS WILL GIVE THESE "TERRORS" A HUGE ADVANTAGE OVER NORMAL MAN.
"CAN YOU IMAGINE A WORLD WHERE HUMANKIND SIMPLY DIES OUT, EXPUNGED BY THE GROWING MUTATION THAT IS 'TERRORISM'?"

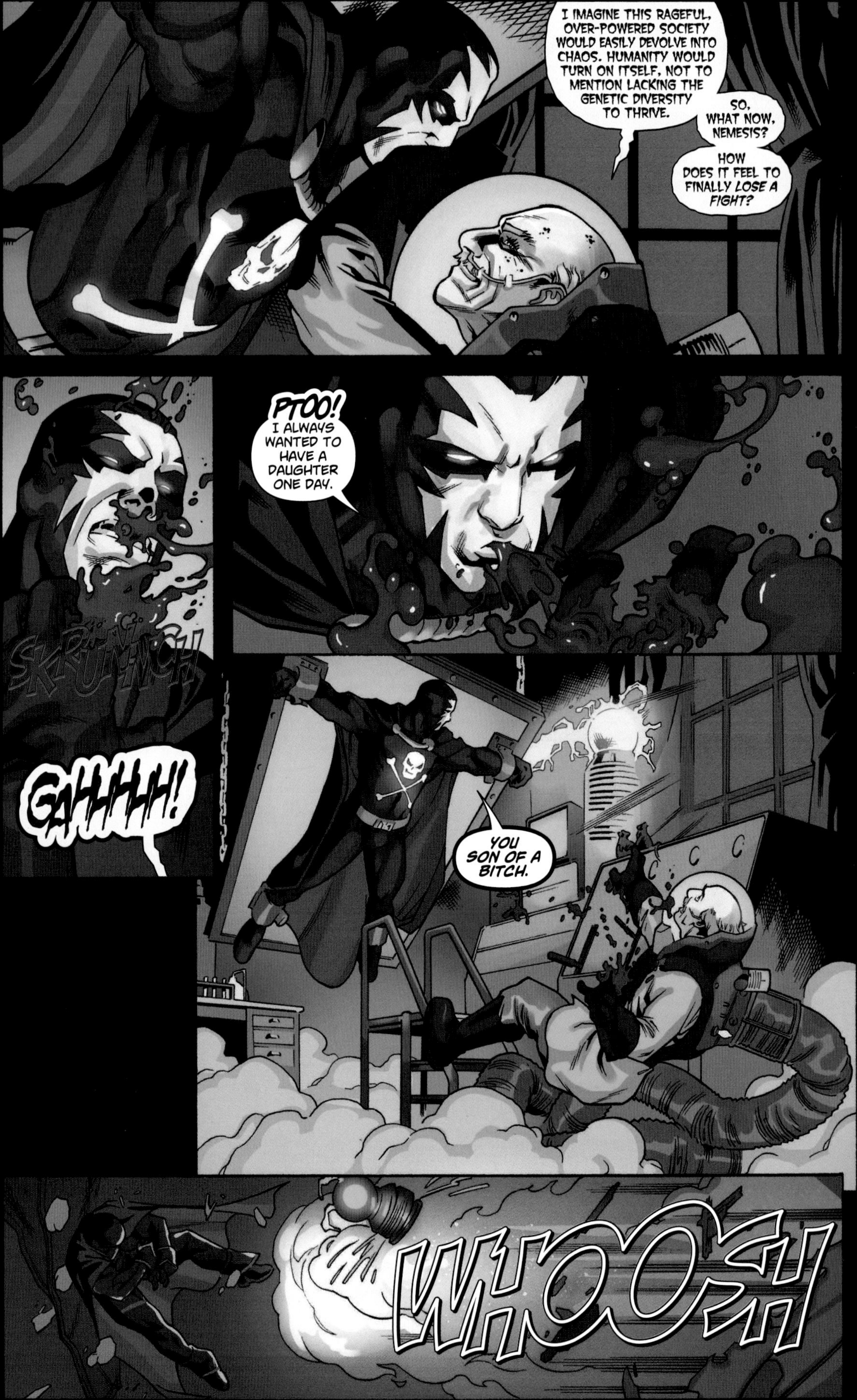
I IMAGINE THIS RAGEFUL, OVER-POWERED SOCIETY WOULD EASILY DEVOLVE INTO CHAOS. HUMANITY WOULD TURN ON ITSELF, NOT TO MENTION LACKING THE GENETIC DIVERSITY TO THRIVE.
SO, WHAT NOW, NEMESIS?
HOW DOES IT FEEL TO FINALLY LOSE A FIGHT?
PTOO! I ALWAYS WANTED TO HAVE A DAUGHTER ONE DAY.
SKRUNCH
GAHHHH!
YOU SON OF A BITCH.
WHOOSH

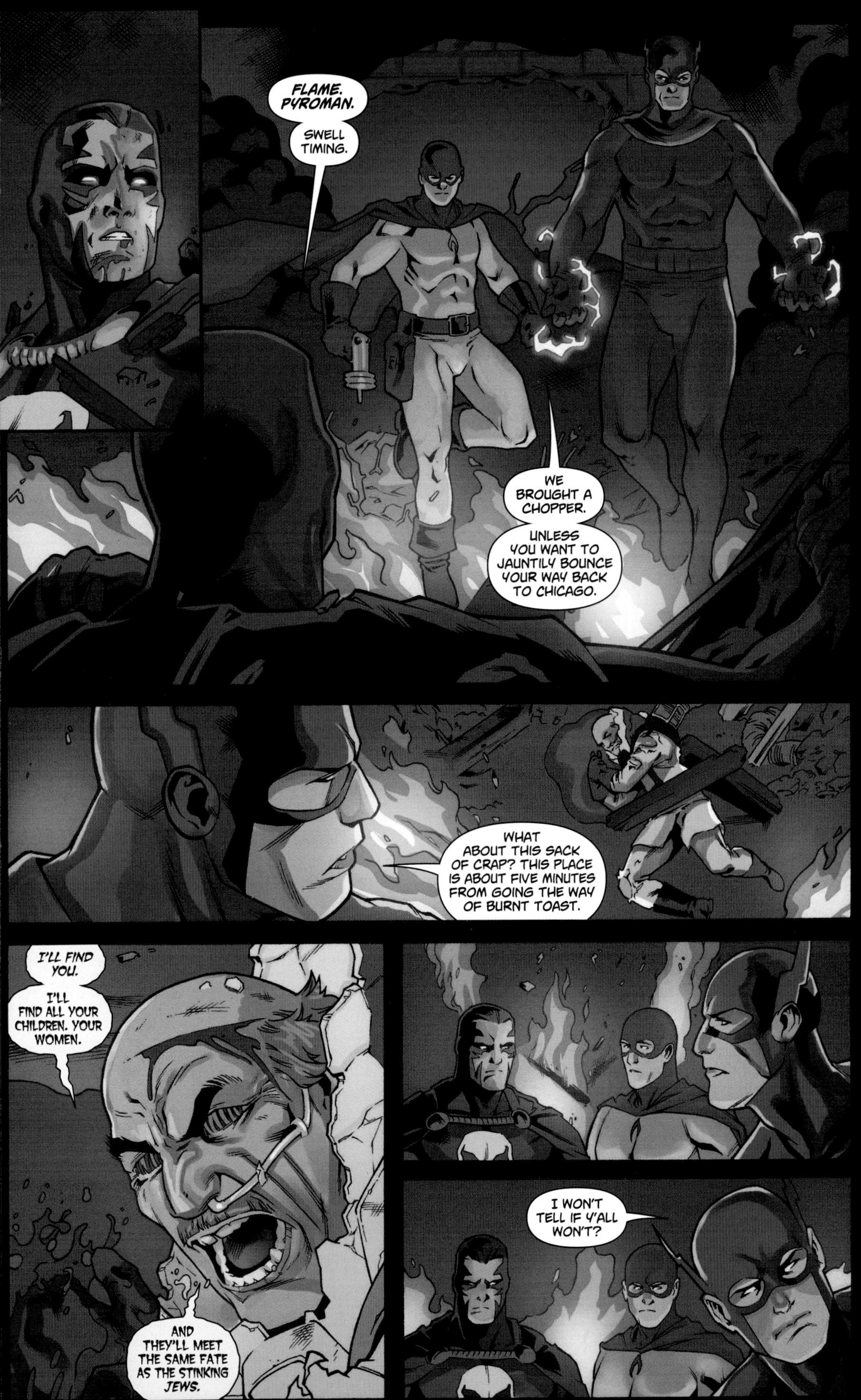

FLAME. PYROMAN.
SWELL TIMING.
WE BROUGHT A CHOPPER.
UNLESS YOU WANT TO JAUNTILY BOUNCE YOUR WAY BACK TO CHICAGO.
WHAT ABOUT THIS SACK OF CRAP? THIS PLACE IS ABOUT FIVE MINUTES FROM GOING THE WAY OF BURNT TOAST.
I'LL FIND YOU.
I'LL FIND ALL YOUR CHILDREN. YOUR WOMEN.
AND THEY'LL MEET THE SAME FATE AS THE STINKING JEWS.
I WON'T TELL IF Y'ALL WON'T?

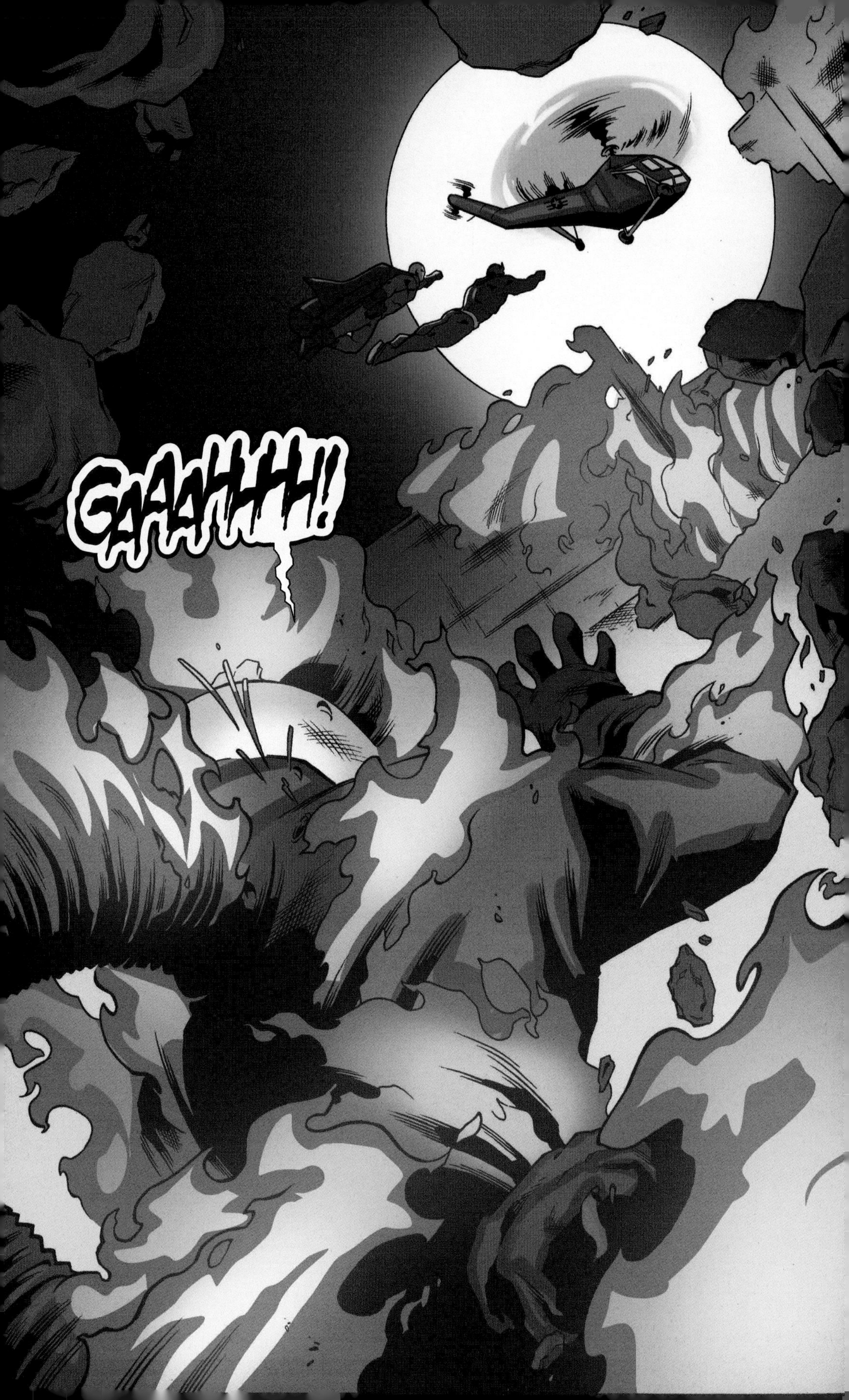
GAAAHHH!

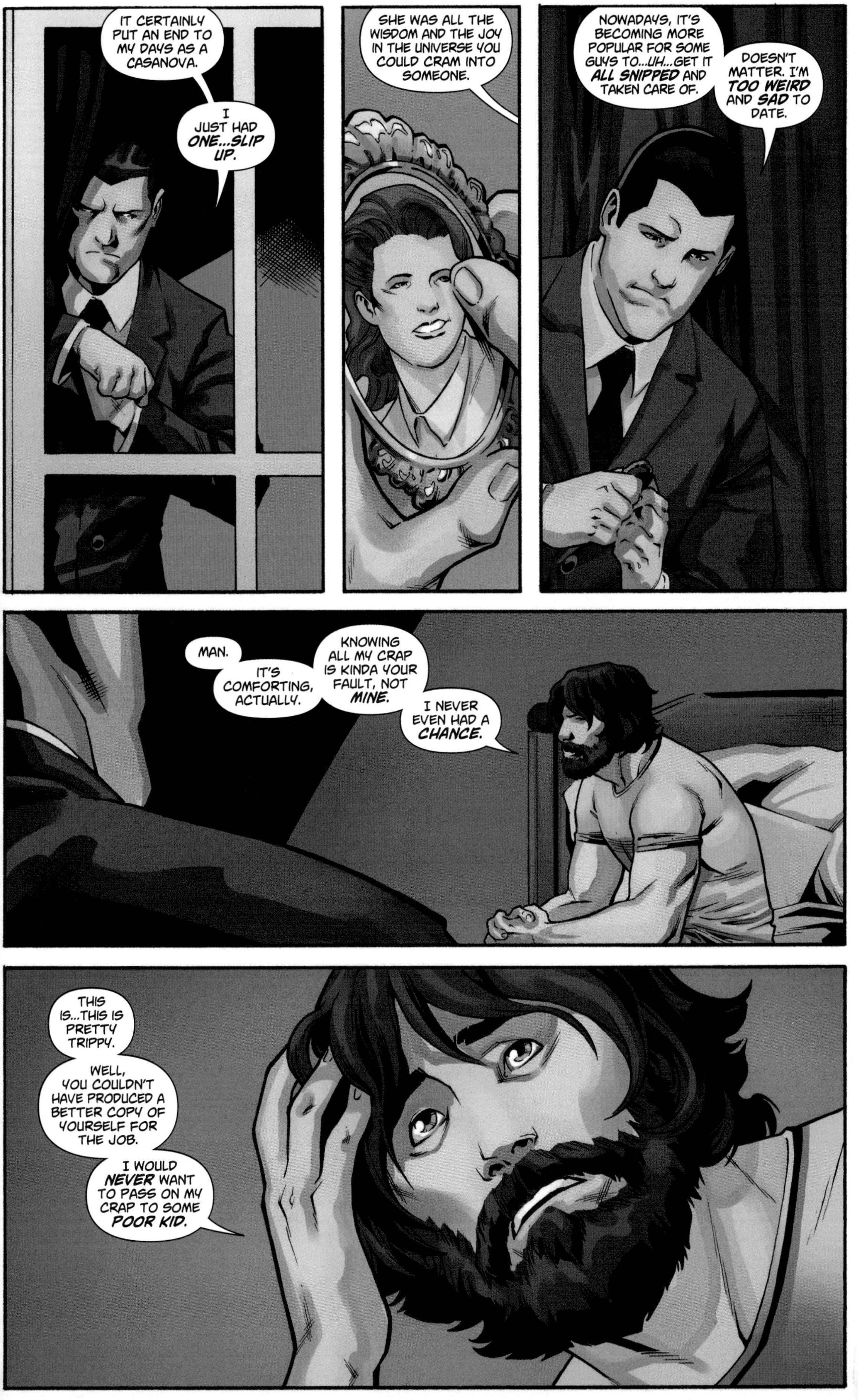
IT CERTAINLY PUT AN END TO MY DAYS AS A CASANOVA.
I JUST HAD ONE...SLIP UP.
SHE WAS ALL THE WISDOM AND THE JOY IN THE UNIVERSE YOU COULD CRAM INTO SOMEONE.
NOWADAYS, IT'S BECOMING MORE POPULAR FOR SOME GUYS TO...UH...GET IT ALL SNIPPED AND TAKEN CARE OF.
DOESN'T MATTER. I'M TOO WEIRD AND SAD TO DATE.
MAN.
IT'S COMFORTING, ACTUALLY.
KNOWING ALL MY CRAP IS KINDA YOUR FAULT, NOT MINE.
I NEVER EVEN HAD A CHANCE.
THIS IS...THIS IS PRETTY TRIPPY.
WELL, YOU COULDN'T HAVE PRODUCED A BETTER COPY OF YOURSELF FOR THE JOB.
I WOULD NEVER WANT TO PASS ON MY CRAP TO SOME POOR KID.

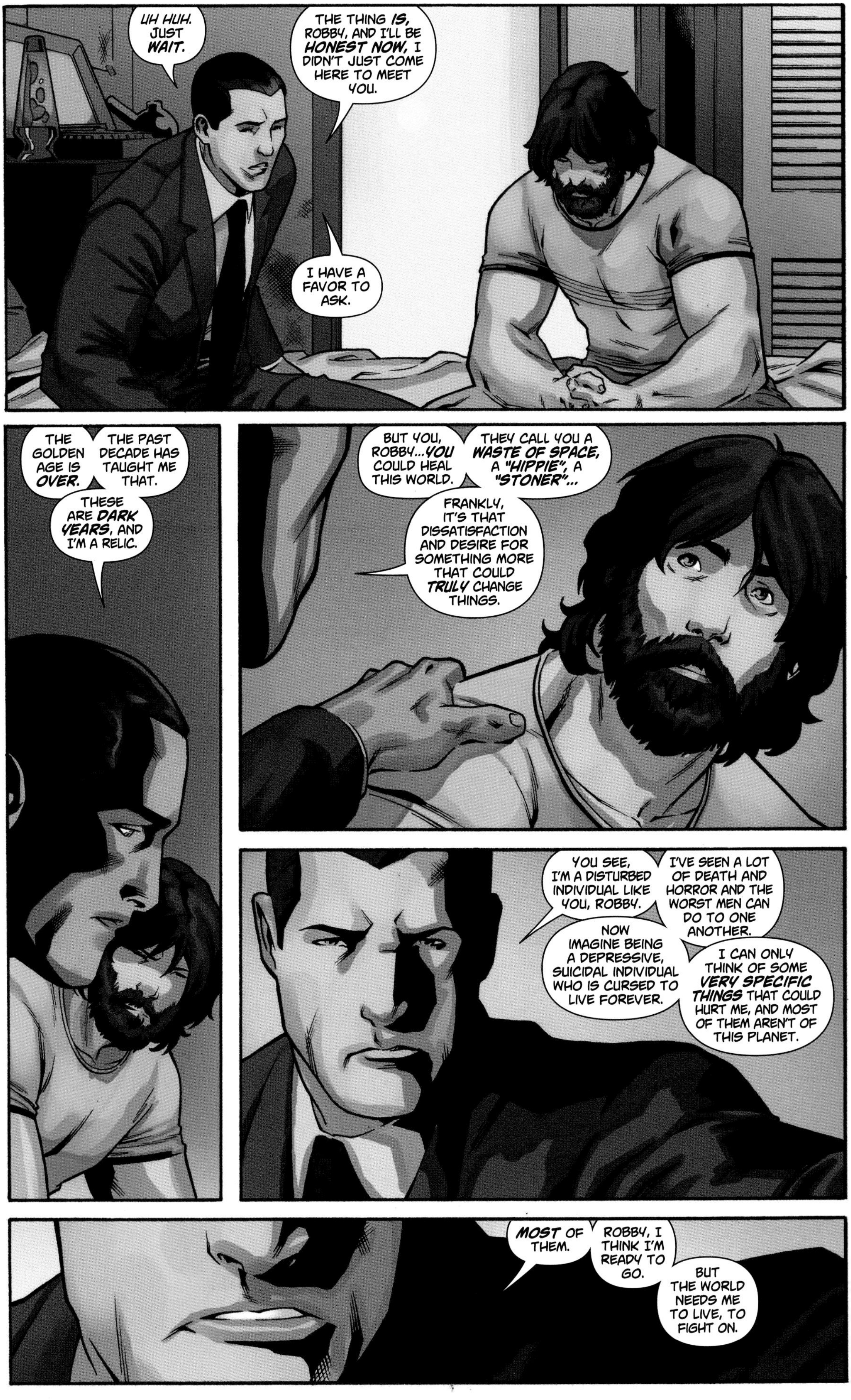
UH HUH. JUST WAIT.
THE THING IS, ROBBY, AND I'LL BE HONEST NOW, I DIDN'T JUST COME HERE TO MEET YOU.
I HAVE A FAVOR TO ASK.
THE GOLDEN AGE IS OVER.
THE PAST DECADE HAS TAUGHT ME THAT.
THESE ARE DARK YEARS, AND I'M A RELIC.
BUT YOU, ROBBY...YOU COULD HEAL THIS WORLD.
THEY CALL YOU A WASTE OF SPACE, A "HIPPIE", A "STONER"...
FRANKLY, IT'S THAT DISSATISFACTION AND DESIRE FOR SOMETHING MORE THAT COULD TRULY CHANGE THINGS.
YOU SEE, I'M A DISTURBED INDIVIDUAL LIKE YOU, ROBBY.
I'VE SEEN A LOT OF DEATH AND HORROR AND THE WORST MEN CAN DO TO ONE ANOTHER.
NOW IMAGINE BEING A DEPRESSIVE, SUICIDAL INDIVIDUAL WHO IS CURSED TO LIVE FOREVER.
I CAN ONLY THINK OF SOME VERY SPECIFIC THINGS THAT COULD HURT ME, AND MOST OF THEM AREN'T OF THIS PLANET.
MOST OF THEM.
ROBBY, I THINK I'M READY TO GO.
BUT THE WORLD NEEDS ME TO LIVE, TO FIGHT ON.

WAIT... WHAT ARE YOU *TRYING* TO...?

OH HELL NO.

NOT HAPPENING.

I SEE.

WELL, I KNOW IT'S NOT SOMETHING I CAN FORCE ON YOU.

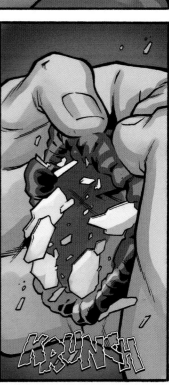

KRUNCH

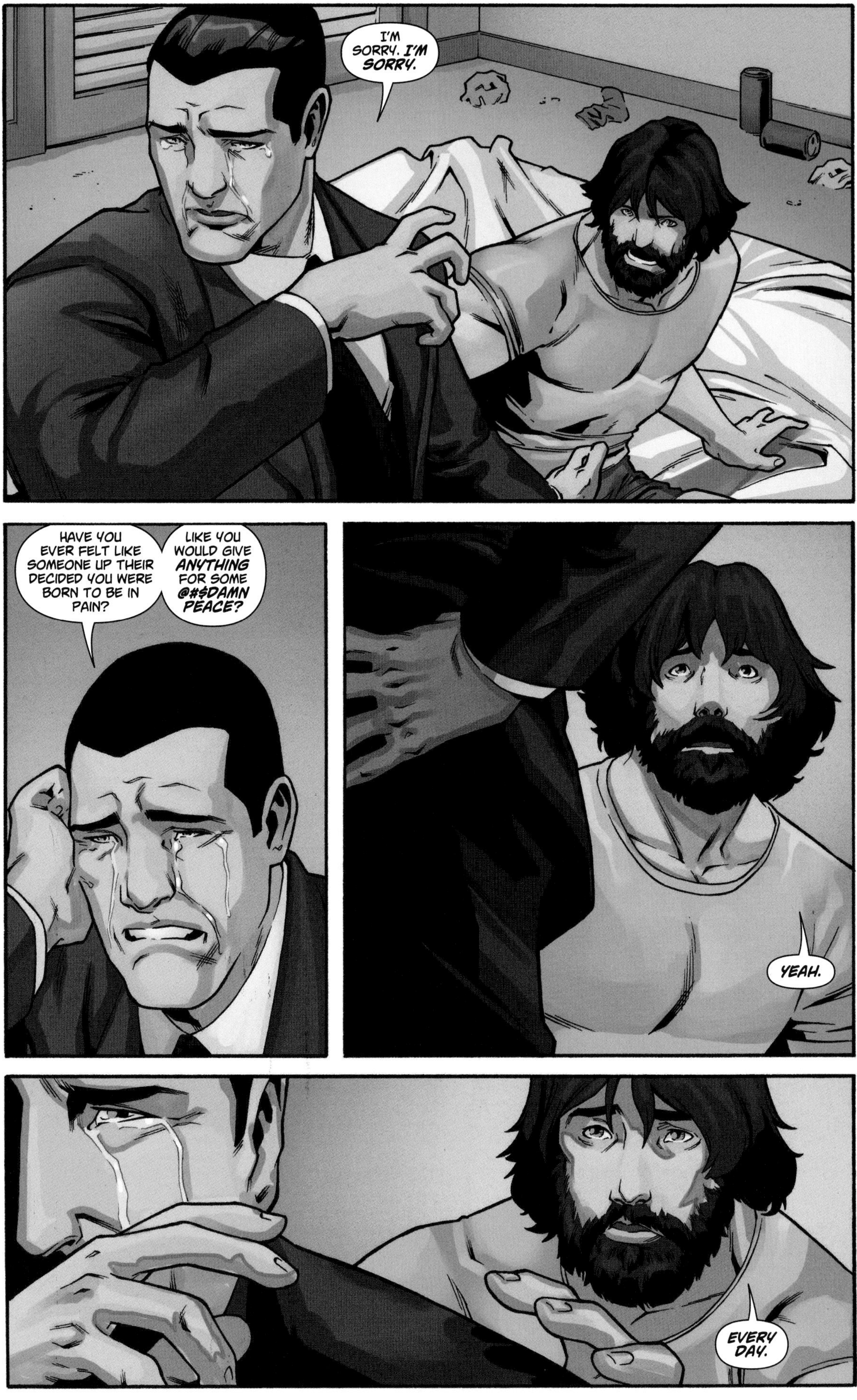
I'M SORRY. *I'M SORRY.*
HAVE YOU EVER FELT LIKE SOMEONE UP THEIR DECIDED YOU WERE BORN TO BE IN PAIN?
LIKE YOU WOULD GIVE *ANYTHING* FOR SOME *@#$DAMN PEACE?*
YEAH.
EVERY DAY.

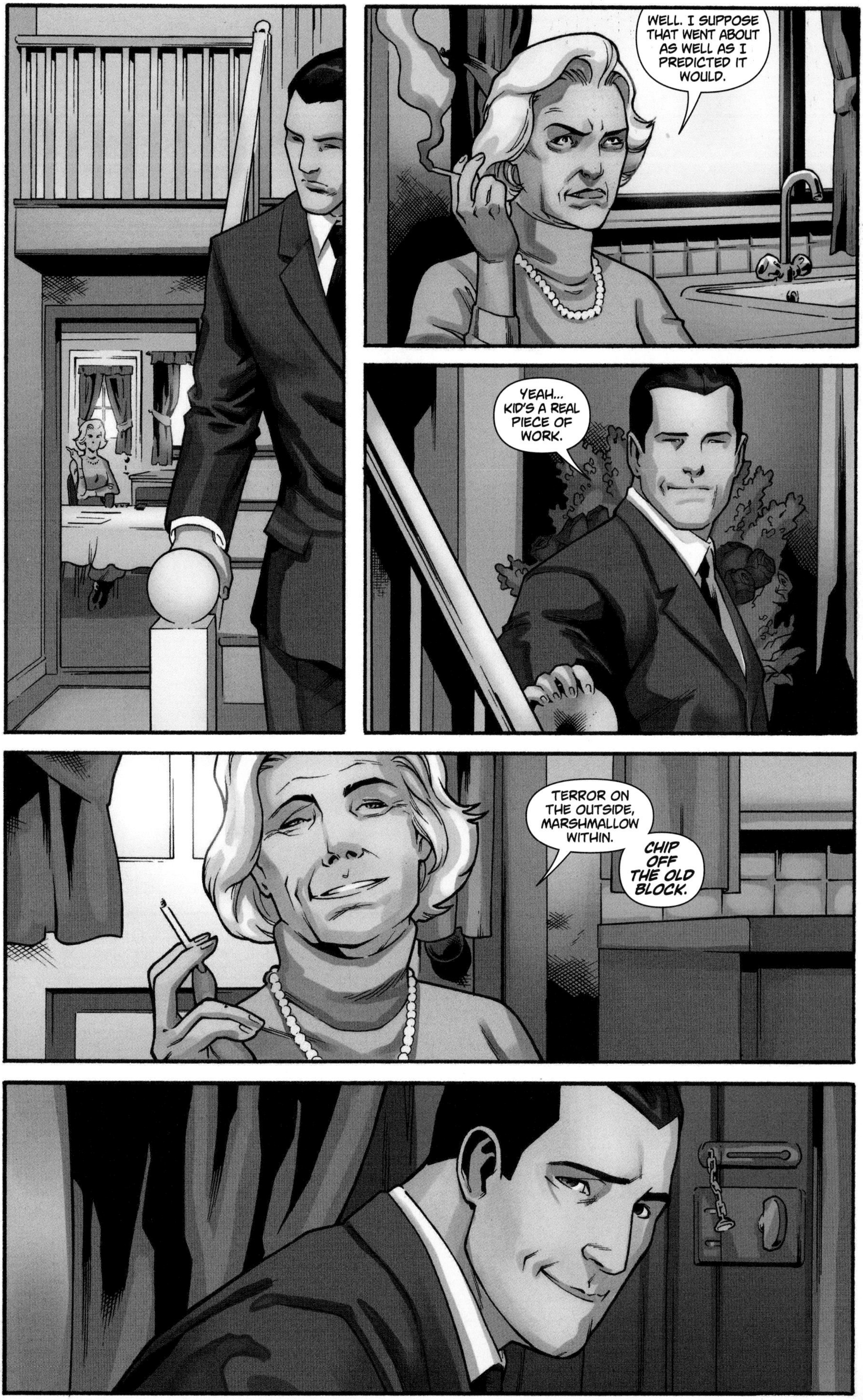
WELL. I SUPPOSE THAT WENT ABOUT AS WELL AS I PREDICTED IT WOULD.
YEAH... KID'S A REAL PIECE OF WORK.
TERROR ON THE OUTSIDE, MARSHMALLOW WITHIN.
CHIP OFF THE OLD BLOCK.

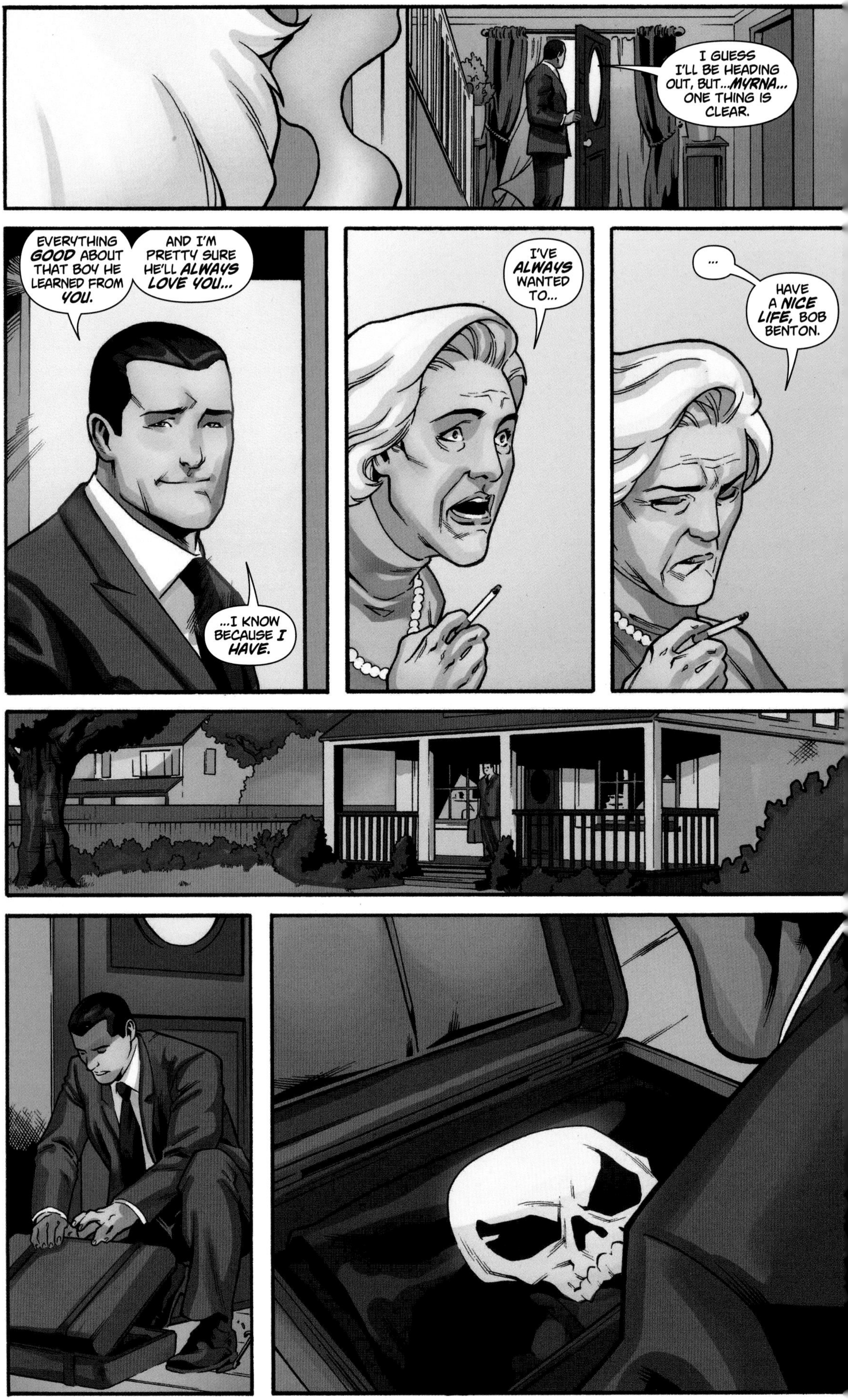
I GUESS I'LL BE HEADING OUT, BUT...MYRNA... ONE THING IS CLEAR.
EVERYTHING GOOD ABOUT THAT BOY HE LEARNED FROM YOU.
AND I'M PRETTY SURE HE'LL ALWAYS LOVE YOU...
...I KNOW BECAUSE I HAVE.
I'VE ALWAYS WANTED TO...
...
HAVE A NICE LIFE, BOB BENTON.

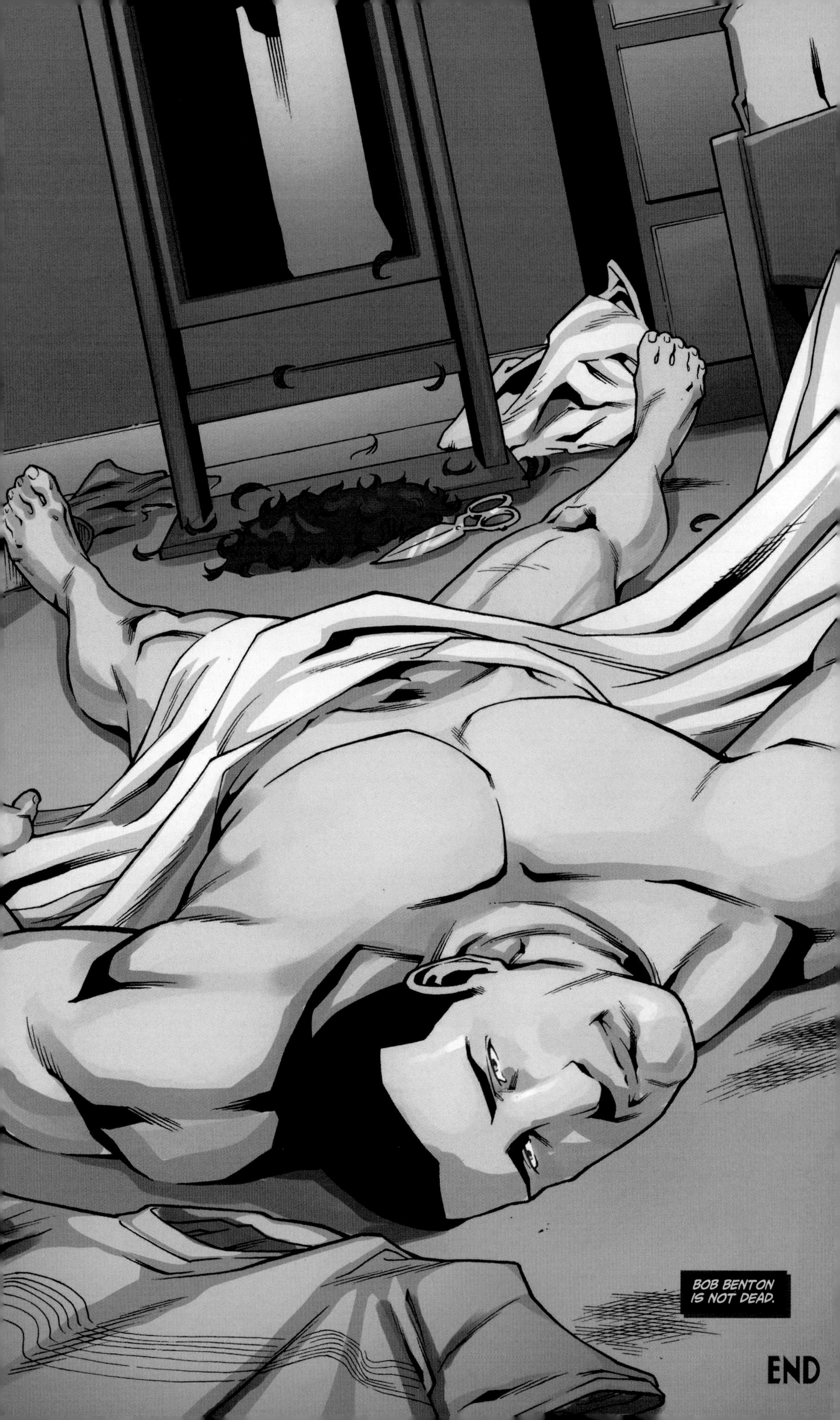
BOB BENTON
IS NOT DEAD.
END

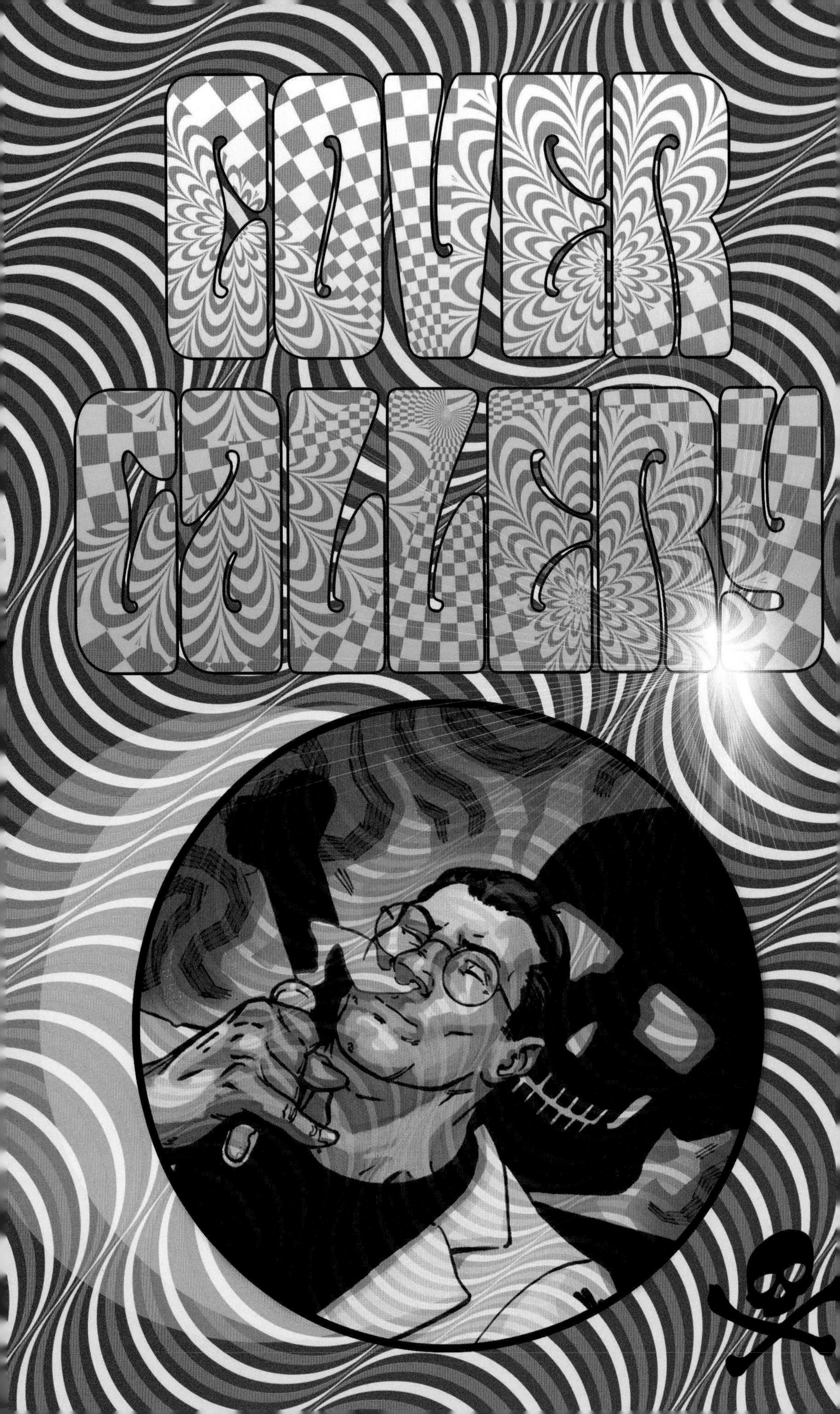
COVER
GALLERY

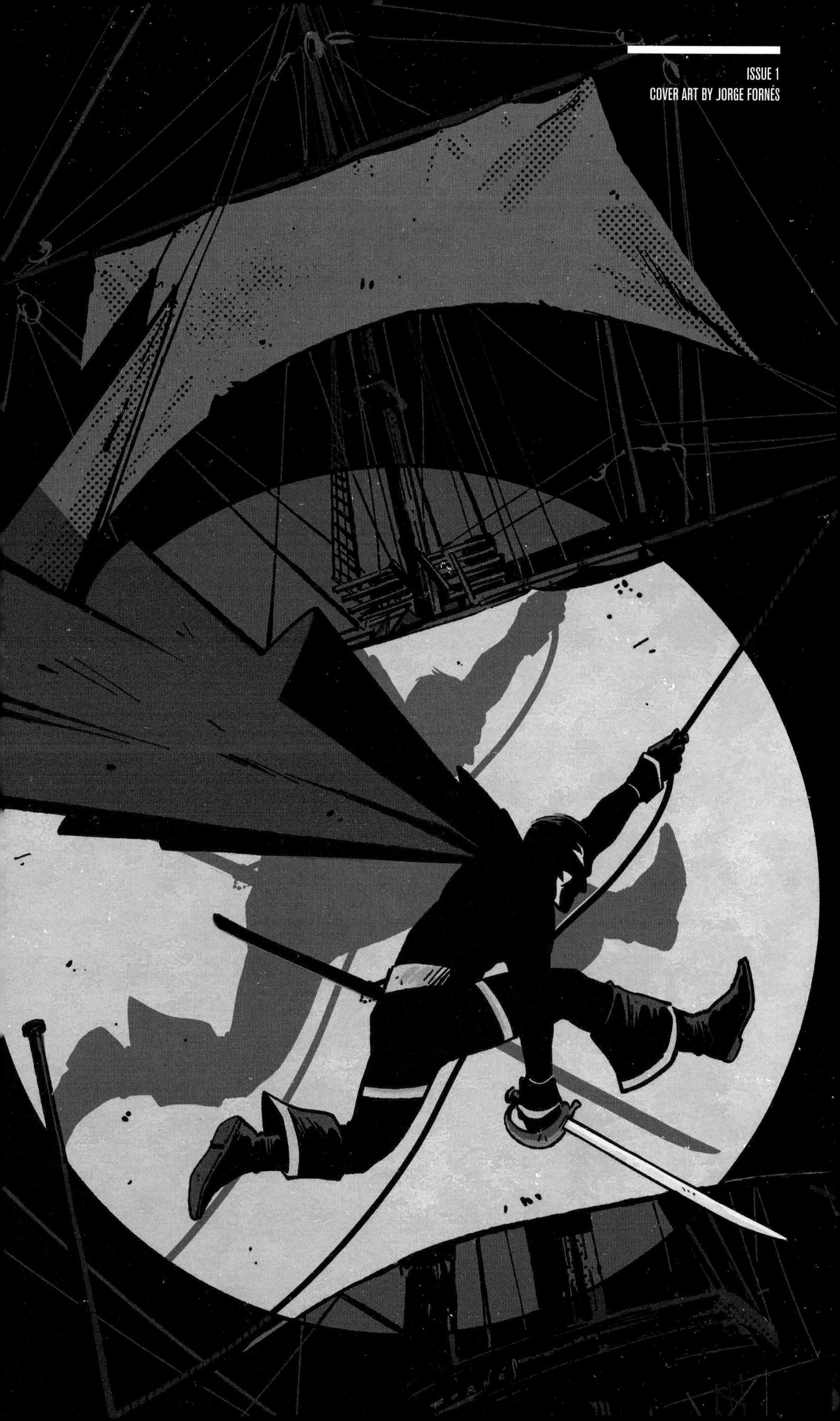

ISSUE 1
COVER ART BY JORGE FORNÉS

ISSUE 1
COVER ART BY DAVID NAKAYAMA

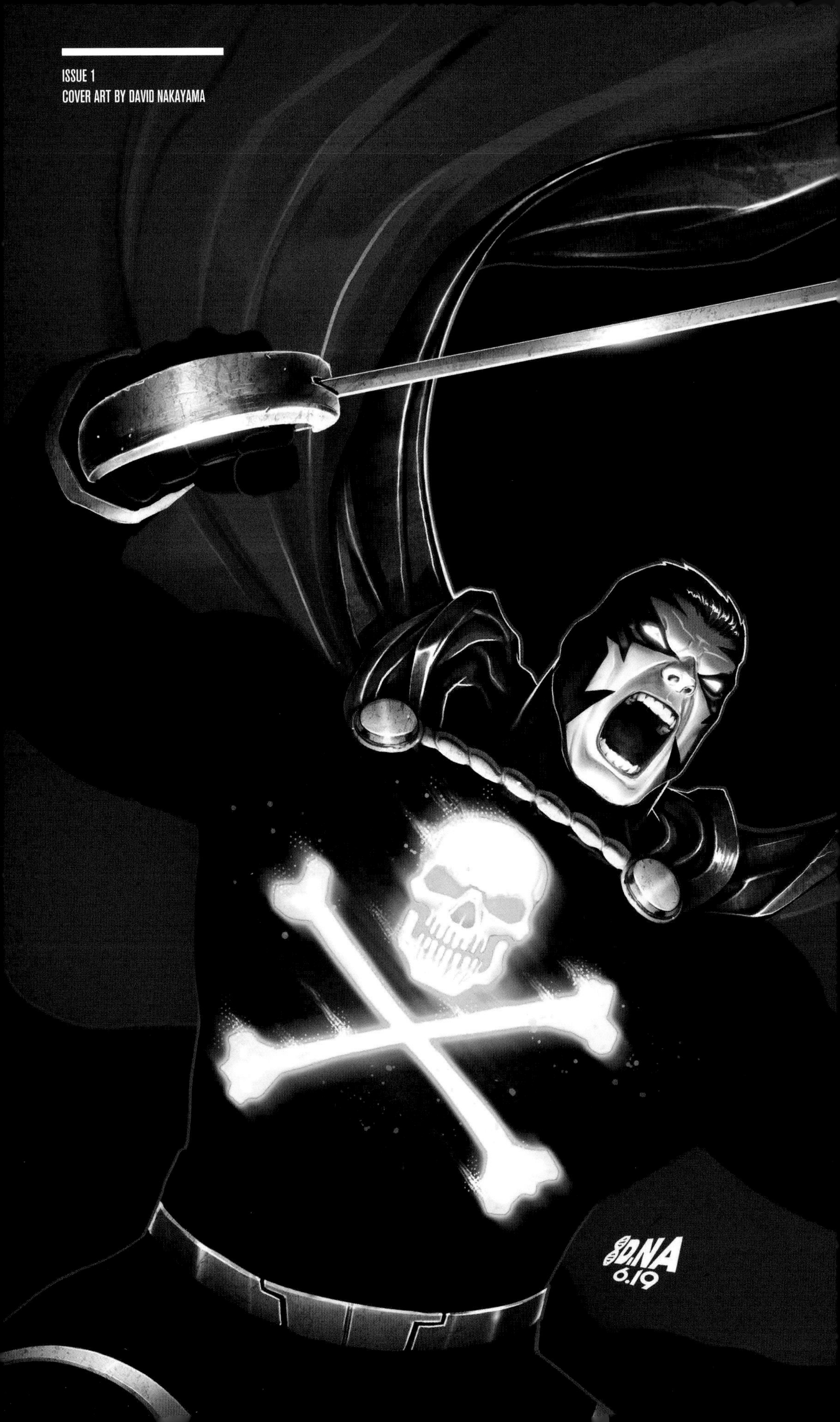
D.NA
6.19

ISSUE 1
COVER ART BY ERICA HENDERSON

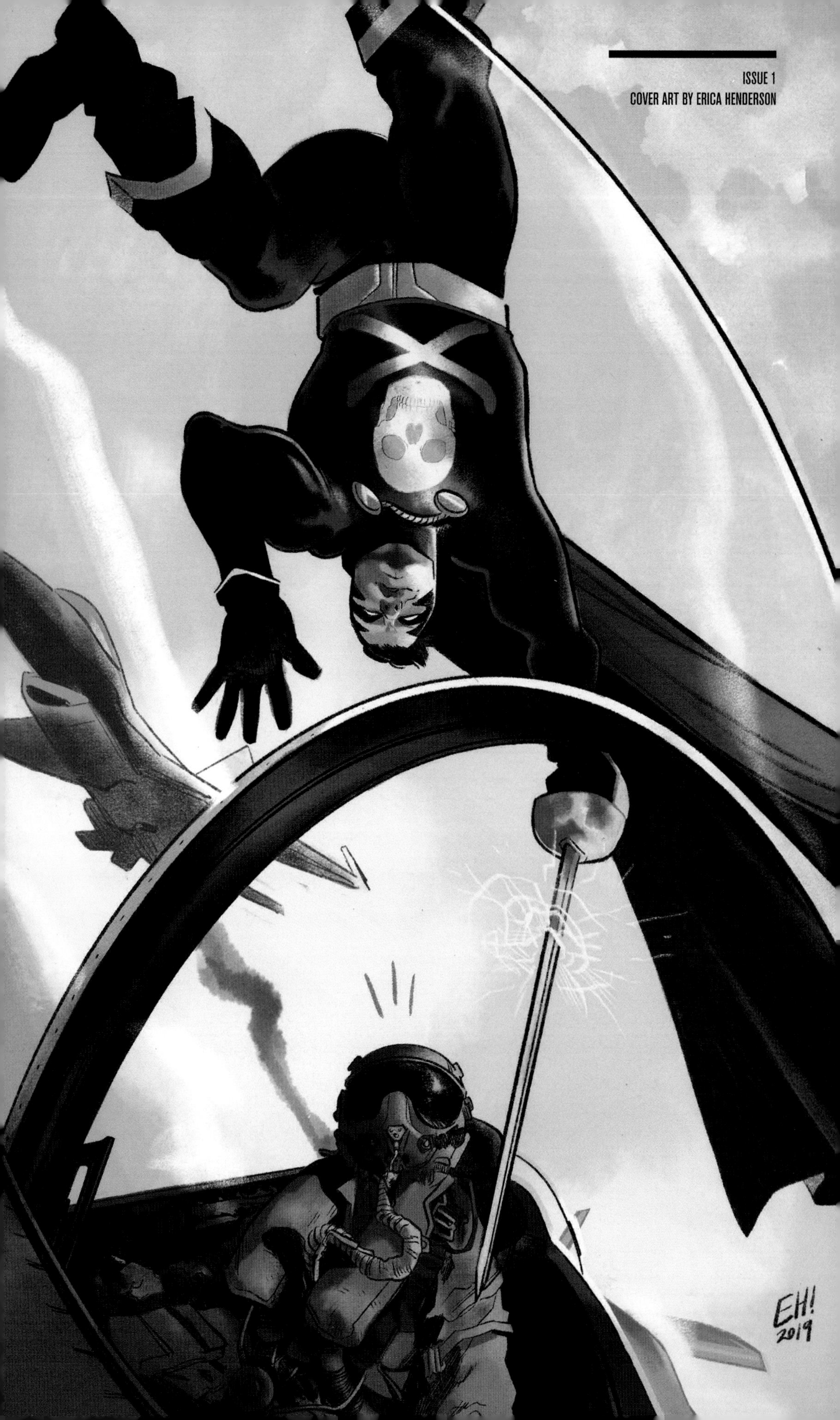
EH!
2019

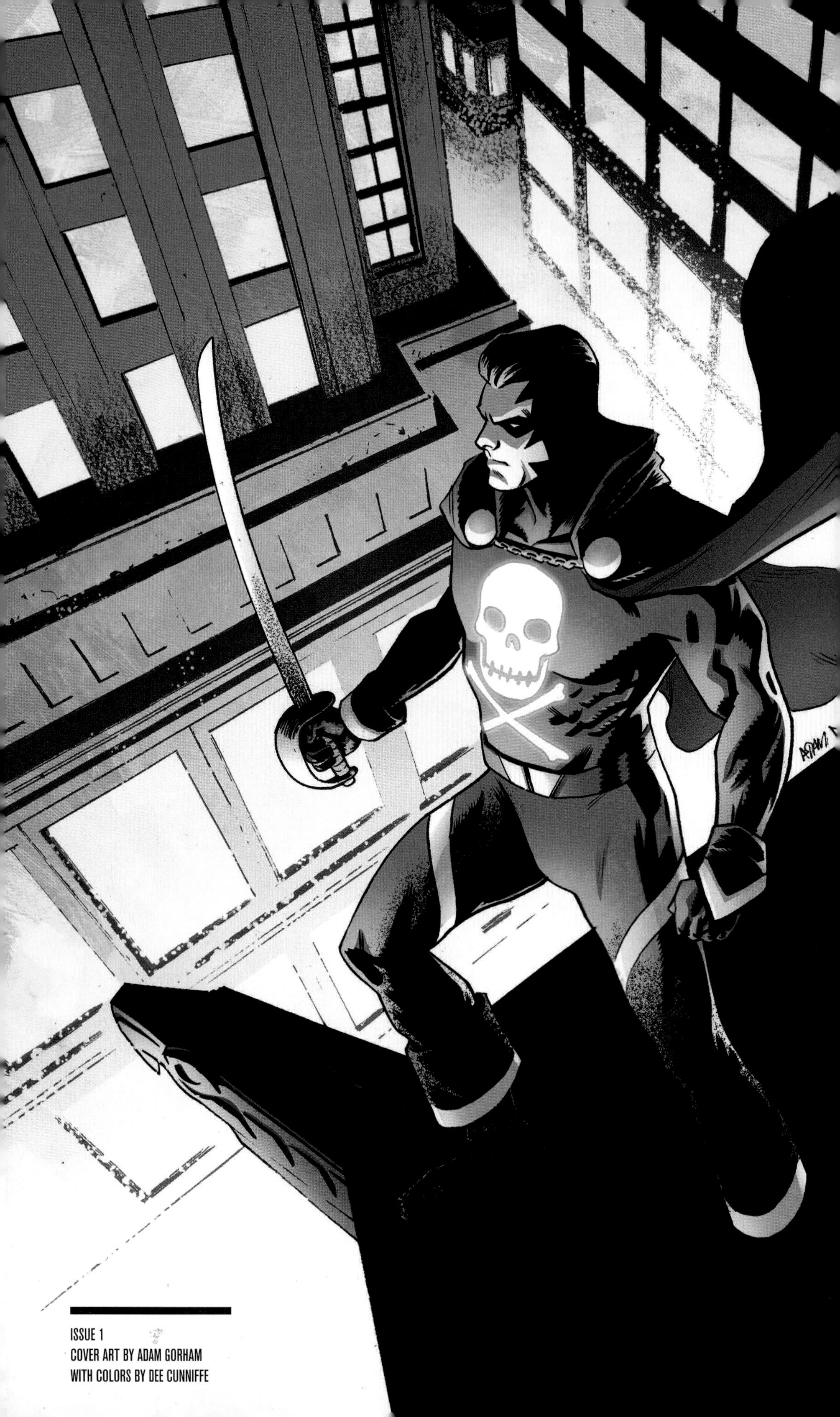

ISSUE 1
COVER ART BY ADAM GORHAM
WITH COLORS BY DEE CUNNIFFE

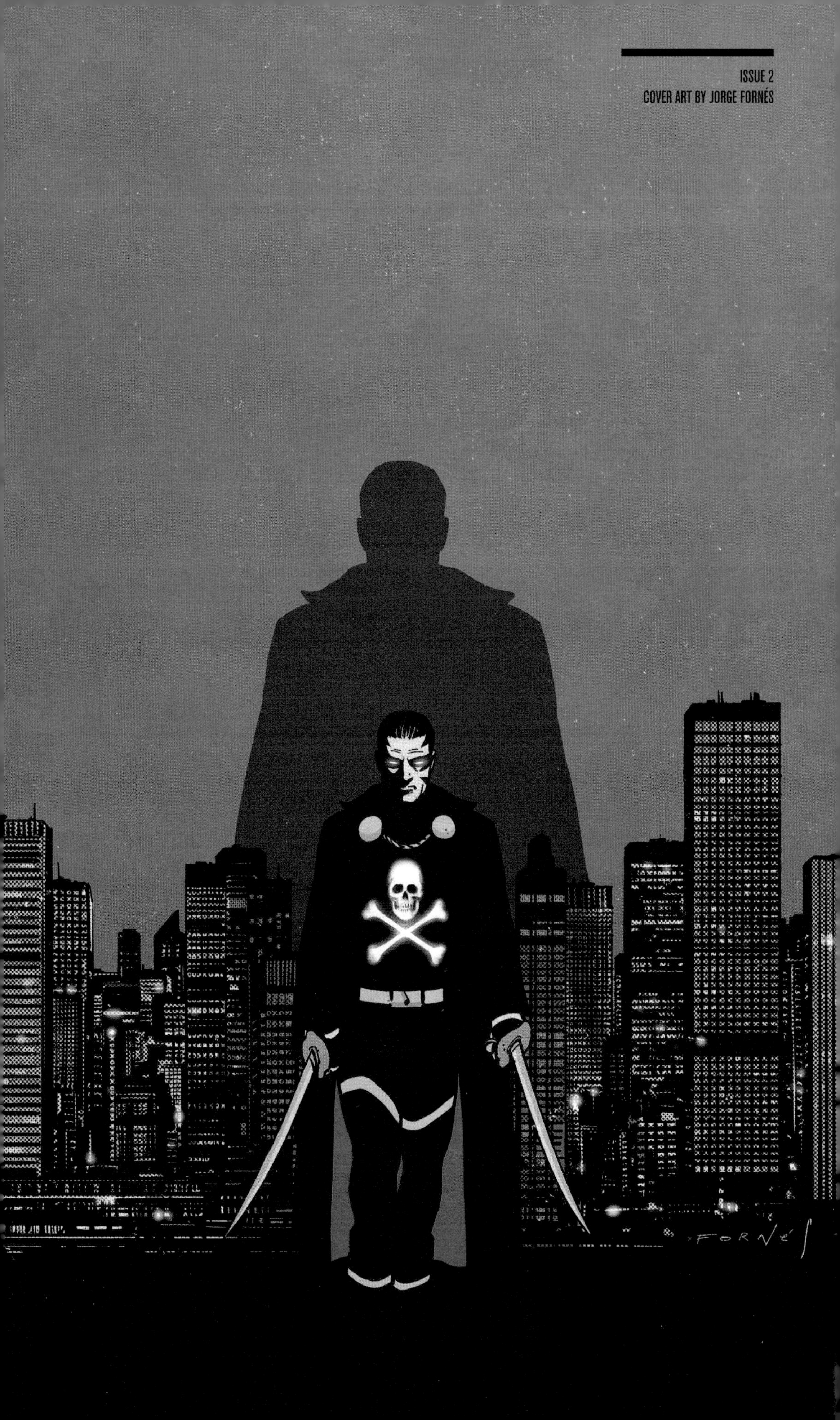
FORNÉS

ISSUE 2

COVER ART BY JORGE FORNÉS

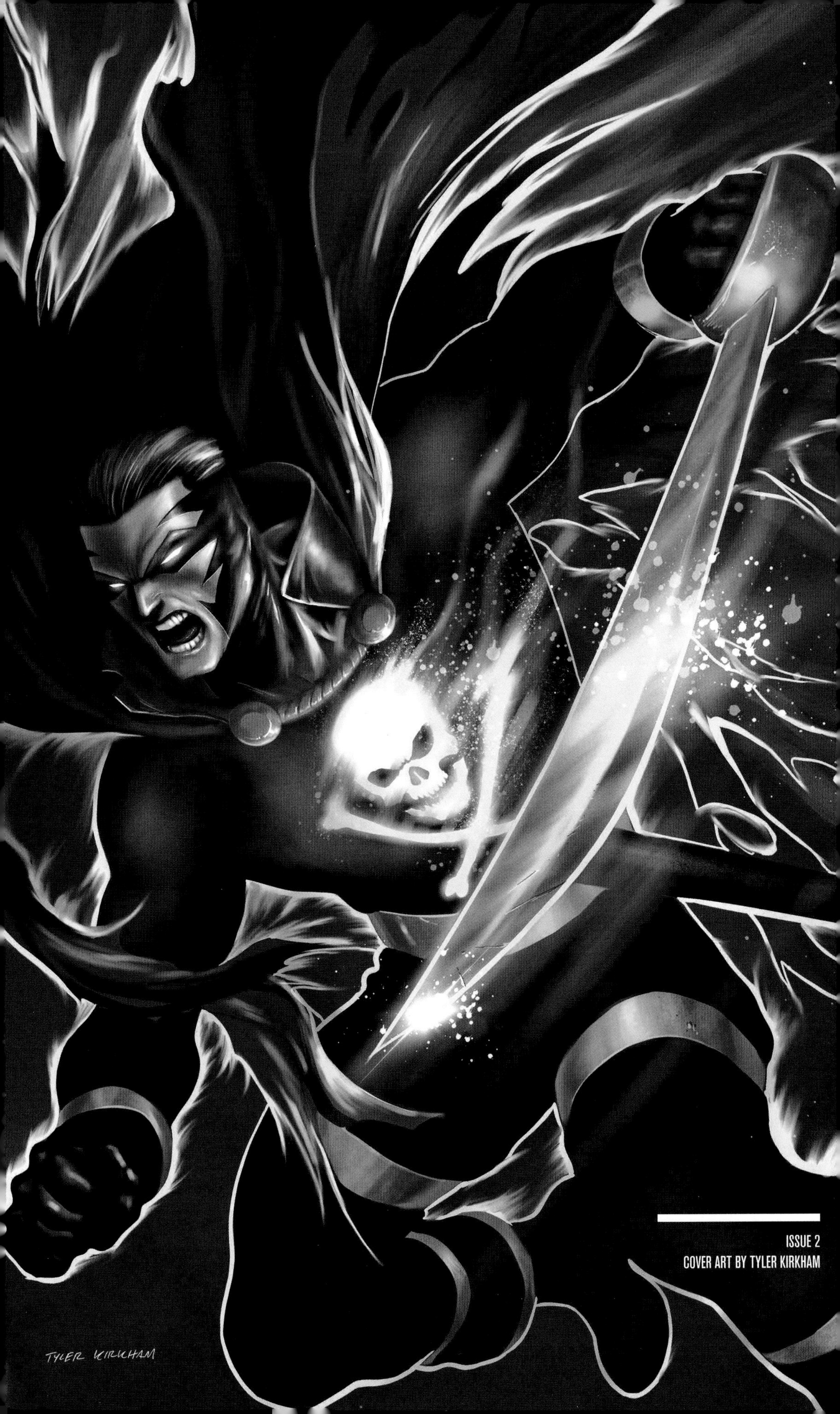
TYLER KIRKHAM

ISSUE 2
COVER ART BY TYLER KIRKHAM

ISSUE 2
COVER ART BY RAHZZAH

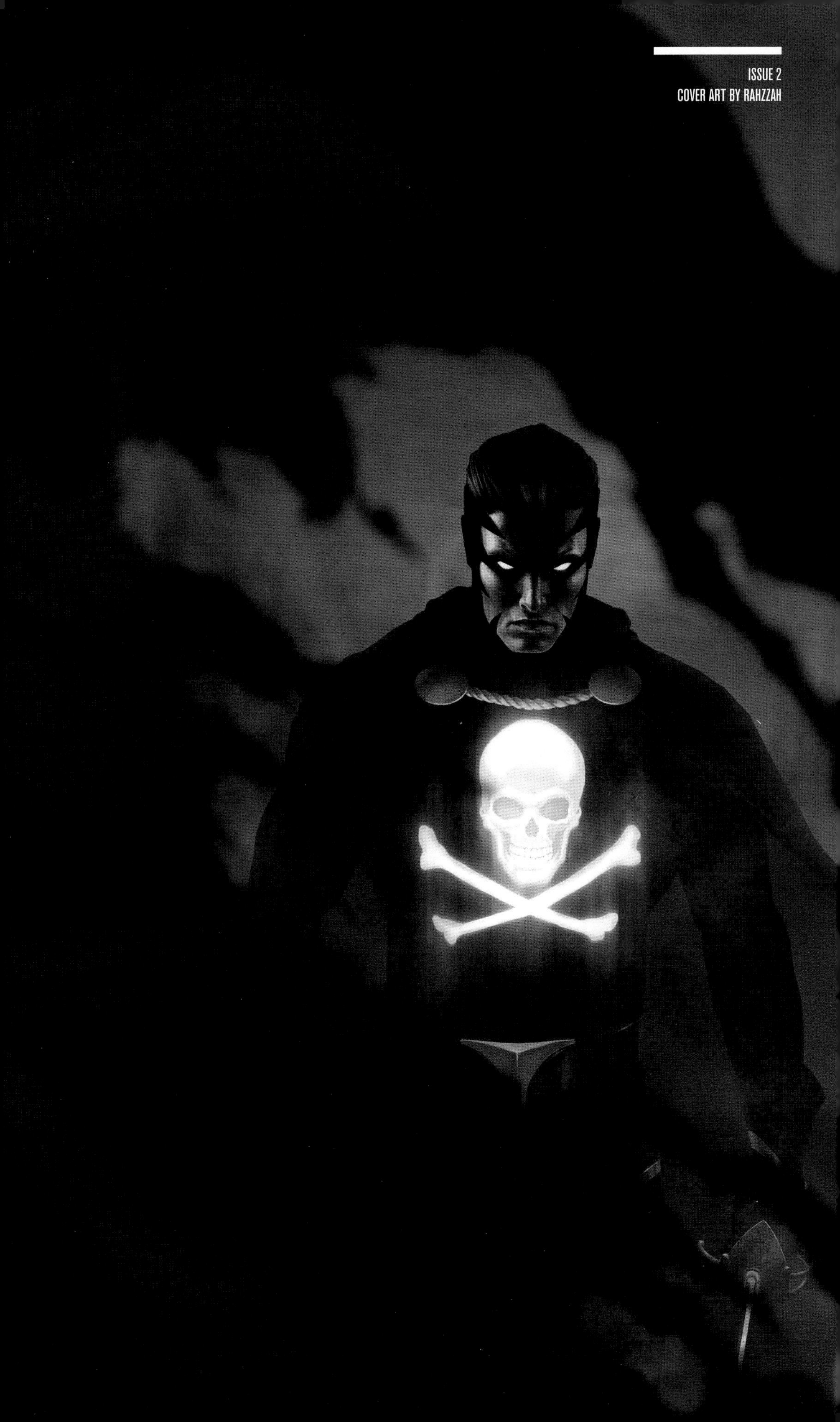

ISSUE 3
COVER ART BY JORGE FORNÉS

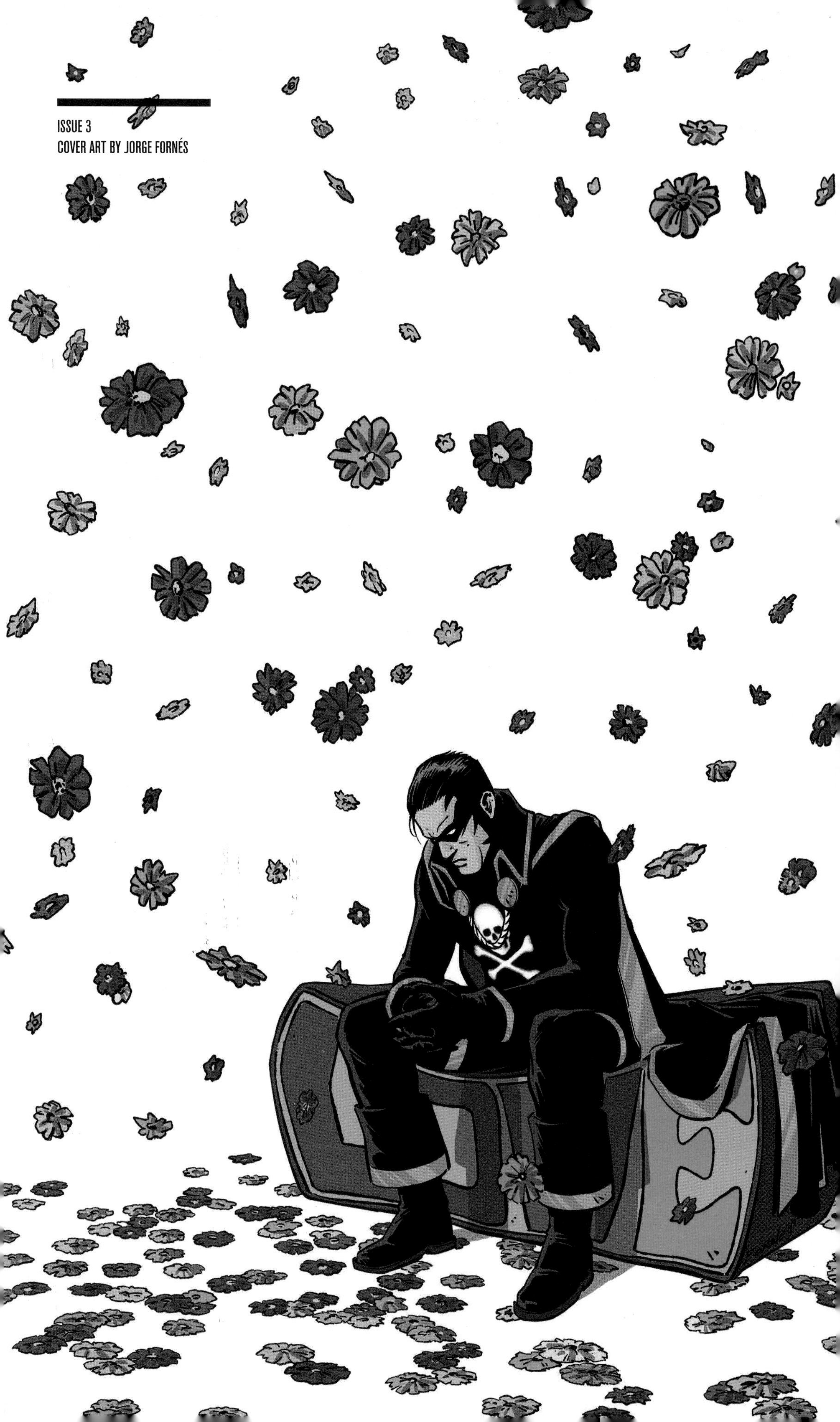

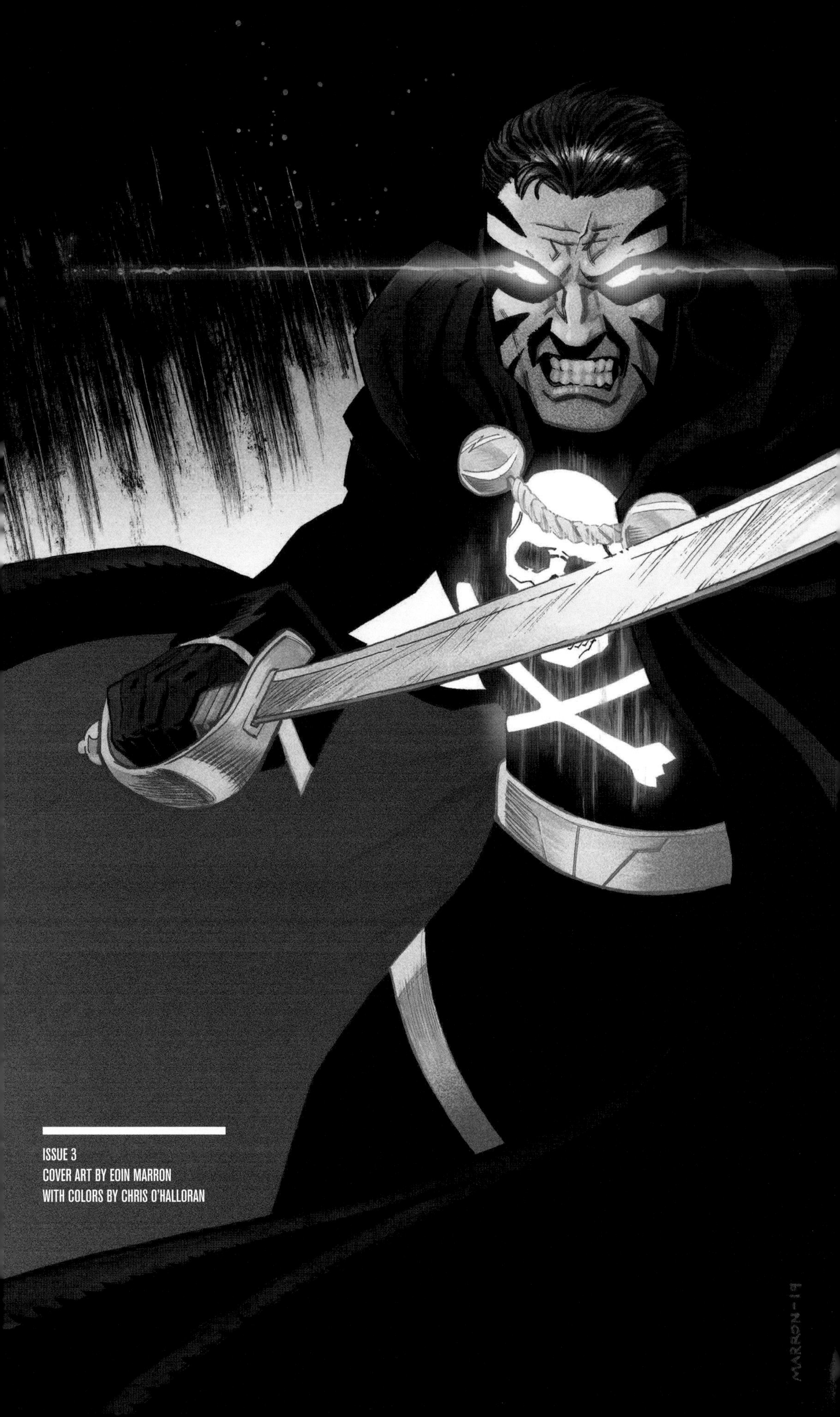
MARRON-19

ISSUE 3
COVER ART BY EOIN MARRON
WITH COLORS BY CHRIS O'HALLORAN

ISSUE 3
COVER ART BY RAHZZAH

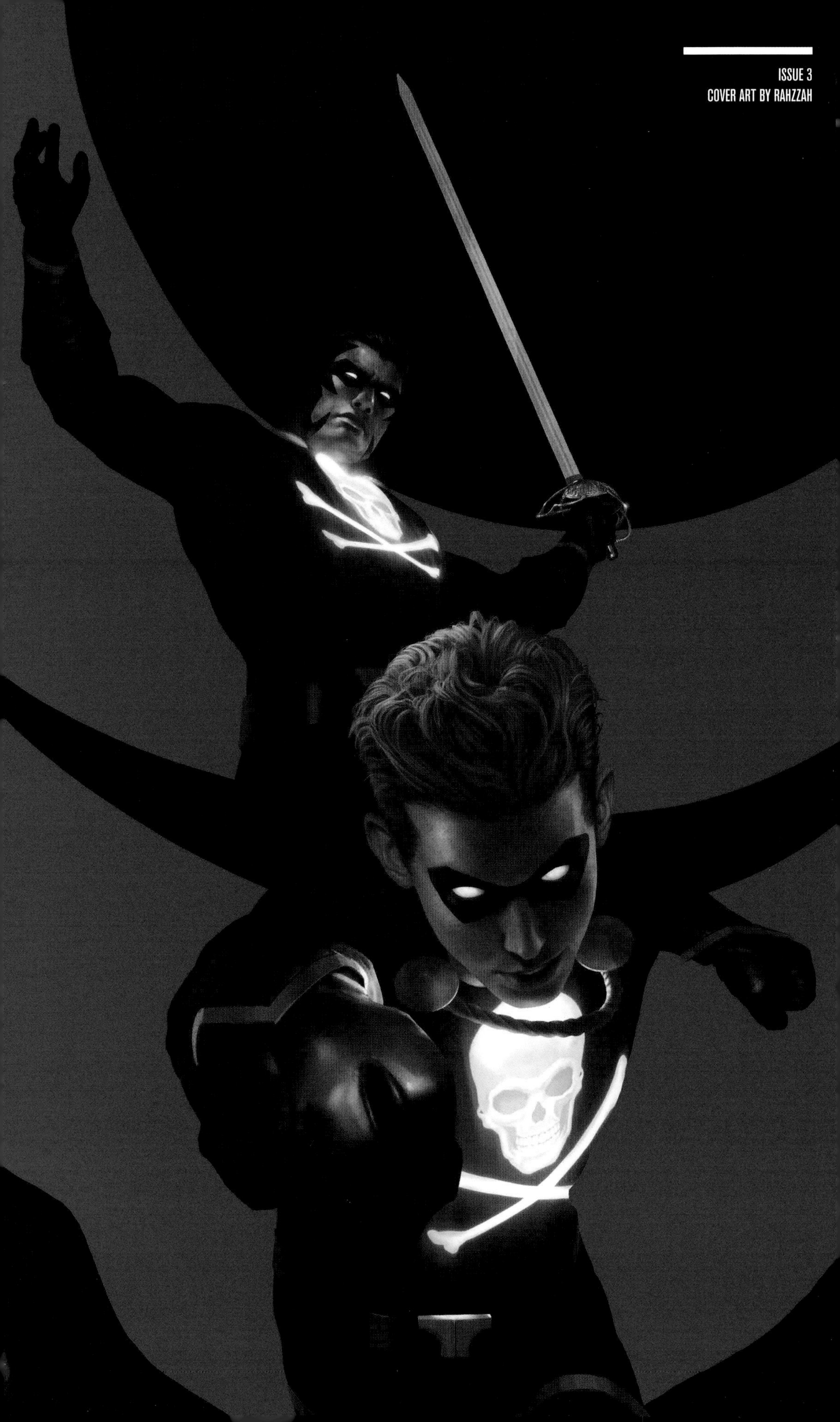

ISSUE 4
COVER ART BY JORGE FORNÉS

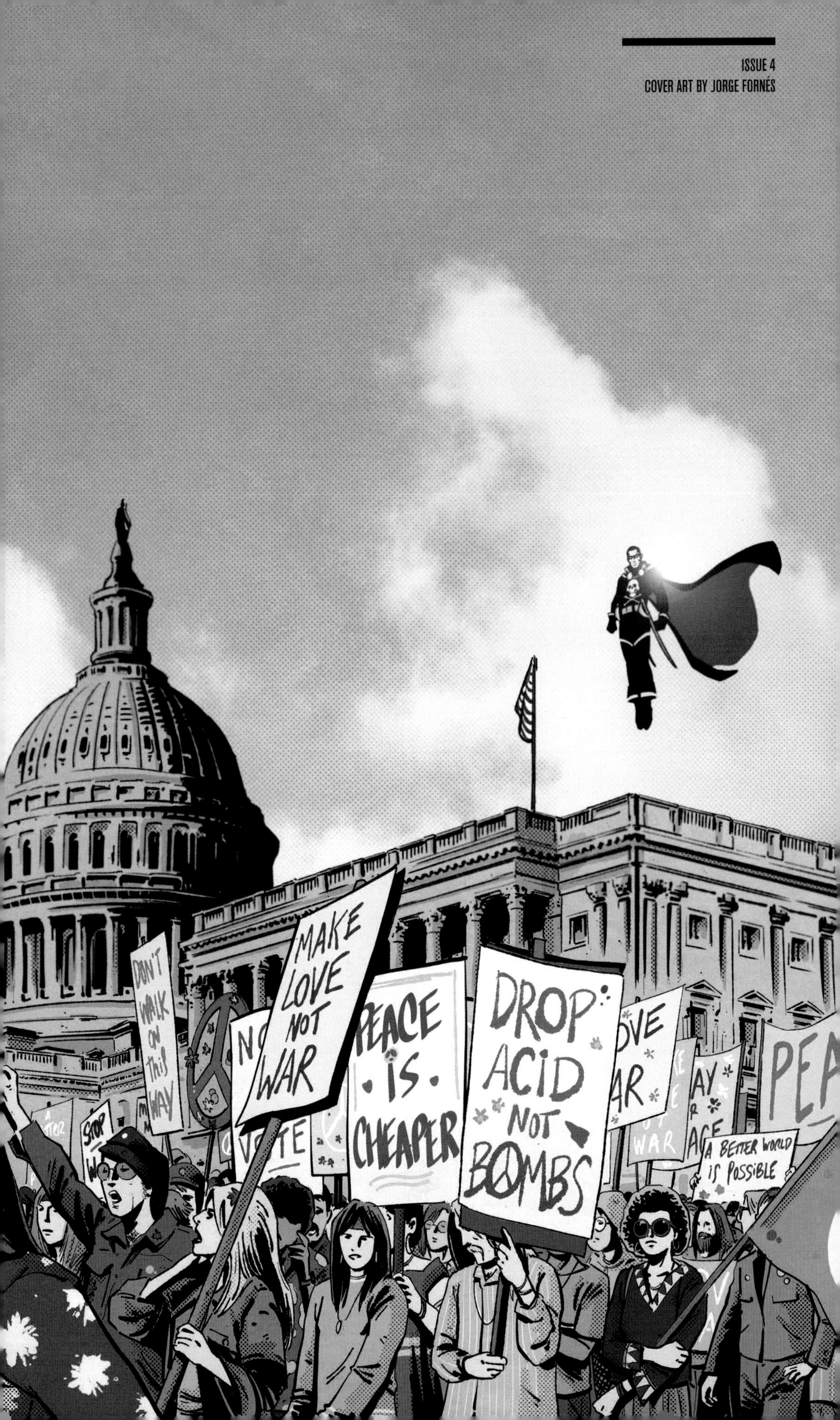
DON'T WALK ON THIS WAY
MAKE LOVE NOT WAR
PEACE IS CHEAPER
DROP ACID NOT BOMBS
VOTE
A BETTER WORLD IS POSSIBLE

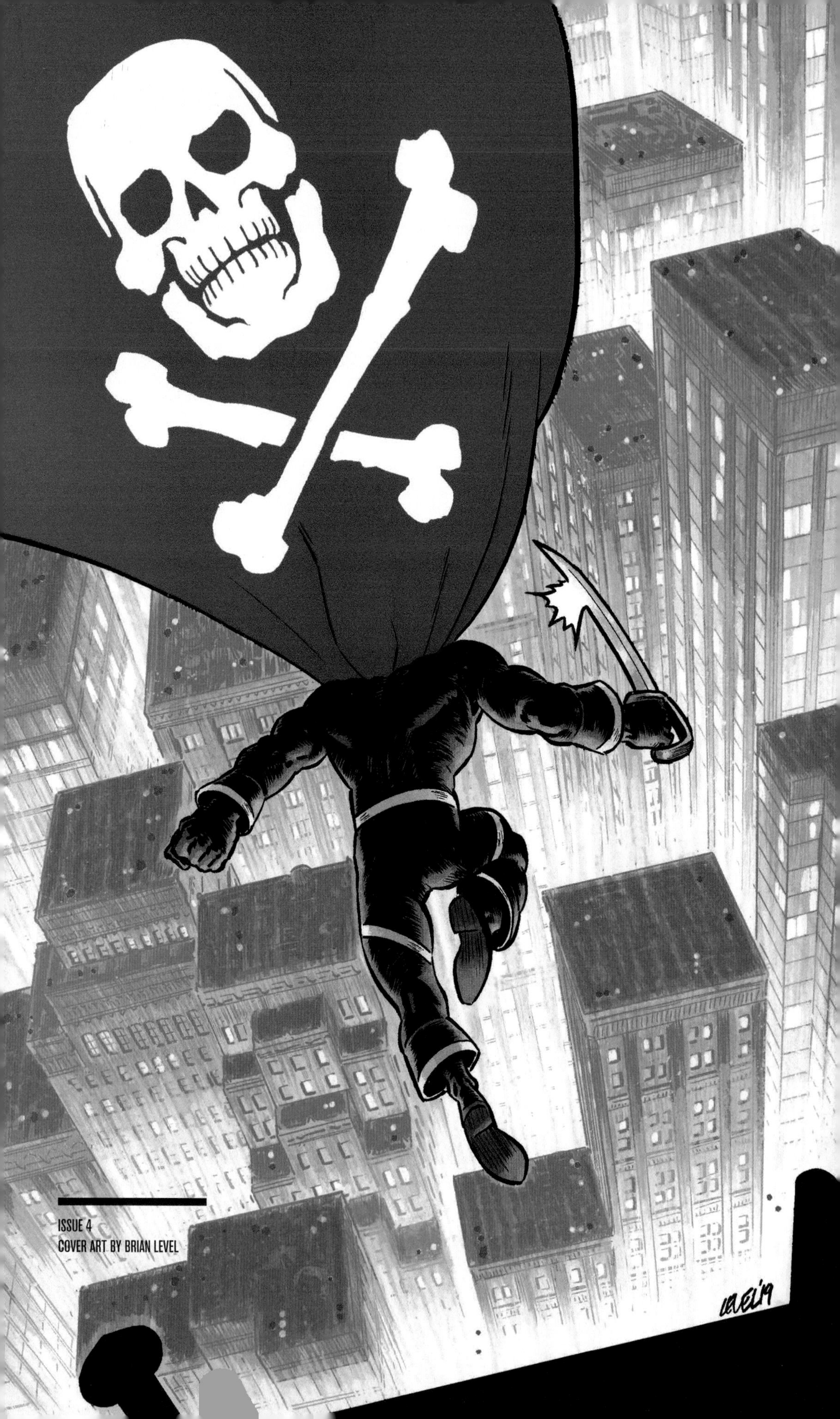
LEVEL'19

ISSUE 4
COVER ART BY BRIAN LEVEL

ISSUE 5
COVER ART BY JORGE FORNES

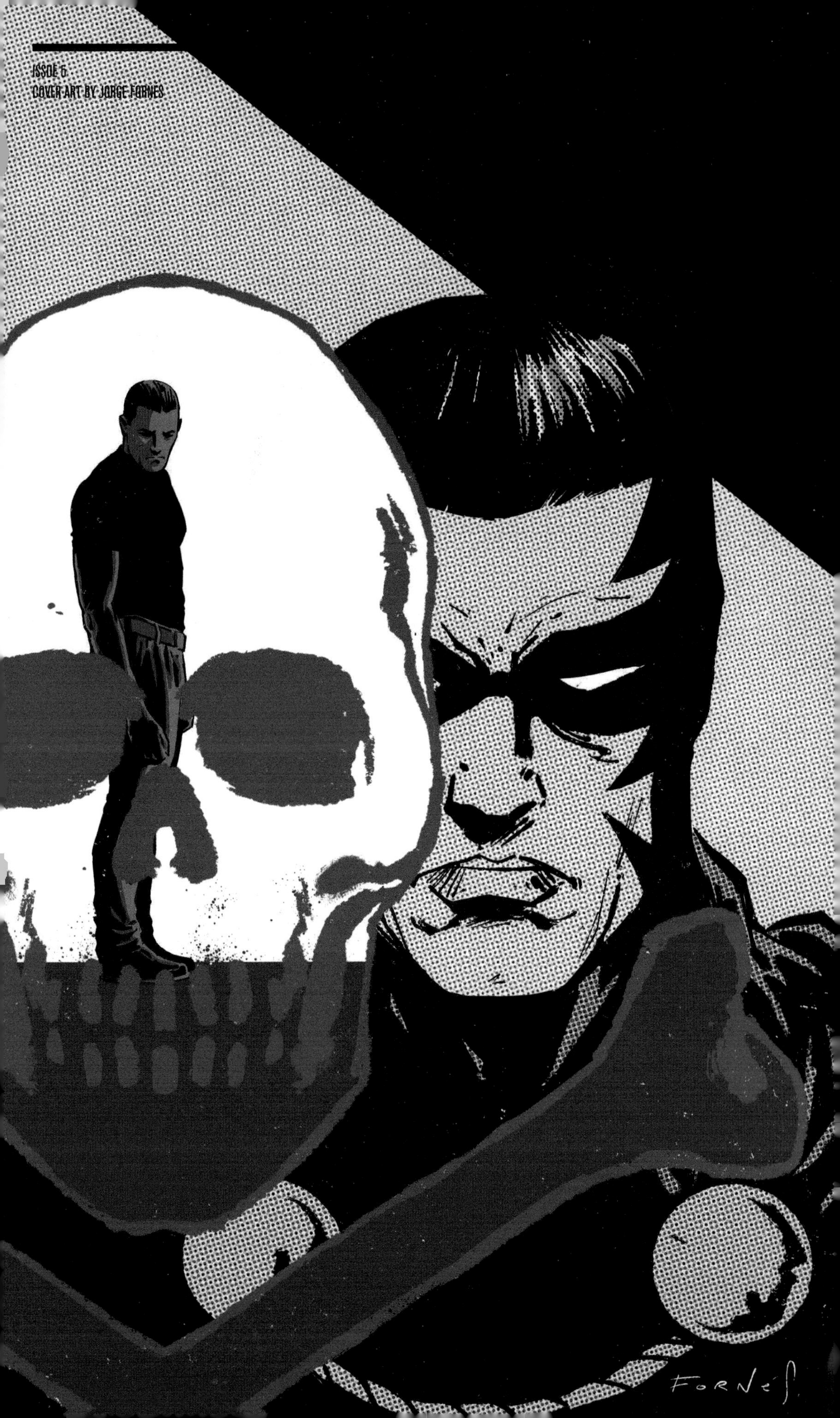
FORNES

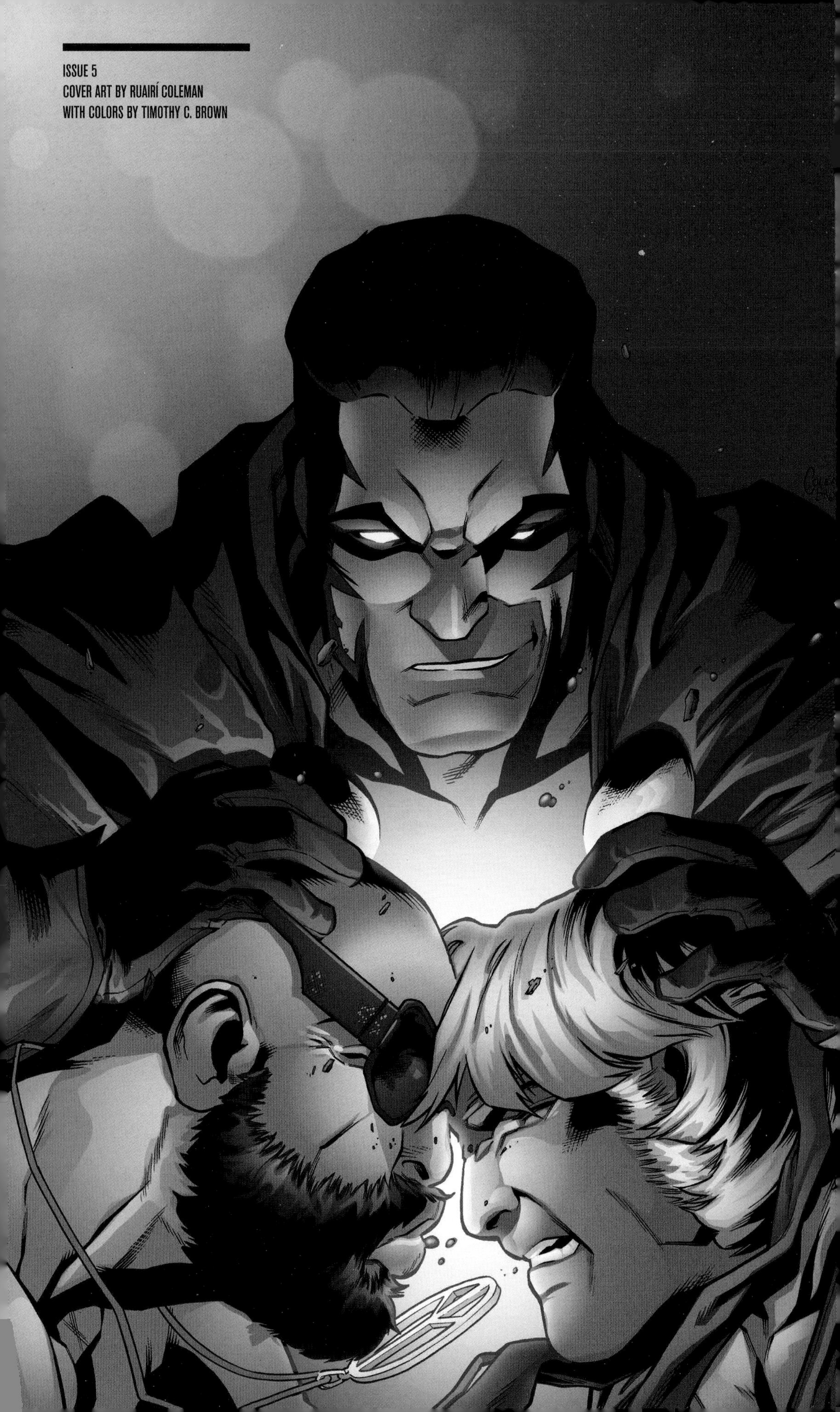

ISSUE 5
COVER ART BY RUAIRÍ COLEMAN
WITH COLORS BY TIMOTHY C. BROWN